Pagan Resurrection

Also by Richard Rudgley

Lost Civilisations of the Stone Age

Pagan Resurrection

Richard Rudgley

<u>C̄</u>

Century · London

Published by Century in 2006

1 3 5 7 9 10 8 6 4 2

Copyright © Richard Rudgley 2006

Richard Rudgley has asserted his right under the Copyright, Designs and
Patents Act, 1988 to be identified as the author of this work

First published in the United Kingdom in 2006 by Century

The Random House Group Limited
20 Vauxhall Bridge Road, London SW1V 2SA

Random House Australia (Pty) Limited
20 Alfred Street, Milsons Point, Sydney,
New South Wales 2061, Australia

Random House New Zealand Limited
18 Poland Road, Glenfield
Auckland 10, New Zealand

Random House (Pty) Limited
Isle of Houghton, Corner of Boundary Road & Carse O'Gowrie,
Houghton 2198, South Africa

Random House Publishers India Private Limited
301 World Trade Tower, Hotel Intercontinental Grand Complex,
Barakhamba Lane, New Delhi 110 001, India

The Random House Group Limited Reg. No. 954009

www.randomhouse.co.uk

A CIP catalogue record for this book is available from the British Library

Papers used by Random House are
natural, recyclable products made from wood grown in
sustainable forests. The manufacturing processes conform to
the environmental regulations of the country of origin

ISBN 9780712680967
ISBN 0 7126 8096 9

Typeset by SX Composing DTP, Rayleigh, Essex
Printed and bound in Great Britain by
Mackays of Chatham plc, Chatham, Kent

Dedication

This book is dedicated to my mother-in-law Dorothy Capitan in thanks for all the inspiration, support and encouragement she has given to me over the years. Her quest to regain her own cultural roots inspired me to do the same and led to the writing of this book.

Acknowledgements

I would like to thank a number of people who have helped in various ways during the research and writing of this book: Graham Butcher for introducing me to the ideas and practices of Stav; David Parry for reading parts of the text and giving me his valuable feedback and enthusiasm; Oliver St John and Grover T. Wickersham for their friendship and support; Matt Turner for dedicating so much of his time to reading the manuscript and providing numerous structural and creative insights that were essential to the successful completion of the manuscript; my editor Mark Booth for his help throughout; Andrew Lownie for getting the book commissioned in the first place; Charlotte Haycock at Random House for her diligence, kindness and invaluable assistance in the latter stages; Anne Kragelund for the line drawings; Robert J. Wallis and Nathan Johnson whose important book *Galdrbok: Practical Heathen Runecraft, Shamanism and Magic* (Wykeham Press) was unfortunately not published in time for me to discuss in the text; I would also like to thank my mother for her help, my daughter Rebecca, my son Benedict and last but not least my wife who has had to listen too many times to the words 'it's nearly finished'!

COVER

The cover picture shows a woodcarving from the facade of the Haus Atlantis building in Böttcherstrasse, Bremen, Germany. This powerful image depicts Odin's self-sacrifice on the World Tree. Around the edge of the circle is a quotation from the *Edda* describing his ordeal which resulted in his vision of the runes. This image was designed by the sculptor and architect Bernhard Hötger and the building completed in 1931. Hötger fell foul of the Nazis and fled to Switzerland in 1933. The building was destroyed in 1944 during an Allied bombing raid (see Nigel Pennick, *The Complete Illustrated Guide to Runes*, Element, HarperCollins, London, 2002, p. 107).

Contents

PART TWO – THE SECOND ODINIC EXPERIMENT: THE
ANGLO-AMERICAN WORLD

PART THREE – VISIONS OF THE WEB

Preface

This book is the biography of a god, a deity who was once the king of the pagan gods of northern Europe before he was dethroned by Christ. He had different names in the various parts of the ancient Germanic world. In the German forests he was invoked as Wotan, among the Anglo-Saxons of England he was Woden and in Viking age Scandinavia he was called Odin. As Christianity loosened its grip on the soul of western man this pagan god rose again. We do not have to believe in Odin's actual existence as a god to track his return to the forefront of the Western psyche.

As this book will make clear, Odin exists in our collective thoughts and has profoundly influenced the course of the modern world. The eminent psychologist and psychiatrist Carl Gustav Jung (1875–1961) described Odin as an archetype – a psychic complex that does not need an independent existence outside our minds to affect changes in the real world. For modern man Odin may be 'all in the mind' but we cannot spirit him away through reason, for he embodies the irrational side of the Western psyche. We do not need to believe in Gods or supernatural entities that have an existence external to the minds and perceptions of human beings. The contemporary relevance of these gods is that they are archetypes and behavioural models and not simply objects of worship. As such they still exert a powerful influence over our imaginations; they are the ancient blueprints in the modern mind.

One of the most widely held illusions of our modern world is that reason can and should rule our lives. In an era when rationality has been exalted by science we are encouraged to believe that irrational forces must be tamed and directed by the exercise of reason. Whilst rationality is both powerful and valuable it is wishful thinking to believe, in the face of so much evidence to the contrary, that it is the most powerful force to emanate from the human mind. The faculty of imagination is often dismissed as merely the source of fantasy and illusion but it is far more than that.

The French scholar Henry Corbin learned from the writings of Sufis (Islamic mystics) that they had a very different understanding of the human imagination. He found his attempt to describe their world of inner experience was hampered by the shortcomings of the overly rational mindset of the modern West. To describe their experiences as 'imaginary' seemed to him to degrade what they were experiencing: 'Despite all our efforts, we cannot prevent that, in current and premeditated usage, the term imaginary is equated with the unreal, with something that is outside the framework of being and existing, in brief, with something utopian.'[1] He also said that to understand such spiritual traditions we must recognise the reality of the world of the imagination because it is: 'A world that is ontologically as real as the world of the senses and that of the intellect. This world requires its own faculty of perception, namely, imaginative power, a faculty with a cognitive function, a noetic value which is as real as that of sense perception or intellectual intuition.'[2]

This book explores how the Odinic archetype manifests itself through our imaginations. On one level it works unconsciously through the shadowy world of political fantasies and strange modern occult mythologies. We will see how, even at this level, it has had profound effects in the real world around us. On a deeper level the archetype works in a conscious way, activating the imaginal reality through a genuine spiritual core of pagan ideas.

The light of reason should complement the fertile darkness of the imagination, not dismiss it. These two primary forces of the mind must both be exercised and given their equal due. The attempt to put reason on a pedestal at the expense of imagination is not only to present a distorted picture of the workings of the human mind, it is also extremely dangerous. If left to its own devices, and without the light of reason, the soils of imagination will spawn strange and some-times dangerous psychic entities – something which is happening in our own time. This book documents psychological and spiritual forces which are alive in modern American and European culture, powers rejected or ignored at our peril.

Introduction

ANCIENT BLUEPRINTS IN THE MODERN MIND

Chapter 1

Jung: The Pagan Prophet

The major cultural figure who must be placed at the very epicentre of the pagan revival is Jung. Carl Jung was a pupil (and later rival) of Sigmund Freud who developed his own system of therapy called analytical psychology. The Jungian system contains two key ideas with implications that extend far beyond the confines of an individual's psychology. While Jung believed that there was an individual unconscious level to the mind, he also described deeper, shared levels which he called the collective unconscious; these can be tapped into by all of us. It is in this unconscious realm of formative ideas that archetypes reside. These archetypes are the blueprints for certain workings of the human psyche. In the various mythologies developed by the ancient mind archetypes are often personified by gods and goddesses with their own distinct personalities and associations. Many of these archetypes are shared by all mankind but others are specific to certain cultures. The subject of this book – the northern god Odin – was identified by Jung as the most important archetype of the Germanic mind.

Jung himself was not merely a detached observer of archetypes but sought to illuminate this world through personal exploration and experiment. In two groundbreaking books – *The Jung Cult* and *The Aryan Christ* – Richard Noll recasts Jung's part in transforming the spiritual life of modern man and reveals his paramount role in neo-paganism. Noll's thesis is so significant that it needs to be outlined in detail for the remarkable influence of Jung over modern spirituality to be fully appreciated. Noll remarks:

> Through years of reflection on Jung's considerable impact on the culture and spiritual landscape of the twentieth century, I have come to the conclusion that, as an individual, he ranks with the Roman emperor Julian the Apostate (fourth century C.E.) as one who significantly undermined orthodox Christianity and restored the polytheism of the Hellenistic world in Western civilization . . . I believe that, for a variety of historical and technological factors – modern mass media being the most important – Jung has succeeded where Julian has failed.[1]

Noll goes on to say that not only was Jung openly against the Judaeo-Christian tradition but that his use of the modern and scientific-sounding language of psychology to communicate his ideas was actually designed 'to make his own magical, polytheistic, pagan worldview more palatable to a secularized world conditioned to respect only those ideas that seem to have a scientific air to them'.[2] Noll is not alone in having identified paganism as the core of Jung's life and work. R.F.C. Hull, the main translator of Jung into English and also someone who was close to him, put it bluntly: 'I am absolutely sure that everything vital and creative came to him out of the depths of his pagan unconscious.'[3]

Jung believed in reincarnation and counted at least two famous Germans among his own previous lives. One was the great Christian mystic Meister Eckhardt (1260–1328) and the other Johann Wolfgang von Goethe (1749–1832). This spiritual link between Carl Jung and Goethe may have also had a more biological basis. As he sometimes liked to recount, there was a rumour that the mother of Jung's grandfather Karl had had an affair with Goethe and it was intimated that Karl was in fact born from this intrigue.[4] Noll has this to say on Jung's beliefs about his own previous incarnations: 'The ethnic pattern of his incarnations is what is so important . . . Jung is the perfected result of the evolution of his ancestors, whose heritage converges in him. And it is always German genius, the genius of his *Volk*.'[5]

Beyond these personal explorations into his own psychic past, Jung developed a more general belief that the ancient mind was still alive in modern man, albeit hidden and suppressed. He also thought this ancient mind represented a deeper and more authentic European spirituality. Much of his professional and personal life was dedicated to bringing this pagan legacy back to light in order to make it conscious once more. Underpinning Jung's psychological system was the belief that Christianity was responsible for the symbolic content of only one layer of the European mind. Beneath it lay another level which was pagan and could show its presence through spiritual imagery which was pre-Christian in origin.

In the light of Noll's powerful analysis of the real nature of the Jungian enterprise we can now begin to see the full significance of Jung's role. He was not only a scientist but also an occultist, a pagan and a prophet. Jung believed that Wotan (Odin) was the true god of the Germanic peoples. He had a number of visions of Wotan throughout his life and, when he had premonitions about both the death of his mother and his wife, it was Wotan who appeared to him in his dreams.[6]

Prophecies on the fate of Europe

In 1936 Jung first wrote of his prophecies on the return of Odin when he published the essay *Wotan*. Odin was seen by Jung as an ancient god who had suddenly and inexplicably awoken from a thousand years of slumber 'like an extinct volcano' and taken over the collective psyche of the German nation under the Nazi party, which was soon to lead them into a catastrophic war. That the old god of frenzy should arise in the very heart of Western civilisation was all the more remarkable.

In *Wotan* Jung said that we are convinced the modern world is a rational place and that we base this opinion that it is so on political, economic and psychological factors (his words ring as true today as they did in 1936). Yet, undermining this whole view of our world, he boldly wrote: 'In fact I venture the heretical suggestion that the unfathomable depths of Wotan's character explain more of National Socialism than all three reasonable factors put together.'[7]

He goes on to claim that the frenzy associated with Odin could be seen at work in Hitler when he gave impassioned speeches as if in a state of unconscious possession. For Jung, Odin is an 'autonomous psychic factor' among the Germanic peoples. He even makes the bold statement, 'the god of the *Germans* is Wotan and not the Christian God'.[8] Jung was himself a visionary figure imbued with pagan ideals and sought to understand, even influence, the spiritual course of a civilisation over which Christianity was losing its grip. He writes: 'An archetype is like an old watercourse along which the water has flowed for centuries . . . the longer it has flowed in this channel the more likely it is that the water will return to its old bed.'[9] And again:

We are driven to conclude that Wotan must, in time, reveal not only the restless, violent, stormy side of his character, but also his ecstatic and mantic qualities – a very different aspect of his nature. If this conclusion is correct, National Socialism would not be the last word. Things must be concealed in the background which we cannot imagine at present, but we may expect them to appear in the next few years or decades. Wotan's reawakening is a stepping back into the past; the stream was dammed up and has broken into its old channel . . . and the water will overleap the obstacle.[10]

Jung seems to have recognised that his own prophetic statements on the return of the pagan spirit were foreshadowed by earlier visionaries for he quotes the following verse from one of the sixteenth-century prophecies of Nostradamus at the very beginning of his essay:

> In Germany shall divers sects arise,
> Coming very near to happy paganism.
> The heart captivated and small receivings
> Shall open the gate to pay the true tithe.[11]

The prophecies of Nostradamus may be obscure and open to many different interpretations but Jung's own prophecy is a crystal-clear prediction concerning the future of Europe – that Odin would outlast the 'thousand-year Reich'. In this respect Jung has been proved right.

The following extract from a letter written by Jung poses vital questions concerning both the present and future states of European and American political, cultural and spiritual life. Jung wrote the letter to his Chilean friend Miguel Serrano on 14 September 1960, in the winter of his life, a few months before he died in the summer of 1961. The true significance of this passage has been largely overlooked and here we set out to explore and understand its implications for the modern world.

> When, for instance, the belief in the god Wotan vanished and nobody thought of him anymore, the phenomenon originally called Wotan remained . . . our consciousness only imagines that it has lost its Gods; in reality they are still there and it only needs a certain general condition in order to bring them back in full force. This condition is a situation in which a new orientation and adaptation is needed. If this question is not clearly understood and no proper answer is given, the archetype, which expresses this situation, steps in . . .

. . . As only certain individuals are capable of listening and of accepting good advice, it is most unlikely that anybody would pay attention to the statement of a warning voice that Wotan is here again. They would rather fall headlong into the trap . . . we are very much in the same predicament as the pre-National-Socialistic Germany of the Twenties, i.e. we are apt to undergo the risk of a further, but this time worldwide, Wotanistic experiment. This means mental epidemy and war. One does not realise yet, that when an archetype is unconsciously constellated and not consciously understood, one is *possessed by it* and forced to its fatal goal . . .[12]

Jung was returning to the subject of Odin, a topic which, as we have seen, had haunted him since the 1930s. Jung had the insight to perceive that far from being simply a dead and ancient god, Odin is an archetype that lives on even to this day among the Germanic peoples. The present book is, on one level, an extended commentary on these remarkable paragraphs from the letter – brief but striking in content. Jung writes of two Odinic experiments. He sees the evidence for the first Odinic experiment in the rise of Nazism in Germany and he warns of a second which could be even more catastrophic.

The psychological profile of a god

To try to understand Odin as a god requires us to alter our mindset, a way of thinking which has developed as a result of our culture's long interaction with Christianity. Even though most of us no longer believe in him, Odin's influence is still there. Odin and the other gods were venerated and honoured but do not seem to have been worshipped in the same way as Christians worship their god. Perhaps the simplest way to understand this pagan mindset is to look at the sheer diversity of roles played by Odin.

As Jung says, the archetype of this Germanic god will remain as long as the Germanic peoples exist. Whether Odin is active or dormant depends upon historical and cultural circumstances; in our time he appears once again very much alive. To trace the growing influence of Odin in the modern world we need to return to his ancient roots. The most important of these are to be found in the Icelandic Eddas, the main source of our knowledge of the Norse myths.[13] Ancient pagan lore was preserved much longer in Iceland than anywhere else in the Germanic world, mainly because the country only officially converted to Christianity in the year 1000.

Incidentally, I have chosen to use the name Odin not only because this is the most familiar to English-speaking readers but also because it is by this name that the Norse poems and other writings refer to him. Whilst the cult of Woden in England, that of Wotan in Germany, and his cults elsewhere may have differed from that practised by the Vikings, as far as we can discover from the historical sources the role of this god across the northern world was fundamentally the same.

Odin is often described as the king of the gods and many of the other deities as his sons. Despite being the king and also being called 'All-father' he is not all-powerful. As pagans the ancient peoples of the north were polytheists, that is to say they worshipped many gods. So Odin may have been the most powerful of the gods but he was not in any way like the God of the Christians, Jews and Muslims. Another way in which he differs from the monotheistic God is that he was not present at the beginning of the world and will not be there at the end of time – Odin dies in mortal combat with the monstrous wolf Fenrir at the Ragnarok, the pagan version of the apocalypse.

Over 200 ancient names for Odin have been preserved. About a quarter of these name him as a god of war, battle and violence; he is Lord of the Spear (his main weapon and an important symbol of his cult), Army Father, Victory Bringer and Battle Wolf (the wolf is one of his animal familiars). He inspires battle and strife on many levels. He is the god of the warriors who are victorious but is also responsible for the slain, whose bodies are eaten by ravens and other carrion birds whilst their souls are transported to the Viking heaven, Valhalla (Hall of the Slain), where they sit in the presence of Odin (see Plate 1).

His connections with the world of the dead go far beyond being Chooser of the Slain and the host in Valhalla. He is both Lord of Ghosts and God of the Hanged and also a necromancer, that is to say a magician who evokes the shades of the dead in order to obtain secret knowledge. He is called Hanging One and Dangler in reference to his great initiation, when he hung on a tree for nine nights without food or water and was rewarded with a vision of the runes, the alphabetical signs which embody the esoteric knowledge of the northern tradition. Myth also records that on another occasion he sacrificed an eye in order to gain wisdom and so became known by the name Blindr, meaning blind.

The puzzle of Odin's multiple personalities does not stop there – he is Sorcerer and Staff Wielder – and because of his shape-shifting powers he is also named Bear, Eagle and Raven God. He is a sorcerer, a shaman and a healer. Many of his names announce him as a master of poetry and wisdom: Grey Beard, Mighty Poet, True One and Much Wise. Yet he is also Riddler, Deceiver, Treachery Ruler and even Evil-Doer. Odin is also *Jólnir*, 'Yule Figure'. This association with Yule (the pagan Christmas) has led to speculation that Odin may be the prototype of Santa Claus. The seemingly endless transformations of Odin mean that he also plays many other roles – Beloved, Lover, Seducer, Cargo God, Wealth Friend and even Hermaphrodite, and is portrayed as a seasoned traveller or outcast, wandering in search of both wisdom and adventure.[14]

These names and the characteristics they imply reveal the complex and contradictory character of Odin. This mysterious aspect is recognised in the myths themselves where he often appears in disguise, prompting one profound student of the myths, Georges Dumézil, to dub him 'both master and spy'. The name Masked One also reveals that his disguise is not merely about physical appearance but also about his hidden nature as a wise man and magician delving into esoteric, secret and forbidden lore.

It seems hard to reconcile these seemingly contradictory traits of the god, either morally or even logically. However, the key that unlocks the mystery is to be found in the name Odin itself. It means frenzy, and Odin is often called the Frenzied One in the myths. This peculiar and powerful state of mind manifests itself in different ways. Firstly it may be found on the battlefield or in other arenas of violence. In these cases frenzy manifests as battle fury, as epitomised by the behaviour of the Viking equivalent of modern-day special forces, the Berserks (from which our word derives) and the Ulfhednar or wolf-skin wearers. The Berserks were said to become invincible in this state of fury and to roar and bite their shields.

Another aspect of Odinic frenzy is the inspiration which often overcomes poets and other artists during their creative acts. Poetry was of profound importance in the northern world, playing a role similar to the mass media of today. Not only were myths transmitted orally through poetry and storytelling but political propaganda was also peddled by bards, hired by kings and chieftains, who extolled their employer's heroic and noble deeds to his entourage and guests alike. In the modern world poetry and fighting are poles apart – most soldiers and other fighters would dismiss poetry as effeminate and many poets would be equally scathing of the martial arts. In the pagan world of the Anglo-Saxons and the Vikings, poetry and song were essential for a leader of warriors to master.[15]

His role as magician is also related to his states of frenzy, for poetry was also spoken magic. English words preserve this understanding: 'enchant' (en-chant) and 'spell' both show the link between magic and the spoken or chanted word. One of the main forms of magic practised among the Norse was called *galdr*, which means 'magic chant'. Magicians and shamans enter trances in which they chant magical words, and whilst these states can often be tranquil and passive they may also be dramatic and violent – for example when the magician himself or his patient is in a state of possession. Similarly, Odin's numerous erotic adventures often have magical elements to them and sexual ecstasy can be added to the types of frenzied activity associated with him. Psychoactive plants also played a role in ancient northern magic, and myth relates that Odin stole the magical mead brewed by a giant and his daughter. Intoxication through alcohol or other drugs may therefore be included.

Battle fury, poetic inspiration, magical trance, sexual ecstasy and drug-induced intoxication are thus all aspects of Odin's embodiment of frenzy and are all altered states of consciousness. So he is the god of altered consciousness, of consciousness heightened beyond the mundane and, as such, potentially dangerous. As a god of altered states of mind, Odin rules not the rational, logical and orderly part of the psyche but the darker irrational side: he is the source of artistic creation, dreams and nightmares, sexual passion, violent rage, magical trance and intoxication. When poets, lovers, warriors or sorcerers are in such ecstatic states of mind they are capable of unimaginable feats; they temporarily gain superhuman powers and become intoxicated with the powers of the god. He is at once dangerous, exciting, wise and cunning. He stands for the instinctual, imaginative, emotional, inspirational and intuitional parts of the human psyche – particularly the northern European psyche. His is divine madness but it may also manifest as terrible and destructive fury. We should seek Odin's influence in our culture where his characteristics tell us to look – in the shadowy world of magical thought, occultism, conspiracy theory and other areas of rejected and esoteric knowledge and in unusual and politically significant outbreaks of violence and psychoses.

This book explores the role of Odin in the ancient north, the mythology that he was part of, and the history of the neo-pagan movement which arose when he returned. It delves into the modern myths concerning Odin and the supposed role of neo-paganism in the rise of Nazism and its offshoots. It looks at the evidence for the second Odinic experiment that Jung predicted – an experiment that could lead to disaster or to spiritual renewal depending on whether it was conscious or unconscious.

Why did this ancient archetype return to cast his spell over the German people? What circumstances occurred in Europe to prompt Odin's return and the ensuing disaster which Jung called the first Wotanistic experiment (the first Odinic experiment as it will be called in the present book) – namely the rise of Nazism and the Second World War? The traumas of these events do not represent the end of the story, for in the present the influence of Odin is also to be found and, as Jung predicted, has grown to global dimensions. The second Odinic experiment has, as this book will show, already begun. How it will end depends partly on our understanding of the effect of this archetype. If we can understand it, then by making its influence clear disaster can be diverted. Yet if we allow it to possess us and let it act through our unconscious then catastrophic events may well lie ahead.

Jung, in his letter to Serrano, predicts that the second experiment will mean 'mental epidemy and war'. This clearly echoes Odin's ancient associations with both war and madness and sounds very much like a pagan version of the apocalypse. In fact this prophecy resonates with the Ragnarok, the end of the world as described in northern myths. Entirely independently of Jung's comments one of the most distinguished scholars of Norse religion, Hilda Ellis Davidson, writes:

> The fight in a narrow place against odds, which has been called the ideal of heroic literature in the north, is given cosmic stature in the conception of Ragnarok, the doom of the gods, when Odin and his peers go fighting against the monsters and the unleashed fury of the elements. The depths and dark mysteries of the subconscious are given full

recognition in the myths. The greatest terror to be faced, that
of the disintegration of the mind in madness or death, is not
pushed to one side. At Ragnarok a rich and wonderful world
was shattered and the monsters had their fill of destruction.
After that facing of reality, it was possible to see beyond the
catastrophe and to imagine a new world built upon the ruins
of the old.[16]

Was the great World War fought as part of the first Odinic
experiment together with the collective madness that brought the
Nazi party to power merely a prelude to another even more
catastrophic era? History and even prehistory will play a part in the
unmasking of Odin's archetypal power but the main thrust of this
book concerns modern history, the present day and the possible
future that awaits us.

Chapter 2

The Pagan Family Tree

The mythology of a people is far more than a collection of pretty or terrifying fables to be retold in carefully bowdlerized form to our schoolchildren. It is the comment of the men of one particular age or civilization on the mysteries of human existence and the human mind, their model for social behaviour, and their attempt to define in stories of gods and demons their perception of inner realities

H.R. Ellis Davidson, *Gods and Myths of Northern Europe*[1]

Throughout history and across the world people have sat at night by the fireside and recounted myths of how the world was created, told of the origins and actions of the gods, of the birth of the sun, moon and stars, of the origins of animals, plants and the first people. The human imagination has always been enthralled by epic tales of cultural heroes, of monsters and fabulous creatures, of hidden treasures and magical powers, of the golden age of mankind, of natural catastrophes, and of the fate of the human soul in the afterlife.

Myths are not simply innocent stories to distract us from our humdrum daily existence; they also have a powerful effect on the political and ideological make-up of society. Their descriptions of the social order, its classes, its moral beliefs and institutions, make myths nothing less than social charters which can both mirror and alter a society's beliefs and institutions. The power of myth is as much about this world as it is about any supernatural realm. For myths are like collective waking dreams shared by whole societies – they live in us and we live in them.

The myths of the Indo-Europeans

As Europeans we must ask ourselves with which myths we have this strong symbiotic relationship. Obviously the myths of Christianity have long been embedded in our minds but beneath them lies another, deeper, level of myth which belongs to our pagan and pre-historic past. Most of the European and many Asian languages belong to a vast family known as Indo-European. In the nineteenth century the peoples who belonged to this language family were called Aryans by linguistics. With the rise of racial theories towards the end of the century anthropologists began to talk of Aryan racial characteristics and bloodlines. Even then linguists protested that such ideas made no sense; the evidence pointed to a common linguistic heritage and nothing more. It was apparent that there were a number of so-called races making up the diverse speakers of the Indo-European language family. But in the fuzzy biological sciences of the time, governed by political and racist motivations, reasonable protests were ignored. And so, when the Nazis appropriated the term Aryan for their own ends it became impossible for others to use this once neutral word, which has now all but been replaced by Indo-European to refer simply to the language family and its speakers.

Linguists have shown that there was an original ancestral language from which all the later Indo-European languages derive. It is called Proto-Indo-European and was spoken at some remote time in prehistory, perhaps as early as 4500 BC. The location of its original homeland is still the subject of great controversy, though it is likely to have been a large territory. But what is clear is that gradually, as the speakers of this language divided and migrated to different parts of

Europe and Asia, different branches of the family developed. Even before the modern era the family had spread all the way from India to Ireland. Among ancient languages Latin, Greek and Sanskrit all belong to this vast extended group. Today it is estimated that two billion people speak Indo-European languages as seemingly diverse as Hindi, Persian, Russian and Italian as well as all the Celtic and Germanic languages.

Those who speak Germanic languages are not only the Germans themselves but also the English, Dutch, Norwegian, Swedish, Danish and Icelandic peoples and their descendants in North America, Australia and elsewhere in the world. Germanic languages have also influenced Irish, Scottish, Welsh and French speakers, all of whom have had close contact with the Anglo-Saxon and Viking worlds. In addition, the Goths, or eastern Germanic peoples, who no longer exist as a separate ethnic group, forged kingdoms in both Italy and Spain as the Roman empire declined, in the process leaving traces of their Germanic legacy in southern Europe.

It is not just languages that link Indo-Europeans but also their common legacy of myth. The myths of peoples as far apart as the Celts and the Indians have been shown by the French savant Georges Dumézil to conform to basic patterns; they share many similar themes and symbols that illustrate a shared ancestry. It is because of these ancient links between seemingly diverse myths that the religious beliefs and practices of a culture as distant as India can still shed light on certain aspects of the pagan European mind. In the Indian tradition we can observe the development of a pagan belief system largely unaffected by the introduction of a foreign proselytising religion. When compared to the thriving and developed pagan tradition of India and its surviving religious practices and texts, the sources for Germanic paganism seem slim indeed. But fortunately a few complete texts and assorted references were written down and have survived in various parts of Europe. The most complete source for the lore and traditions of Germanic paganism has been left to us by the Vikings of

Scandinavia, in what is commonly referred to as Norse mythology.

According to Dumézil, the various mythologies of the Indo-Europeans all show what he called a tripartite ideology, that is to say, an ideology in which both gods and social order are organised into three groups or hierarchical classes. This pattern can be clearly seen in a myth of the Scythian nomads, an ancient Indo-European people, preserved in the writings of Herodotus, the early Greek historian. In this myth Kolaxaïs, the youngest son of the primeval being Targitaos, recovers three golden objects that fall from the sky – a cup, an axe and a plough. He seizes the cup for himself and becomes the ruler of the dominant tribe of the Scythians while his two older brothers become the subordinate rulers of their respective tribes. The axe and the plough are unambiguous symbols of the warrior and agricultural classes whilst the cup represents the highest order, the vessel from which the sovereign gods and their earthly representatives consume a divine drink.[2]

Dumézil discerns the same basic pattern throughout the Indo-European world. The highest class, who dwell in the heavens, the uppermost part of the cosmos, consists of the sovereign gods. Their human counterparts in the world, those concerned with the maintenance of social order through law and those in charge of religious affairs, are the political rulers and the magicians and priests. In the heavenly order these two roles also needed to be filled – among the Indian gods the first of these was played by Mitra and the second by Varuna. In the Norse pantheon it was Tyr who filled the first role, the god of justice, law and social order, whilst Odin ruled over magic and the supernatural order.

The second class of gods in the tripartite system resides below the heavens in the atmosphere. These are the gods of battle and conflict – the Indian war god Indra and Mars in the Roman pantheon. In Norse mythology this role is played by Thor, son of Odin. Thor is patron of the martial arts and the god of thunder, protecting the world from the forces of chaos as embodied by giants and monstrous beings. These gods are represented in the social order by the warrior class, which ensures that the whole community is protected from dangerous outside forces.

The third, lowest and largest class of the system is represented by the gods and goddesses of the earth. They rule over human, animal and plant fertility and general physical and material well-being. Some of these Indo-European deities are portrayed as twins, for example the Asvins of Indian myth, twin horsemen associated with healing. The Norse deity Frey, closely linked to a horse cult, is the god of plenty and pleasure. His sister Freya is the goddess of love and sexuality. In the social world such gods are mirrored in the lives of farmers and craftsmen.

The ideology of tripartition as seen among the ancient Indo-Europeans did not die out but continued to exert its influence even when paganism gave way to Christianity. As C. Scott Littleton has suggested, the idea of the Trinity only arose after the new religion had developed in Greek- and Latin-speaking cultures. He even sees this archaic code at work in scientific and other academic schemes of classification, which, as he rightly points out, usually involve three successive stages or periods. Among the examples he gives are the philosopher Hegel's notion of thesis, antithesis, synthesis and the anthropologist Lewis H. Morgan's scheme for the evolution of human culture from savagery to barbarism and finally civilisation.

Littleton also notes that both geologists and archaeologists have tended to divide their objects of study into three stages. As examples from archaeology we may note the scheme of Stone Age, Bronze Age and Iron Age as the three great epochs of prehistory. The Stone Age has itself been divided into three – the Palaeolithic (Old Stone Age), the Mesolithic (Middle Stone Age) and the Neolithic (New Stone Age). Again, the Old Stone Age is internally divided into Lower, Middle and Upper Palaeolithic. Littleton concludes: 'it seems clear that Europeans and Americans are conditioned to think and categorize in threes'.[3]

Family feuds

The mythology contained in the Eddas, our most complete record of the pagan deities of the north, is not a straightforward one. It tells us that the ancient Norse gods consist of two groups or families – the Aesir and the Vanir. The larger of the two groups, the Aesir, are mainly gods of government and war whilst the Vanir are gods of fertility, peace and earthy pleasures. Odin is among the Aesir, along with other well-known gods such as the mighty warrior Thor, and Tyr (the English variant Tiw gave his name to Tuesday) and the trickster Loki. Highly honoured among the Vanir are Frey, the fertility god, and his sister Freya, who is said to be the most beautiful and exalted of the Norse goddesses.

This unusual mythology with its two families of gods may contain insights into the historical processes of the Indo-European migration. According to the Lithuanian archaeologist Marija Gimbutas, the prehistoric people who spoke the Proto-Indo-European language were the Kurgan people of the late Stone Age, mounted warriors from the steppes of Russia. They possessed a warlike and patriarchal society and a mythology based on warrior gods. The cultures they encountered when they reached Europe were seemingly more peaceful with a mythology based around a multifaceted goddess. In the Norse myths the Aesir and the Vanir, after warring with each other, finally made peace and learned to coexist and cooperate. It seems likely that this narrative preserves some vestiges of the collision between these two cultures. Gimbutas characterises the northern European mythology as 'hybrid' – containing elements from the older and indigenous Vanir alongside those traits that derive from the Aesir, the incoming family of gods. It is the Vanir family who therefore represent an earlier and deeper level of European consciousness, epitomised in the concept of the web of Wyrd, as we shall see.

Northern cosmos: the countdown to creation

The division of gods and social order into three classes is by no means the only symbolic use of numbers in the northern pagan tradition. As in many mythologies around the world, there is in fact a complex cosmological system with numerical correspondences. Such numerical symbolism recognises that the world around us is made up of many classes of phenomena. Within each class there are many varieties. For example, the category 'tree' includes numerous species all of which have certain features in common – leaves, branches, trunk and so on. What these systems of numerical categories seek to do is divide the world into smaller and smaller classes of qualities. Conversely, as the number of classes *decreases* they include *more* phenomena within them; the qualities that define the class become more abstract and gradually they transcend the phenomena of the material world, eventually arriving at a trinity, then a duality and finally unity and the void.

In any symbolic numerical system various numbers have their correspondences, and the Norse pagan system is no exception. Ancient Norse lore is particularly concerned with the number nine, which, being three times three, has particular magical significance. Nine appears as a significant number again and again in Norse symbolism and myth. One of the key symbols of the northern tradition is the Valknut, (see Figure 1) drawn as an interconnecting set of three triangles. With nine lines in total it is associated with magic and is therefore of special significance to Odin.

It is in the lives of the gods and those who worshipped them that we can see the great symbolic significance of the number nine in the northern tradition. In the pagan counterpart to Christ's crucifixion Odin endures great suffering whilst hanging on the world tree for nine nights. Odin's son Hermod travels for nine consecutive nights to retrieve another of his sons, the god Balder, from the underworld realm of Hel.[4] At the Ragnarok, the pagan apocalypse, the god Thor slays his old adversary the world serpent but can only stagger back

Figure 1: The Valknut symbol

nine paces before falling down dead from the poison that the serpent
has blown on him. We can also discern the special significance of the
number nine in pagan religious practices. For example, at the pagan
cult centre of Uppsala in Sweden the god Freyr was worshipped every
nine years with a nine-day-long cycle of sacrifices.

Unlike Christianity, with its concept of one all-powerful God
ruling a single universe, pagan Norse cosmology recognises a
plurality not only of gods but also of worlds. There are nine worlds in
Norse cosmology, born out of a primal void called Ginnungagap – the
nothingness that existed before creation or, in numerical terms, zero.
The world of men is in the middle of this multiverse in a place called
Midgard (Middle Earth). At the top, in the realm of the heavens, is
Asgard, home of Odin and the Aesir gods. The various other worlds
are homes of giants, dwarves, elves and spirits and the dead.
According to Norse mythology all these realms are connected by
Yggdrasill, the World Tree. Other Germanic lore describes the
Irminsul, a great wooden pole which was the focus of worship.
The World Tree and World Pole are both images of the *axis mundi* –
the sacred centre of the cosmos analogous to the poles of the Earth
and the spine which holds the human body upright.

In order to understand how these nine worlds came into existence our survey of numerical symbolism takes us to the concept of duality, the number two, which may be said to be the northern European equivalent of the Yin and Yang of traditional Chinese cosmology. In Norse mythology the whole cosmos is generated out of the interaction between the two opposite principles of Fire and Ice. On one side we have Niflheim, the dark world, an icy realm in the far north, and on the other we have Muspellzheimr, the fiery realm of the far south – two primal forces in polar opposition separated from one another by the void of Ginnungagap. It is when these two forces combine that the entire cosmos is generated – in the form of a giant called Ymir, who begets the gods and from whose body the gods fashion the worlds and all living things, including humanity.

From the magical and mythical significance of the number nine to the duality of Fire and Ice from which all creation is born out of the void, our examination of numerical correspondences in Norse cosmology has now reached the number one – the unity of all things. Everything in existence is included in symbolic oneness: all the gods, giants and spirits; the nine worlds connected by the tree Yggdrasill; humanity, plants, animals, and everything else in Midgard and all the nine worlds. And so, out of the nothingness of Ginnungagap, when the world comes into being, a primal layer of reality emerges, a concept representing the totality of all things, a unity or oneness – the Web of Wyrd, wherein all the numerological and mythological strands of the pagan cosmology that we have been discussing are woven together.

The Web of Wyrd

The word wyrd means fate in Old English and has survived in modern English as 'weird'. However in Anglo-Saxon times it meant much more than simply weird. Wyrd was depicted as a primeval goddess who had power even over the gods. The word appears a number of times in the Old English epic poem *Beowulf*, where it means omnipotent fate or destiny, but elsewhere in the poem the Christian

God is also described as all-powerful thus showing the old pagan tradition surviving alongside the new religion. Wyrd weaves her spell in another Old English poem, *Dream of the Rood* (rood being another word for cross), in which she makes an appearance:

> At the crucifixion, after describing Christ's hanging on the cross and his wounding with nails, the Rood says, 'I was dripping with blood shed from the Man's side after he had given up the ghost,' and most significantly, immediately afterwards, 'I have endured many terrible Wyrds upon the hill' . . . modern translators usually render the word *Wyrds* as 'trials' or 'experiences'; but when it comes, as it does, immediately on the mention of Christ's death, it is reasonable to suppose that the poet was remembering the old power wielded by Wyrd over the gods.[5]

The pagan goddess Wyrd and the Christian God lived side by side in the Anglo-Saxon mind for some time but gradually Wyrd began to sink into the unconscious as Christianity took control over the old ways. But Wyrd was not to fade away completely and resurfaced through the greatest poetic minds in England, in the form of Wyrd and her two sisters – the three Norns, triple goddesses of fate. Chaucer wrote in the *Court of Love* (1345): 'I mene the three of fatall destine that be our Werdes'. They reappear, of course, in Shakespeare's *Macbeth*, first performed around 1605, as the three 'Weird Sisters'.

Wyrd is the Anglo-Saxon version of the Norse goddess Urd. In Norse myth Urd sits beside a spring, known as the Well of Urd, at the base of the world tree, Yggdrasill. Odin comes here to visit her for guidance and sacrifices one of his eyes to obtain wisdom from her. These myths also tell us that Urd is one of three goddesses known as the Norns. The Norns are rulers of time – Urd rules the past, Verdandi the present and Skuld the future. Whether in the form of Urd alone or the three Norns, the goddess(es) of fate are often described as spinners, as weaving webs.[6] This web is the fabric of fate, the pattern that underlies life itself and within which all things are entwined.

Chapter 3

Ancestral Visions

I know, I hung on the wind-swept tree
for nine nights in all
wounded by a spear and dedicated to Odin
Given myself to myself
on the tree, of which no-one knows
from which root it grows.
With nothing to eat and nothing to drink
I bent my head down
and groaning took the runes up
and fell down thereafter.

Hávámal (*Sayings of the High One*), stanzas 138–41[1]

The notion of the Web of Wyrd underpins the whole philosophy and cosmology of the northern pagan tradition. The web describes a cosmic network of relationships that exist between all things. Understanding what the Web of Wyrd signified for the pagan mind requires us to examine the weaving metaphor used in the myth of the Norns. The Norns are weavers, carefully crafting an endless fabric, a complex tapestry of interconnections, knots and threads which represents all of reality. For pagan magicians and visionaries the ultimate goal would be to somehow learn to decipher the patterns of the weaving, the crossing of various strands and the locations of knots – to understand the web that expresses the reality of the cosmos.

With this knowledge would come great power, for the magician would be able to see into the past, to see a greater portion of the present, and, of course, to divine the future. In order to attempt to understand something so vast and complex, the magician requires a special language, a system of symbols and codes. As we shall see many such systems have been used in cultures around the world, systems of symbolic analogy and classification. In the northern pagan world the runes are the main system used to understand the vast Web of Wyrd.

Analogy: an ancient system of symbolism

Symbolism is a form of classification. There are two basic ways in which things can be classified – hierarchically and analogically. The rational faculty, the left hemisphere of the brain, typically works by ordering things hierarchically. We can see this clearly in the way an army is organised. Power flows from the top down; each rank has its own place in the scheme. Apart from the field marshal and the private every other rank has levels both above and below it. The right hemisphere of the brain, the faculty of imagination, orders things by analogy. Analogy is not simply a vague way of referring to things – like the rational mind it has its own rules.

The various different cultures of the world, both past and present, follow the same basic rules of analogical classification. But each has its own version of the system, which, whilst working on the same basic principles, is different to that of other cultures. Analogical classi-fication is the underlying system which gives shape and structure to the workings of the imagination. Today, we tend to believe that we can imagine whatever we want. But traditional societies show that a more holistic process may be involved, where those belonging to the same culture share a common language of the imagination, a collective consciousness, a group mind. The collective symbols of the group mind are communicated to the individual members of that culture. The group mind is contacted by using the analogical and symbolic language of the culture. If this symbolic language is understood then the individual can share in the workings of the group mind. The symbolic and analogical language of the northern European mind is intimately bound up with the runes. The runes were the central symbolic code of this pagan past. Their role in northern European pagan culture was similar to that of the *I-Ching* of ancient China.

Joseph Needham, the world-renowned historian of Chinese science, had this to say about the use of analogical classification: 'This intuitive-associative system has its own causality and its own logic. It is not . . . primitive superstition, but a characteristic thought form of its own . . . the symbolic correlation system was exactly what the magicians needed for carrying on their operations.' [2]

Fundamental to each of these cultural codes is a mystical numerology in which certain numbers take on special significance, such as the numbers nine, two and one as we have already seen in the Norse myths. There are also divisions into symbolic zones of time and space usually combined with a mythical and symbolic geography, such as the nine worlds of Yggdrasill and the tripartite scheme of Dumézil where the various gods, spirits and other supernatural beings are placed within these basic structures. Sensory information is also a key part of such systems with, for example, colours, sounds, smells and tastes all classified according to the rules of the particular cultural scheme.

Beginning with the system of the ancient Chinese tradition, we find that everything unfolds from the underlying principle Tao. From this comes the doctrine of Yin–Yang, the two principles that pervade the cosmos. Symbolically the Yin and the Yang provide the labels for the two fundamental categories of the system. One of the most obvious divisions in human life is that between male and female, and from this example of an apparent oppositional relationship one can see how a system of these relationships can be constructed.[3] A few of the symbolic correspondences are given below but in theory the list of things that could be added to each row is endless.

YIN	black	female	night	moon	dark	north	weak
YANG	white	male	day	sun	light	south	strong

Elaborating on the comparison made earlier with the two worlds of Norse mythology in Chapter 2, we can extend the analogy. Niflheim, the dark world, the icy realm in the far north of the land, would correspond to the Yin category, whereas its opposite, Muspellzheimr, the fiery realm of the far south, would correspond with Yang.[4]

Techniques of destiny

A further and more complex numerological and symbolic system of correspondences is to be found in the *I-Ching*, or Book of Changes, which has become widely known as a means of fortune-telling in the Western world. It is the most complex and sophisticated example of what the Chinese call the 'techniques of destiny' – systems of divination similar in function to the runes. The basics of the *I-Ching*

Figure 2: I-Ching diagram

system are as follows. Two types of lines make up the basic building blocks of the system and correspond to the Yin–Yang doctrine. Unbroken lines (——) are Yang lines, broken lines (— —) are yin lines. By using all the various combinations and permutations of these two types of line the eight trigrams (symbols made up of three lines) are formed (see Figure 2).

These in turn are combined to form the sixty-four hexagrams (symbols made up of six lines) used in divination. Each of the hexagrams in the book is accompanied by detailed information on its individual meaning. Both the trigrams and the hexagrams are also part of an extremely complicated system of correspondences.[5]

The runes: a key to the northern mind

As we have pointed out the northern European pagan equivalent of the *I-Ching* of China are the runes. With their own system of correspondences, associations with magic and religion, and use in divination, the runes were the most important symbolic system used by Norse sages to explain the worlds within and around them. The runes provide us with a psychic map to the pagan landscape of the collective northern psyche with each rune marking a particular aspect of this group mind.

The myth of Odin's pagan resurrection is the archetypal image concerning the origin of the runes. Odin voluntarily sacrifices 'himself to himself', undergoing an ordeal which parallels many spiritual practices all over the world. Through a stringent fast – no food or water for nine nights – he achieves his goal: acquiring the wisdom of the runes and their use. His ordeal also bears striking similarities to initiatory practices of shamanic traditions – hanging from a tree, wounding himself with a spear – practices involving the endurance of pain and suffering.

That they appear to him at the culmination of his ordeal shows that in northern myth the runes are the most important set of symbols and that they embody the wisdom of Odin. But before we explore the mythology, magic and mysticism that surround the runes as they are used in the Norse pagan system it is necessary to look at the origin of these enigmatic symbols.

The runes first emerged as an alphabet in the first or second century AD. One theory suggests that they originated in Denmark.[6] But wherever the first runes were carved most researchers believe that the actual idea of using an alphabet was not a Germanic invention but was taken from a more southerly script. Researchers indicate a possible northern Italian origin for the runes and the Greek and Latin alphabets have also been suggested as sources. As our word alphabet is made up of the first two letters of the Greek alphabet (alpha, beta) so the name of the runic alphabet (there are actually a number of runic alphabets as described below) was constructed out of the first six letters f, u, th, a, r, k.

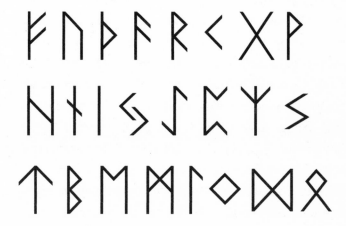

Figure 3: The Elder Futhark

The oldest runic alphabet, known as the Elder Futhark (or Common Germanic Futhark), has twenty-four letters (see Figure 3) divided into three groups known as *aettir* (*aett* is an Old Norse word meaning family and refers to a group of eight; the *aettir* can thus be described as three families or groups within the futhark). Scholars have suggested that number mysticism may have been involved in this dividing up of the futhark with the numbers three and eight having a special significance.

In Viking age Scandinavia (c.AD 800–1100) the runic alphabet was reduced to sixteen letters. This is known as the Younger Futhark and exists in two main forms. The first, and probably the older, is the Danish Futhark while the second is known as the Swedish–Norwegian Futhark. These runic alphabets share the same letters in the same order, the only real difference being that the latter represents some letters in a shorthand form. Unlike the Vikings, the Anglo-Saxon settlers of Britain and their cousins in Frisia (Friesland in the northern Netherlands) did not reduce the number of runes but increased them. This probably happened even before the Anglo-Saxons reached Britain in the fifth century, for there are fifth-century examples of runes in Frisia which are unknown in the Elder Futhark. There are a number of versions of this Anglo-Frisian Futhorc (the use of the alternative spelling reflects linguistic differences) which have as many as thirty-three letters and as few as twenty-seven.

The angular shape of runes is largely the result of the kind of materials they were carved into, especially wood, straight rather than curved lines being much easier to carve. Often runes were coloured red, sometimes using blood, partly to make them more visible but also for magical reasons. They were used for both practical communication – for example, to denote ownership over some object or other and for spiritual and magical purposes. This dual usage reflects the dual origin of the futhark. The practical idea of using runes as a script was, as has been noted, due to outside influences from the south. On the other hand the magical and religious significance of the runes:

had its origin in the pre-runic pictures and pictorial symbols carved into the rocks and stones of ancient Teutonic lands and [was] closely linked with the religious beliefs and ritual practices of pagan Germanic antiquity. The symbolism of these primitive designs attached itself to alphabetical characters derived from quite another source, certain formal affinities facilitating the fusion. It was in this way that the runic 'alphabet' came to be primarily an instrument of magic and the storehouse of pagan Germanic rite and religion.[7]

The rock carvings of both Bronze Age and Iron Age Scandinavia depict numerous motifs such as circles, spirals, swastikas and other forms of cross, along with a number of symbols which bear more than a passing resemblance to the runes of later times (see Figure 4). Although we do not know exactly what these images mean it does seem clear that they provide the symbolic background to the magical use of runes.

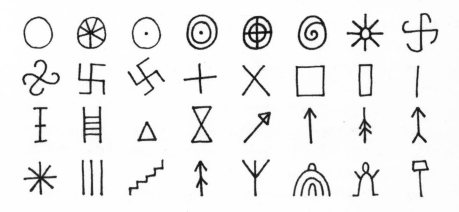

Figure 4: Symbols used in prehistoric Scandinavian rock art

The magical use of runes, although widely practised, was no simple matter. In *Egil's Saga*, one of the best-known stories in Norse literature, the main character Egil comes across a bedridden young woman. He asks her family what is wrong with her and discovers that a local farmer's son, wishing to make her better, has written runes on a whale bone and placed this amulet in her bed. Egil removes the amulet from the bed and inspects the inscription written on it. Having read the runes he scrapes them off the whale bone and then burns it. He orders that her bedclothes be thrown away and then makes up a poem:

> None should write runes
> Who can't read what he carves:
> A mystery mistaken
> Can bring men to misery.
> I saw cut on the curved bone
> Ten secret characters,
> These gave the young girl
> Her grinding pain.[8]

Egil then carves his own runes and places them under the girl's pillow after which she soon recovers.

There is considerable evidence to suggest that runes were widely used as a means of divination. In the tenth chapter of his *Germania* the Roman historian Tacitus describes how the ancient Germans practised divination by using strips of wood marked with different signs. These were thrown onto a white cloth and the diviner – who could be either a priest or the head of a family – would then look to the sky, say a prayer and pick out three strips, one after the other. On looking at them, the diviner would learn the answer to his question.[9] It seems fairly safe to assume that the signs on the strips of wood were probably runes.

The word rune refers not only to the letters themselves but also means mystery and secret. The private meetings of Anglo-Saxon chieftains with their counsellors were also called runes. The Old English word *rūn* means mystery, secrecy and hidden knowledge. A number of other words also reveal such meanings, as Stephen Pollington, an expert on both Old English and runes, has shown by giving both literal and normal translations of such words. *Rūnwita,* usually translated as counsellor or adviser, has the literal meaning rune-knower; *rūnian,* normally rendered as 'to whisper' or 'to tell secrets' is literally 'to rune'; *rūncofa,* meaning chamber of secrets or innermost thoughts, literally means rune chest.[10] The modern German word *raunen* means mystery, secret and whisper, thus preserving the occult connotations of the runes.

Much of a culture is embodied in its language and runes are embedded in Old English and other early Germanic vocabularies. The runes themselves were, before being replaced by the Latin alphabet, the written forms this language took. The patterns made by the runes are part of our cultural code, embedded in the languages of our past and cemented in the pagan strata of our collective minds. For it was from Odin that 'the secrets of runic wisdom passed to men and with them the firm belief in the magic efficacy of the complete futhark and its separate runes'.[11] In a more earthly sense, there were others whose task it was to transmit the wisdom of the runes. One early runic inscription carved onto a spearhead has been translated as, 'I belong to the Heruli.' The Heruli were a Germanic tribe whose name lived on after they faded from history; a number of inscriptions point to them being specialists in the knowledge and wisdom of the runes. This led to their tribal name being transformed into a name for a pagan priest or wise man skilled in the way of the runes. Another runic inscription on the Lindholm amulet from Sweden translates as, 'I am a Herulian, I am called the cunning one.'[12]

We will return in detail to the subject of the runes in Chapter 23, where we will look at each individual rune and its correspondences as well as examine the ways runes have been understood and made use of by pagans in the modern era. One such modern application has been the development of the shapes of the various runes into physical postures, which may be described as a northern European version of the yoga practices of India. But is there any evidence suggesting that such practices existed in the pre-Christian, pagan era?

Yoga in prehistoric and pagan Europe?

It is a historical fact that the Vikings travelled at least as far east as Baghdad on their numerous trading expeditions and some have speculated they may have gone further – to India or even China – although there is no evidence for any such extended journeys to the east. Yet even before the dawn of the Viking era some knowledge of the east, however vague, is suggested by the discovery of a small statuette of the Buddha unearthed at Helgö not far from Stockholm.[13] Its presence probably signifies little more than an interest in exotic curios and should neither be taken as evidence of any real understanding of Buddhism nor proof that its Scandinavian owner collected it directly from its cultural source; it is more likely to have been traded through a number of middlemen.

Whilst we may dismiss the Helgö Buddha as little more than a curiosity there are intriguing examples of northern art not so easily explained away. The most important of these was found among the numerous treasures unearthed by Norwegian archaeologists excavating the remains of one of the most spectacular Viking vessels ever found – the Oseberg ship, which belonged to a Viking 'queen'. Found in Oslo Fjord in 1903, the ship was built in AD 820 and in AD 834 it was buried along with its owner and her lavish personal property.[14] Among the objects found in the burial was the so-called Buddha pail, a finely wrought bucket adorned with two strange identical ornamental attachments. These are small figures which show a Buddha-like figure meditating in the lotus position (see back cover). Significantly, the legs of the figure are not simply crossed but drawn up into the full yoga position. The chest of each figure is decorated with an enamel panel with four *runehakekor*s (rune swastikas) separated by an equilateral cross. It is interesting to note that *svastikasana* is the name given in India to a particular yoga posture almost identical to the one depicted on the Oseberg artefact.

Rejecting any direct connection with the east, archaeologists once thought the object might have been made in Britain or Ireland.

However, the discovery of a similar figure from Myklebostad in Norway indicates that it is almost certainly of local origin. This other figure, whilst standing rather than adopting a yogic posture, has a very similar chest panel displaying *runehakekor*s. If these objects are Norwegian in origin – and all the indications are that they are – and if we reject the possibility of such an early northern European knowledge of Indian yoga then how are we to explain them? The answer appears to lie in the practices of *útiseta* (literally sitting out) and *útilega* (lying out) recorded in Old Norse literature, which may be described as techniques used in a kind of meditation practised in the northern pagan world. According to the sources the practitioner would typically go to a 'place of power' such as an ancestral burial mound and go into a state of trance which would result in visions or other spiritual insights. Could the Buddha-like figure from the Oseberg burial show someone practising *útiseta*?

Whilst the Oseberg 'Buddha' figure is the most dramatic example of its kind there are a number of other archaeological finds which indicate that some kind of yoga may have been practised in pre-historic Europe independently of any Indian influence. One of the most famous of all Iron Age archaeological treasures is the Gundestrup cauldron, which was found in a Danish bog. This vessel, made in either the first or second century BC, is richly decorated with various scenes, some drawn from ancient Celtic mythology, but details of its workmanship show that it was probably fashioned by a Thracian craftsman from the Balkans. One of the decorative panels on the cauldron shows the god Cernunnos sitting cross-legged, his head adorned with antlers. In one hand he holds a torque (a kind of neck ornament worn by Celtic warriors) and with the other he grasps a ram-headed snake firmly by its neck.[15]

The Hindu tradition describes a spiritual energy which exists within the body. It is known as the *kundalini* and is represented either as a snake or a goddess or sometimes both, in the form of a she-serpent. The kundalini is said to lie dormant, coiled like a serpent at the base of the spine. In most people it never really awakes, but once aroused by the spiritual exercises of the yogi it travels up the spine through the various *chakras* (a series of mystical centres in the body), creating a mystical heat or fire in its wake. On reaching the seventh and highest centre, the *kundalini* has attained its final destination after its journey through the other six.[16] We may speculate that the grasping of the snake by Cernunnos symbolises his mastery of this inner source of energy.

Other enigmatic artefacts have been found amongst the relics of the ancient Celtic civilisation. A bronze plaque discovered in southern Poland and dating from the Late La Tène culture of the last centuries BC shows a human figure in an unusual posture. One arm is bent at the elbow with the forearm and hand raised up whilst the other arm, also bent at the elbow, points down to the earth. Above the head of the figure is a row of what appear to be snakes and below the feet is another creature, perhaps a frog. This posture may symbolise the union or correspondence between the sky above and the earth below.[17]

There are even earlier signs of a prehistoric European yoga, some dating back to the Neolithic period or New Stone Age. A number of sculptures of a snake goddess were found in Crete and nearby islands of the Aegean from the period 6000–5500 BC, many representing her sitting in a yoga-like posture. One of these is a clay figurine which shows the snake goddess in a yogic posture with human facial features and snake-like legs.[18.]

According to the archaeologist Marija Gimbutas, 'a vertically winding snake symbolized ascending life force, viewed as a column of life rising from caves and tombs, and was an interchangeable symbol with the tree of life and spinal cord'.[19] If Gimbutas is right, what we have here is a vestige of an archaic kind of analogical classification, the correspondences in question being: tree of life/plant world; snake/ animal world; spine/human body.

The snake symbol also appears around the same time in the

Neolithic art of Anatolia (modern Turkey). One figurine excavated there shows a snake-headed goddess whose back is adorned with serpentine lines painted in red, symbolising, according to Gimbutas, the pulsating life energy (*kundalini*) surging through her divine body. Again there are clear parallels with the Hindu tradition of the *kundalini*, which is described as a snake or a goddess or both – in other words a snake goddess.

Along with these artefacts, which seem to show the *asanas* or ritualistic body postures of a Neolithic snake goddess, is evidence from an actual Stone Age body – that of Ötzi the Iceman, whose 5,300-year-old corpse was found almost perfectly preserved in the Alps in 1991. Study of the medicinal tattoos found on Ötzi's body reveals that a sophisticated kind of acupuncture was in use in central Europe during this remote time.[20] This is particularly remarkable as Ötzi predates the known origins of acupuncture in China, showing that it was an independent system developed without eastern influence. In the Chinese tradition acupuncture is part of a wider system of medicine and spiritual practices which includes martial arts and t'ai chi, and it seems likely that the Stone Age acupuncture of Europe was also part of a wider system that probably included specific postures and exercises.

The seeress of the north

So it appears that the evidence for a European form of yoga may be related to a pre-Indo-European culture dominated by the feminine principle in the form of Gimbutas' primal goddess. We have seen how the most primal layer of pagan mythology is the Web of Wyrd woven by three female goddesses, which, when deified, comes closest to a single all-powerful deity, a female version of the Christian God. We have already seen from the ideas of Dumézil that Indo-European mythologies (including that of the northern Europeans) can be understood as a tripartite scheme. However the evidence suggests that way back in prehistory before the coming of the Indo-Europeans to the north there was an earlier religious system based on belief in a powerful feminine deity. This primal tradition was preserved in the later visionary practices of women in the northern pagan world.

The myths and sagas, as well as the archaeological material, provide us with evidence of female magical practitioners utilising trance and clairvoyance as a means of divination. There were a number of practical techniques which they used to achieve this. Today the crystal ball is associated with New Age bookshops and fairgrounds where those who claim to see into the future ply their trade often to people as superstitious as any medieval peasant. Yet the use of crystals, though much debased in our modern consumer society, has played an extremely important role in human affairs since prehistory. Crystal-gazing is just one method of scrying, a means of fixing the gaze and so stilling the mind in order to make it receptive to the seeing of visions. Although scrying in its fairground setting should not be taking seriously, those who laugh the whole subject out of court are mistaken.[21]

In the context of northern Europe, archaeology has revealed that as early as the fifth century AD Anglo-Saxon women as far afield as Kent and the Rhineland wore crystal balls suspended from their waist by cords.[22] It is likely that these Anglo-Saxon wise women used their crystals for scrying, and according to Thomas Karlsson the name of the Hagal rune (usually associated with hail and hailstones) originally meant stone, crystal or crystal-stone.[23] In many ancient cultures the sky was believed to be made of stone or crystal, thus quartz and other stones were valued by shamans and magicians because they were believed to be of heavenly origin.[24] Many traditions believed the various crystalline stones to be solidified light and associated them with enlightenment and seeing in the sense of scrying – inner sight or insight.[25]

The wise women of the Anglo-Saxon world who used both crystals and other means of entering trance were the foremothers of the witches of later European history, who became outcasts in a male-dominated world. But before showing the links between these pagan visionaries and the witches we shall explore the traditions of female pagan magic which continued in Scandinavia after the Anglo-Saxon world had succumbed to Christianity.

Seidr is the Old Norse term for the practice of entering a trance to gain knowledge and visions. It was another way in which pagan people made contact with the inner world that today we may choose to call the unconscious. *Völva* is the Old Norse word for a seeress or a prophetess but it literally means wand-bearer, and it was she who practised *seidr*. The wand or staff was an essential part of her ritual equipment. Although the *völva* might make house visits to give predictions and personal consultations this was not her central role in pagan society; she conducted ceremonies to which the gathered members of the community were invited. She would sit on a raised seat or platform where she entered a trance state. Sometimes such performances would be accompanied by singing or chanting. After her visions were over she would take questions on the future of the community and then respond to individual enquiries.

In *seidr* we can see the female practice of divinatory trance, which can be both compared and contrasted with the runic divination more typically associated with men. Both seek to understand the workings of the Web of Wyrd but they do so in very different ways. The runes, as part of the *galdr* system of male magic, are a systematic code through which the Web and its meanings can be divined. Trance, as part of the *seidr* practices of female magic, is a more direct and intuitive path to understanding of the Web, one that men typically find difficult to enter.

The visionary powers of the seeress play a very important part in the Eddas. The opening poem of the poetic Edda, *Völuspá* (meaning prophecy of the seeress), takes the form of a *seidr* ceremony in which she answers questions: 'Yet it may be noted that the *völva* is not shown as revealing the will of the gods . . . or speaking as their mouth-piece, as an oracle, it is the gods themselves, as well as men, who wait upon her, and seek to know what is hidden from them by a greater power still, that of Fate.'[26] The visionary myths contained in *Völuspá* tell of both the beginning of the world and its destruction at the Ragnarok and hint at what comes after.

The staff which was part of the ritual equipment used in *seidr* has sexual connotations and it has been suggested by the American academic Jenny Jochens that such trance-inducing ceremonies might have involved the woman using the staff as a penis substitute to reach orgasm.[27] There is evidence to support such an idea from a number of sources including phallic artefacts, Old Norse stories about phalluses as fertility symbols and suggestions regarding the Viking use of dildos detailed by the British archaeologist Neil Price.[28]

An archaeological discovery which seems to link drug plant use in the pagan north with the later witch cult of Christian times (in which drug use was common) is the burial of a wise woman dating from the tenth century at the Viking fort at Fyrkat in Jutland, Denmark. During the excavations at the fort, which took place in the 1950s, archaeologists made a number of unusual discoveries, including a small silver pendant in the form of a chair. This may be a clue that she was a seeress, for the *völva* would, as has already been noted, perform her trance either on a special platform or a chair. Also in the grave were hundreds of henbane seeds. Henbane is a powerful hallucinogenic and narcotic drug which was used by the witches of later times. Both henbane and belladonna (deadly nightshade) contain three psychoactive tropane alkaloids – hyoscyamine, atropine and scopolamine. Belladonna is a plant of many names – the devil's herb, sorcerer's cherry, witch's berry, among others. Such epithets give us a clear picture of the sinister reputation and uses of the plant. *Dwale,* another English name for the plant, is derived from an Old Norse term for sleep, torpor or trance. To the Germanic tribes it was *walkerbeere,* the berry of the Valkyries. Valkyries were female spirits who delivered warriors slain in battle to the heavenly castle of Valhalla, where they would feast with Odin. The berries may, perhaps, have contributed to the legendary battle frenzy of the Norse warriors known as Beserks.

Útiseta: European meditation?

The intuitive urge that modern witches and neo-pagans have to make pilgrimages to Stonehenge, Avebury, the Extersteine and other prehistoric monuments is often looked at askance by archaeologists and others who doubt the authenticity of such impulses. But in identifying with the ancient builders of these monuments such pilgrims are following in a continuous tradition which goes back itself to prehistory. Long before the neo-Druids of the eighteenth and nineteenth centuries others were drawn to these ancient places of power.

Even before the Christian era the pagan Anglo-Saxons would often place their settlements and cemeteries on the site of Neolithic mounds and other monuments – for example, at West Heslerton in Yorkshire and Lakenheath in Suffolk. The Hill of Tara, seat of the high kings of Ireland, was a place of power at least as far back as 3500 BC. The evocatively named Mound of the Hostages – the name given to it by the poets of early medieval Ireland – is actually a Neolithic passage tomb built 5000 years ago. Irish myth describes it, aptly, as a gateway to the underworld. Numerous other examples could be given but these will suffice. What we see from the time of the Celts and Anglo-Saxons to the neo-pagans of today is a continuous re-mythologising of the monuments of earlier cultures. These ancient places of power remain in use today.

In the northern world there are many references to kings and seers practising a form of *útiseta* – 'sitting out' on burial mounds to communicate with the dead.[29] In one story a shepherd named Hallbjörn seeks poetic inspiration by sleeping on the burial mound of a renowned poet. Whilst asleep he dreams that the poet comes out of the mound and teaches him how to compose his verses.[30] This association with ghostly presences at the site of pagan burial mounds has continued into our own era. Sutton Hoo in Suffolk is a pagan burial ground of Anglo-Saxon kings and princes. In the 1930s stories of a spectral horseman and ghostly figures wandering through the mounds at night were rife.[31] Soon after these ghostly visions, excavations began at Mound One, resulting in the dramatic discovery of a rich ship burial.

Ships not only played a fundamental role in the practical life of both Anglo-Saxons and Vikings but also a symbolic one. Boat and ship burials were a common feature of both cultures.[32] This is a tradition which can be traced back at least as far as the Bronze Age in northern Europe.[33] In parts of Sweden, especially Gotland, there are monuments which consist of groupings of stones in the shape of a ship. About 2000 have survived to this day and many are found in groups, sometimes even in rows of four or five. They are the size of real boats and are typically between 4.5 and 9 metres in length with a ratio of length to width of three or four to one. Originally many would have been covered by barrows, and many contain evidence that they were burial sites – usually cremations. Others, clearly not burial sites, seem to have had another symbolic purpose for their builders.[34]

The stone ships belong to an era before the Vikings and some are thought to date back to the Bronze Age. Thomas Karlsson, a historian of religion and a practising rune magician, has made the interesting observation that these monuments can be seen to have a crystalline form – perhaps connecting them with crystal-gazing.[35] Karlsson believes that the stone ships may have been used for *útiseta* – meditating and contacting ancestors or spirits – and, given the well-documented examples given above, this is totally plausible.[36]

A seventeenth-century report from Iceland specifically singles out the practice of *útiseta* as an illegal activity which promotes heathenism by trying to wake up trolls.[37] Clearly by this time, and no doubt much earlier, the practice had been culturally denigrated and translated into the language of Christian demonology. The same thing had also occurred with the whole system of female pagan magic, which had been transformed into the 'evil' practices of witchcraft.

Chapter 4

Heathen Altars

We earnestly forbid any sort of heathenism. Heathenism it is when someone venerates an image of the devil, that is when someone worships heathen gods and the sun or moon, fire or water, springs or stones or any kind of tree, or loves witchcraft, or commits harmful acts in any fashion, either in a sacrifice or in divination, or takes any part in such impropriety . . .

Laws of Cnut (translated by Bill Griffiths)[1]

Having outlined the fundamental beliefs and practices of the pagan era, it is now necessary to explore the survival of these traditions after the arrival of Christianity. Far from being completely obliterated they gradually went underground in the new era. The lore and legends of the pagan myths were transformed into folk and fairy tales, and integrated into everyday life (as in the names for days of the week), surviving in oral form amongst the populace right to the present day. And they survived in literal ways as well, some of the old gods still being worshipped and the old ways still being practised throughout the centuries. It is amongst the witches and occultists of the Christian era that we are able to discern traces of the pagan legacy.

Under the Christian axe

The conversion of the Germanic peoples was neither easy nor peaceful. The turning point – at least as far as the continental tribes were concerned – occurred in the year AD 772 when the Frankish Emperor Charlemagne ordered the wholesale massacre of some 30,000 Saxons who refused to convert. The victory of the new faith over the old was made even more emphatic when the Irminsul, the sacred pole of the pagan Saxons (the symbolic equivalent of the Scandinavian world tree Yggdrasill), was cut down at Charlemagne's command. As the archaeologist Marija Gimbutas has said, this act of desecration would have had the same impact as the demolishing of St Peter's would have for Catholics.

The conversion of the Germanic tribes was achieved by trying to explain the Gospel in terms that the pagans could understand. This is made clear in an Old Saxon manuscript dating from around 830. This text, known as the *Heliand* (Saviour), was the first translation of the Gospel for the Saxon world. The figure of Jesus is portrayed with many of the features of the god Odin. He is a magician, a master of the runes and the chieftain of a band of twelve warriors (counterparts of the twelve disciples). Instead of the two ravens named Huginn and Muninn that perch on the shoulders of Odin (representing thought and memory) the new saviour has the dove, representing the Holy Spirit, in their place.[2]

Once conversion had been successfully achieved this temporary synthesis of the old pagan god and Jesus faded away. During the long era in which Christianity was dominant, Odin's previous pre-eminence in the pagan pantheon made him a prime target for the Church's propaganda. He became transformed into the devil of Christian belief. Sorcery in some form or another continued to be practised surreptitiously throughout the Christian era, usually in the form of ritual magic or witchcraft, and Odin, as the master magician of the pagan tradition, was sometimes implicated in such practices. Usually, but not always, ritual magic was performed by men and witchcraft by women.

Broomsticks and flying ointments

Amongst the European witches of the Christian era the most popular means of entering altered states of consciousness was to mix a host of psychoactive plants together to make an hallucinogenic paste known as flying ointment. Henbane and belladonna were key ingredients in these ointments. These pastes when smeared on the body of the witch caused her to experience wild hallucinations and a narcotic trance.

The anthropologist and neo-shaman Michael Harner has pointed out that the psychoactive effects of the ointment would have been intensified if the ointment were introduced through the sensitive vaginal membranes by means of an anointed staff or broomstick. Not only does this help to explain how the ointment worked on a chemical level but also explains the frequent sexual fantasies of the sabbats – ritual gatherings of witches and 'demons'. Another common experience of the witches, at least according to their accounts before their inquisitors, was that when they had sexual intercourse with the devil his penis was painfully cold. This peculiar fact, incidentally, was one that Sigmund Freud, much to his annoyance, could never decode. However, it may refer to the insertion of the broom accompanied by rapid changes in body temperature caused by the initial effects of the drugs.

There do not seem to be any accounts of accidental self-poisoning by witches using these ointments, which is quite remarkable bearing in mind the great number of potentially toxic plant extracts contained in them. This suggests that the preparation of the ointments must have been very exact, particularly as both henbane and belladonna can be lethal in too high a dose.[3] What is clear from a number of accounts and reported cases is that the women who were using these drugs went into powerful trance states in which they (or at least their spirit bodies) flew to sabbats.[4]

There are a number of features which link the visionaries of Viking times with the later witches of Christian Europe. Firstly, and most obviously, those who practised *seidr* were almost all women and most witches were also female. Secondly, both the *seidr* ceremony and the witches' flying to the sabbat (where she meets demons and participates in imaginary orgies) involve trance states. In both cases these trances often have a strong sexual element. Thirdly, the staff of the Norse seeress has its counterpart in the broomstick of the witch. There is an interesting twelfth-century mural of the Norse goddess Frigg in Schleswig cathedral in northern Germany. She is shown astride a broomstick in the manner of a witch. Both the staff and the broomstick may have been used as phallic substitutes during magical practices. Lastly, henbane was used by both seeresses and witches and its psychoactive properties induce trance states. It is hard to believe that all these parallels are simple coincidences.

Hallucinogenic drugs and sexual ecstasy were not the only means of entering trance states; other techniques were also used either separately or in conjunction with these. There are a number of features of ancient spells designed to bring about trance. One of these is repetition, as important to the seeress as repetitive drum beats are in bringing about shamanic trance. For it is equally important to the seeress to repeat the same words or the same or similar phrases over and over again. This is the power of suggestion at work or what we may call auto-hypnosis. Many people today when they are 'psyching themselves up' for some task will repeat their own private mantras. The text of any spell can be compared to the script of a play. However potent or profound the written words may be, it is up to the actress to bring them to life by the emotional power of her performance. Like-wise, the seeress must make her spell reach a similar emotional pitch; she must enter into an altered state of consciousness to attempt to realise her, or her client's, goal.

We can also discern a possible survival of pagan meditation and *útiseta* in the same period. In Dorset in the year 1566, during the course of the examination of a man named John Walsh, it came to light that he had learnt witchcraft from 'iii kindes of Feries, white, greene, and black'. He was said to have spoken with them 'upon hyls, where as there is great heapes of earth, as namely in Dorsetshire'. We may deduce that the 'great heapes of earth' are the prehistoric barrows that still survive in great numbers on the hills and heaths of this county. In other cases the local people shunned these places of power. Robert Kirk in his *The Secret Commonwealth of Elves, Fauns and Fairies* wrote: 'there be many Places called Fairie-hills, which the Mountain People think impious and dangerous to peel or discover, by taking Earth or Wood from them: superstitiously believing the Souls of their Predicessors to dwell there'. The folklore of France also reveals the close association in popular belief between menhirs, dolmens and the witches' sabbat, with monuments named the Sabbat Stone and the Witches' Kitchen.[5]

The *Galdrabók* and the wizards of Iceland

As we have seen so far, vestiges of the old ways lived on in the secretive practices of the witches, practices dominated by women in most parts of Europe. But the survival of paganism in Iceland is quite different and it illustrates a further link with the pagan past. In Iceland the victims of witch hunts were predominantly men and the evidence for their practices shows them to be clearly distinct from those of their female counterparts in the rest of Europe.

The end of the old northern pagan tradition took place in the year 1000 when Iceland officially became a Christian country. It was the last of the Germanic countries to take up the new faith. Out of the 120 recorded witch trials only ten involved women and of the twenty-two witches who were burned to death only one was a woman.[6] The first witch burning in Iceland took place in 1625. The man in question was executed when a page of runes was discovered in his house. By this time runes were widely associated with the workings of the devil.[7]

The discovery of magical manuscripts (known as grimoires) reveals that some traces of paganism persisted among the sorcerers of Iceland. Grimoires are basically practical manuals for magicians or sorcerers. The word grimoire is derived from grammar so such

manuscripts and books may be described as grammars of sorcery –
containing the structures of the language of magic. The earliest such
books derive from the Jewish tradition and are thus structured on
the Hebrew language, particularly on its mystical expression, the
Kabbalah. Typically a grimoire contains tables giving the symbolic
connections between angels, demons, planets, colours, numbers and
so on; these provide the theory behind the practice. The actual
practices of ritual magic given in the grimoires include conjurations
and evocations of both good and evil spirits, spells to locate treasure,
to gain knowledge of the identity of a thief, to work love magic and
so on.

Many of the later grimoires of Christian Europe contain elements
of folk belief preserved alongside material derived from the Kabbalah.
It is also often the case that these later grimoires are less
systematically organised, having lost much of the structure of the
earlier works. In Iceland, which has traditionally had a higher level of
literacy than most other European countries, the links between folk
magic and the magic of the learned members of society seem to have
been stronger. Thus the Icelandic grimoire known as the *Galdrabók*
('magic book') contains more material of pagan origin than perhaps
any other work of this peculiar literary genre. That Iceland was the last
country in the Germanic-speaking world to be converted to
Christianity was also a major factor in the presence of pagan elements
within its pages.

The *Galdrabók,* like most grimoires, is a compilation of spells,
sigils and conjurations drawn from a number of different sources. The
contents of this particular magical book were put together between
about 1550 and 1680. What is clear is that the book passed through
the hands of four different people, each of whom wrote his own spells
after those of his predecessor(s). There are forty-seven spells in all and
the name of Odin appears in six of them, that of Thor in three.[8] It
would probably be wrong to think of references to Odin, Thor and
other pagan deities in the Christian period as evidence of the intact

survival of the heathen faith. The pagan gods were never fully forgotten but banished to the fringes of society; they had become outlaws in their own culture.

Forms of rune magic appear to have survived also and played a role in the traditional form of Icelandic wrestling known as *glíma*. In 1664 a *Galdrabók* was found in the possession of a student and its contents were subsequently described in detail by Bishop Brynjúlfur Sveinsson. Among the spells and magical sigils contained in the book were four signs to be used in wrestling.[9] One of them was known as *ginfaxi* (see Figure 5) and was hidden in the wrestler's shoe.[10]

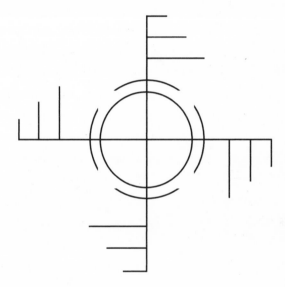

Figure 5: The *ginfaxi* sigil

While *glíma* wrestlers were still using sigils incorporating runes, it is unclear whether they were familiar with runes themselves. Whilst Icelandic traditions of sorcery show that fragments of the old pagan faith persisted, the first historical traces of a neo-pagan revival are to be found in Scandinavia. For although the use of runes died out in most of the Germanic world it never did entirely in Scandinavia. On the large island of Gotland in the Baltic Sea runes were still carved on gravestones as late as the sixteenth century, while in certain districts of Sweden the runic script survived among the people almost to the present day.[11]

We have seen a continuous thread of northern European paganism, extending from prehistory all the way into relatively recent times, and although some beliefs and practices have been forgotten and the survivals driven underground, Europeans have never completely forgotten the old gods or the old ways. We have seen clear continuities between the pagan female magic of *seidr* and the later practices of witchcraft. Furthermore, the largely male rune magic of pagan times is echoed by the practices of later magicians who used grimoires and sigils. Iceland was an important repository of pagan lore and knowledge, a source that continues down to the present day. As Iceland had been the last 'official' bastion of old Germanic paganism so it also became a herald of its official modern revival when, in May 1973, the Asatruamenn, a neo-pagan movement founded by its chief priest Sveinbjörn Beinteinsson, was given government recognition as a religious organisation.[12]

Chapter 5

Hyperborea: Lost Continent of the European Imagination

Neither by ship nor on foot could you find the marvellous road to the meeting-place of the Hyperboreans.

Pindar, *Pythian Odes*

It seems to me that there has been another spiritual stream in the West, parallel to Christianity, that I call the 'Polar Tradition'.

Joscelyn Godwin, *Arktos: The Polar Myth*[1]

Legends of lost continents peopled by advanced races of beings had long been a theme of the European imagination when J.R.R. Tolkien created his intricate fantasy world of Middle-earth. The legend of Atlantis has remained embedded in the European mind and even today is the subject of numerous speculations. The legend has been expanded with further lost continents such as Lemuria and Mu being added to this mythical geography. In creating these realms modern writers have followed an extremely ancient tradition. Its roots can be traced far back into the prehistoric period of the Indo-Europeans. Legends of a homeland in the far north are preserved in the most ancient scriptures of both India and Iran.

The ancient myth of Hyperborea

The oldest sacred texts of the Iranian tradition are known collectively as the Avesta and have many parallels to the ancient Vedas of the Indian tradition. This clearly shows that much of the mythology contained in these two sets of scriptures belongs to a common tradition which existed before the Indians and the Iranians split into two separate cultural streams in the second millennium BC. In the Iranian *Avesta* we are told of a place known as the Airyanem Vaejah – the original homeland of the Aryan Iranians. Much ink has been spilt trying to find a geographical location for this mythologised place with little agreement among the scholars. Henry Corbin, an orientalist and specialist in the spiritual traditions of Iran, has put forward his reasons for this confusion: 'Those who have attempted to determine its position on geographic maps have run into great difficulties; no convincing solution has been obtained in this way, for the first and good reason that the problem of locating it lies in the realm of visionary geography.'[2] Corbin goes further, describing it as a primordial and archetypal image. In other words, this lost northern homeland is part of the psychic map of the Indo-European peoples, existing within rather than without – it is to be found not on the map of the earth but the map of the soul.

The ancient Iranian myths tell of Yima, the greatest of mortals, who was commanded by the gods to create an enclosure within which the most spiritual beings would take refuge from a lethal winter to be released by demonic forces. When this catastrophe had finally passed those humans within the enclosure could re-enter the world outside and people it anew. This northern refuge of the Iranians is described as a fortified citadel within which houses and storerooms allow its occupants to survive through these terrible times. Corbin tells us that it has 'Luminiscent windows *which themselves secrete an inner light* within, for it is illuminated by both uncreated and created lights. Its inhabitants see the stars, moon, and sun rise and set only once a year, and that is why a year seems to them only a day.'[3] As has been mentioned, Corbin sees the citadel as a spiritual rather than an earthly location, but this passage does seem to preserve some folk memory or knowledge of the earthly realm of the far north, for at the poles there is only one day and one night per year – six months of darkness and six months of light. This is fascinating but here is not the place to pursue this line of enquiry; our present interest is to outline the mythical dimensions of this polar paradise.

Some features of this Iranian myth echo those of northern European mythology. Asgard, the home of Odin and the other members of the Aesir family of gods, is a fortified enclosure. The unusual mythical account of a lethal winter preserved by the Iranians can also be found in Norse myths. The Fimbulwinter (from the Old Norse *fimbulvetr* meaning great or terrible winter) is said to last for three years with no break in its harsh monotony. Throughout this time there are constant snowstorms and frost. It is said to herald the coming Ragnarok and in some versions of the myth even to be identical to it.

Corbin sees this lost northern homeland of the Iranians as an archetypal symbol:

> The threshold of a supernatural beyond: there are uncreated lights; a world that secretes its own light . . . a shadowless country peopled with beings of light who have reached spiritual heights inaccessible to earthly beings. They are truly beings of the beyond; where the shadow which holds the light captive ends, there the beyond begins, and the very same mystery is enciphered in the symbol of the *North*. In the same way the Hyperboreans symbolize men whose soul has reached such completeness and harmony that it is devoid of negativity and shadow.[4]

There are parallels with such legends in the Indian tradition. Hindu myth speaks of the people of the northern sun, the Uttara-kurus, who inhabit a polar paradise and whose perfection is symbolised by their being formed as twins joined together.

One of the most prominent figures in the quest for Indian independence from the British empire was Bâl Gangâdhar Tilak (1856–1920). In 1897 he was imprisoned as a result of his anti-British activities. Whilst incarcerated he was allowed to spend his time writing on a less seditious subject, thanks to the intervention of the orientalist Max Müller. The result of his literary labour was *The Arctic Home in the Vedas,* completed in 1897 and published in 1903, in which he proposed that the original homeland of the Aryans was not somewhere in central Asia, as received wisdom had it, but in the far north. He claimed that many otherwise inexplicable passages in ancient Hindu scriptures became clear once this polar homeland was accepted. For example, the mythical imagery of the Vedas speaks of 'Thirty Dawn-Sisters circling like a wheel' and the 'Dawn of Many Days' which precedes the rising of the sun – both of which reflect conditions at the poles.[5]

Greek literature abounds with references to Hyperboreans. Sometimes these passages are couched purely in mythical terms whilst others attempt to locate them in a more mundane geography. Hecataeus wrote that 'the Land of the Hyperboreans lies on the Atlantic sea, opposite the land of the Celts'. Most sources are vaguer but all agree that Hyperborea is in the far northern zone of the world, understood to be either part of continental Europe or beyond it further towards the north pole. Others tried to locate them in relation to other semi-mythical races. Some sources talk of a people called the Arimphians who were said to dwell to the south of the Riphean Mountains. These mountains were envisaged as a vast stone girdle encircling the earth. To the north of this mountainous barrier was the homeland of the Hyperboreans. This mention of a circular stone barrier echoes the citadel of the Iranian homeland.

The Greek historian Herodotus of the sixth century BC noted that his writings on the Hyperboreans were not based on eye-witness accounts of this northern civilisation since neither he nor anyone he knew (or had even heard) of had actually been to Hyperborea (*Histories*, 4.16). The name Hyperborea means 'beyond the north wind'. It is described as a fertile country with a temperate climate. The Hyperboreans are said to live in a state of perpetual bliss in their utopian country, to worship Apollo (the Greek name for the sun god) and to have built circular temples. Although it is possible to draw parallels between the Bronze Age peoples of northern Europe – which the Greeks had a vague awareness of – and the Hyperboreans it is clear that most of their accounts contain more mythic imagery than fact. The sun-worshipping Hyperboreans also present us with a close parallel to the spiritually enlightened beings of the Iranian tradition.

The archetypal symbol of the far north has many layers of meaning. Fundamental to the symbolism is the underlying idea of a vertical ascent. The Hyperboreans, the perfect beings who dwell at the pole, represent those who have attained enlightenment. The spiritual journey expressed in these mythical traditions is one of travelling up to the north, the way to enlightenment. In many archaic cosmologies the heavens are symbolised as being held up by a pole or a pillar and we find such beliefs in the Norse tradition. The Old Norse term *áss*, meaning god – hence the Aesir family of gods – also means pole.

Among the pagan Saxons the huge pole or pillar of the Irminsul was central to their religion. It symbolised the mystical centre of the world and its felling by the Christian Charlemagne was seen by them as an act of great sacrilege. As a symbol the Irminsul seems to be closely connected to Yggdrasill, the world tree of Norse myth, and probably to the veneration of poles and tall wooden idols, which can be traced back at least to the Bronze Age. All these symbols show the importance of the vertical axis in northern paganism; the Norse gods were invoked facing north. The Hyperborean myth was still current at the time of the Vikings. Even as late as the eleventh century the historian Adam of Bremen, who wrote about the pagan rites he witnessed in Sweden, repeated the myth that the most northerly people in the world were the Hyperboreans.

So in these various ancient Indo-European mythologies a northern homeland and paradise was a common feature; we can say without exaggeration, that this polar myth can be traced back to the peoples of prehistoric Europe and parts of Asia. In northern Europe it was integral to Germanic myths and thus part of the inner geography of the northern imagination. Hyperborea is indeed the lost continent of the European imagination. It was the union of this concept of the lost continent of Hyperborea along with an in-depth study of the culturally dormant runes which marked the origin of a conscious pagan revival in Europe.

The Rune Cross

The origins of the pagan revival and the resurgence of the ancient symbolism of the runes can be traced to Johannes Bureus (1568–1652), the greatest Swedish scholar of his day. His studies ranged far and wide but his central focus was on the esoteric. Alongside his mystical interests Bureus was also a fervent antiquarian with a desire to understand the ancient Swedish past. He was the first to make a systematic study of rune stones and the other monuments which adorn the Swedish countryside. The runic revival was not just an esoteric matter for the learned Bureus and his circle; it was also a much larger social project. The Reformation was a cultural reaction to the dominance of the Roman Catholic Church and in Sweden some Protestants planned to replace the Latin alphabet with runes. In 1611 Bureus published his runic ABC, designed for use in schools across Sweden.[6] He also revolutionised printing in Sweden by designing runic typefaces. He became director general of the national archives and director of the royal library and exerted a powerful intellectual and spiritual influence over his monarch Queen Christina (1626–1689), who was herself a practitioner of alchemy and an avid collector of magical manuscripts.

During his lifetime the Rosicrucian movement, a mystical and alchemical fraternity, was sweeping across Europe, radically transforming the face of Western esotericism. Bureus was also a profound student of the Kabbalah. The Kabbalah involved the mystical study of the Hebrew letters in conjunction with their symbolic and numerical significance in order to decipher the hidden meanings of the Bible and other religious and mystical texts. Bureus thought that the runes, like the Hebrew alphabet, contained esoteric knowledge. As the Kabbalah revealed the way to read the inner teachings of the Bible, so Bureus hoped that he could decipher the spiritual meanings contained within the runes.

Figure 6: Bureus' Rune Cross

The influence of both the Kabbalah and the Rosicrucians (also known as the Brotherhood of the Rosy Cross) can also be seen in the symbol that Bureus created at the centre of his magical and esoteric system – the Rune Cross.[7] The cross is made up of fifteen runes (see Figure 6). These are the first fifteen runes of the Younger Futhark, the runic alphabet used in Sweden and other parts of Scandinavia. The two arms of the Rune Cross each consist of four runes in a horizontal line – the right arm spelling out T-R-O-N (faith) and the left arm Å-F-U-L (honourable). Faith and honour are the essential requirements on the spiritual journey of ascent up the vertical axis of the cross. The eight runes of the arms of the cross are complemented by seven runes on the vertical axis. These symbolise seven symbolic steps on the spiritual path and should be viewed both as an ascending and a descending sequence. The aim of the initiate is to travel from the lowest rune, Byrghal/Berkano (B), to the highest, Thors (Th), which represents the pagan god Thor. At the centre of the cross where the horizontal axis (called the nine-rune width) and the vertical axis (the seven-rune height) intersect is the rune Haghal, which represents the god Odin. Odin is seen as the connector – linking upper and lower, left and right.

The Rune Cross is also to be viewed as a symbol of the body of Odin. The nine-rune width represents his outstretched arms, whilst the seven-rune height represents his upright body. The lowest rune Byrghal symbolises his feet and the highest, Thors, his head. The five runes in between are named the five-rune ladder and represent the spiritual rungs by which man (Byrghal) is linked to God (Thors). The five steps are linked together to make another symbol – the arrow which Bureus connects to Abaris, the Hyperborean sage of Greek myth. This arrow is also described as a *gandr* (a wand or magical staff) inscribed with runes. By modifying the rosy cross symbol of the Rosicrucian Brotherhood into the Rune Cross it is clear that Bureus was attempting to synthesise the pagan and Christian traditions. As Thomas Karlsson put it, 'Bureus equates Odin on Yggdrasill [the world tree of Norse myth] with Jesus on the cross.'[8] We may note a similar synthesis on the cover picture of the present book.

Bureus also found much inspiration in the work of the French mystic Guillaume Postel (*c*.1510–81). Postel's mythological ideas on the spread of the Hyperborean peoples were entwined with his belief that alongside the prophetic tradition of the Old Testament there was another line of prophecy. This second line was that of the Sibylline Oracles. The Sibylline Oracles is the name given to various collections of prophecies widely read in antiquity. The sibyls were seeresses whose visions were said to be divinely inspired. Among them was one named Alruna, the northern Sybil, said to have been born in 432 BC. To rediscover the tradition of Alruna, Bureus investigated the ancient monuments of his country, finding connections such as evidence of solar worship and the mystical meanings of the runes, which he sought to reconcile with biblical prophecy and the Kabbalistic traditions which derived from it.

He believed that the Swedish people had, in ancient times, descended from their northern homeland and colonised Europe, bringing their runic mysticism and writing with them. He also believed that his rediscovery of the spiritual tradition of the runes was a partial fulfilment of Rosicrucian prophecies for the transformation of European civilisation. What Bureus did was to combine the myth of Hyperborea with the inner meaning of the runes and revive the northern pagan tradition in a prophetic vision of the spiritual and cultural renewal of Europe. He never claimed to be a pagan but his revival of the northern tradition, symbolised by the Rune Cross, was the beginning of the pagan resurrection.

Part One

THE FIRST ODINIC EXPERIMENT: GERMANY

Chapter 6

The Wanderer Returns

'Wodan' in Old Germanic expresses the idea of the 'All-transcending'; in the various old idioms it appears as 'Wuodan', 'Odan', and 'Odin', signifying the power penetrating all nature which is ultimately personified as a Germanic deity. 'Od' is consequently the word to express a dynamic or force which, with a power that cannot be obstructed, quickly penetrates and courses through everything in the universe.

Baron von Reichenbach, *The Odic Force: Letters on Od and Magnetism*[1]

We have seen the survival of northern European paganism throughout the Middle Ages and beyond, driven underground and pushed to the fringes of European society, transformed into the practices of witches and sorcerers. In the work of Bureus we have seen the revival of the runes and the myth of Hyperborea. Although others continued this work it was not until the rise of romanticism in the early nineteenth century that interest in ancient Scandinavia became more firmly established in mainstream culture. By this time the brothers Grimm and other leading figures in German romanticism were also reviving interest in the Germanic past.

In October 1817 a group of young idealistic German students gathered together at Wartburg castle in the medieval town of Eisenach to celebrate a *Thing* – the name given to a pagan tribal assembly. Neither the date nor the location were arbitrarily chosen – this was the site of Martin Luther's excommunication resulting from his protest against the Catholic hierarchy and its dogma in 1517. A great bonfire was built and hymns sung to commemorate the liberation that had taken place exactly 300 years earlier. Speeches were made and it was explained to the congregation that the oak represented the German forest and its people. The oak was invoked as a powerful symbol of Germany's pagan past and identified as the cross upon which Odin had made his visionary self-sacrifice. Oaths were taken to mark allegiance to the group and to the purity of the *Volk* (people) and, foreshadowing the literary holocausts of the Nazi era, books considered 'un-German' were cast into the flames of the bonfire. Among those present was the twenty-three-year-old Karl Gustav Jung, who cherished the memory of that night as one of the best and most meaningful experiences of his life.[2] He was a Freemason and a member of another esoteric fraternity, the Illuminati, and was also the grandfather of Carl Gustav Jung.

It was not just the romantic movement and the revival of pagan ceremonies that heralded the return of Odin.[3] He was also to reappear early on in the first Odinic experiment in the laboratory of one of Germany's leading scientific researchers, who risked his career and reputation when he announced his discovery of a new type of energy as shadowy and elusive as Odin himself.

Odin and the Odic force

It is odd to think that Odin seems to have re-emerged through the unlikely channel of a German scientist named Reichenbach. Baron Karl von Reichenbach (1788–1869) was born in Stuttgart and became a widely respected scientist who is best known for two innovations as far removed from mystical reverie as can be imagined – the development of paraffin and creosote. However, at the height of his career his researches took him into uncharted waters which would alienate him from the scientific elite of his age. In 1845 he first published his theory on a mysterious and intangible force which he believed permeated the whole of nature. Terrestrial magnetism, animal magnetism and the magnetism of the human body were all seen by him as manifestations of a universal energy which he named Odic force.

That Reichenbach chose to make Odin the patron god of the force he believed to pervade the universe was no mere whim. Drawing on his knowledge of the links between the various Indo-European languages he noted that the Sanskrit word *va* means move about, which he linked to the Latin *vado* and the Old Norse *vada* meaning, I go quickly, hurry away or stream forth. He saw this Old Norse word as intimately connected to the god Odin.[4]

According to Reichenbach, the very nature of Odic force made it imperceptible to ordinary scientific instruments. No device such as an odometer or odoscope could measure and record its workings. This inability of Reichenbach to demonstrate the existence of the mysterious force he claims to have discovered (or rediscovered) made his position within the scientific community increasingly uncomfortable. His earlier solid scientific work began to be overshadowed by his obsession with a force which seemed to have no place within the confines of the science of his age.

From science to science fiction

As science gained ground from religion during the nineteenth century it was accompanied by a parallel trend in the collective imagination of Western culture – the rise of the written genre of science fiction. Among the most famous of such works is *Journey to the Centre of the Earth* (1864) by Jules Verne (1828–1905). Many of Verne's adventures have inevitably been turned into Hollywood movies – *20,000 Leagues Under the Sea, Around the World in Eighty Days* and *Journey to the*

Centre of the Earth itself. Known largely to the anglophone world through the bowdlerised and abridged children's editions of his works Verne is usually looked down on by English-speaking literati. In France however his literary reputation is well established. Interestingly, Verne's *Journey to the Centre of the Earth* is imbued with northern themes.

It is set in the year 1863 and the story begins in Hamburg at the home of Professor Otto Lidenbrock, a brilliant but irascible mineralogist. The story is narrated by his nephew Axel, who also acts as the professor's assistant. Lidenbrock is an avid collector of rare books and manuscripts and one day Axel comes home to find the professor enthusing about a leather-bound volume he has just acquired. It is a copy of the *Heimskringla*, a work recording the lives of Norway's kings from the sixth to the twelfth centuries by Snorri Sturluson, the most famous of all Icelandic writers, who also wrote down for the first time many of the Norse myths in his *Prose Edda*. Lidenbrock explains that the manuscript is written in runes, seeking to excite his nephew's curiosity by telling him, the runes 'were letters of an alphabet used in Iceland in olden times, and legend has it that they were invented by Odin himself. Look at them, irreverent boy, and admire these characters sprung from a god's imagination!'[5]

As he is waxing lyrical a fragment of old parchment falls from the volume onto the floor. Eagerly picking it up, Lidenbrock unfolds it to reveal three columns of seemingly indecipherable runes. He is able to deduce that it is at least 200 years younger than the book itself and finds a small inscription revealing the name of one of the book's previous owners – Arne Saknussemm, a sixteenth-century Icelandic alchemist whose books were burnt in 1573 after he was accused of heresy. After the professor has tried and failed many times to unlock the mysteries of this cryptogram– although he realises that the runes translate into Latin – it is Axel who finally solves the riddle. The deciphered message on the parchment reads: 'Descend into the crater of Snæfells Yocul, which the shadow of Scartaris caresses before the calends of July, O audacious traveller, and you will reach the centre of the Earth. I did it. Arne Saknussemm.'[6]

Snæfells Yocul is an actual extinct volcano in western Iceland and the place where Lidenbrock, Axel and their stalwart Icelandic guide Hans descend into the earth's interior to begin their subterranean adventures. At the bottom of the volcano's crater the travellers discover Saknussemm's name carved in runes on the rock and much later in their journey find his knife and carved initials on the shore of a desolate chthonic sea deep inside the earth.

Whilst the novel may be enjoyed simply as an adventure story it does not just describe a physical journey into the interior of the earth. It is also a journey back in time, an atavistic journey back through the cultural layers of the European past to a prehuman prehistoric world. The modern scientist Lidenbrock, an expert on the properties of minerals and stones, discovers the way to the middle of the earth from a sixteenth-century alchemist. The alchemist, whom Lidenbrock praises as a precursor of his own scientific quest, was concerned to discover the philosopher's stone (sometimes simply referred to as the stone), the mysterious goal of his hermetic art. The alchemist's parchment is written in runes, ancient pre-Christian symbols which encode the way to the inner world. The entrance to the inner world is geographically in Iceland – psychologically the Hyperborea of myth. This world is an inner world, projected into geological terms but essentially atavistic and psychological.

Verne's book can also be read as an individual psychological journey. The scientist Lidenbrock can be interpreted as symbolising the mind and rational enquiry, the hero Axel as representing emotion, and the almost characterless stalwart Hans as symbolising the body. When through their joint labours the three successfully complete the psycho-spiritual journey and return to the known world Axel is united with his lover Gräuben who can be said to represent the soul.

Although Arne Saknussemm is a fictional character invented by Verne the theme of a hollow earth can be found in genuine alchemical writings. In a book named *Azoth*, published in 1613 and attributed to the mysterious German alchemist Basil Valentine, there are a number of complex symbolic emblems. One of these (see Plate section 1, page 4) shows a bearded face at the centre of a seven-pointed star. Between each of the points of this star are words making up an inscription in Latin. When translated it reads, 'Visit the interior of the earth, by rectifying you discover the hidden stone.' The hidden stone is the philosopher's stone – the mystical goal of the alchemist. By this time the medieval idea that the interior of the earth was the location of hell had clearly been replaced, at least among alchemists and like-minded mystics. Guillaume Postel (who, as has been said, wa an important influence on Johannes Bureus) suggested that in order to make paradise inaccessible to mankind God had hidden it beneath the North Pole.[7] Thus the ancient myth of Hyperborea, the earthly northern paradise, returned to European consciousness. Could it be that Verne was aware of these mystical beliefs, that were current around the time his invented alchemist Arne Saknussemm was said to have flourished?

Frenzy and the overman

The philosopher Friedrich Nietzsche (1844–1900) also drew on the Hyperborean myth. He opens the first book of *The Antichrist* with: 'Let us face ourselves. We are Hyperboreans; we know very well how far off we live. "Neither by land nor by sea will you find the way to the Hyperboreans" – Pindar already knew this about us. Beyond the north, ice and death – *our* life, *our* happiness. We have discovered happiness, we know the way, we have found the exit out of the labyrinth of thousands of years.'[8] Nietzsche has had a profound effect on modern Western thought. His extolling of the Dionysian side of life – the dark, ecstatic, orgiastic and irrational – at the expense of the Apollonian realm of reason and light revealed the influence of Odin despite Nietszche's conscious preference for the mythological language of ancient Greece.

A key feature of Nietzsche's philosophy is his prophetic idea of a new and more evolved kind of human being, which he named the overman or superman. This is the subject of his most celebrated book *Thus Spoke Zarathustra*. In this work Nietzsche chose the ancient Iranian prophet Zarathustra (Zoroaster) as his alter ego and mouth-piece for a radical philosophy rather than draw on his own northern heritage. According to Jung, Nietzsche was not well versed in Germanic literature but the influence of Odin is unmistakably there, beneath the masks of Greek and Persian influence. In the first part of *Thus Spake Zarathustra* he makes an explicit connection between the overman and frenzy, which, as we have seen, is the meaning of the name Odin: 'Where is the lightning to lick you with its tongue? Where is the frenzy with which you should be inoculated? Behold I teach you the overman: he is this lightning, he is this frenzy.'[9]

The strident nature of Nietzsche – who said that he philosophised with a hammer – is closer to that of Odin the warrior and wise man than that of the Greek god Dionysus. The name of his patron god seems to have eluded Nietzsche, as his poem 'To the Unknown God' reveals:

> I shall and will know thee, Unknown One,
> Who searchest out the depths of my soul,
> And blowest through my life like a storm,
> Ungraspable, and yet my kinsman!
> I shall and will know thee, and serve thee.[10]

Jung also reports a powerful and shocking nightmare that Nietzsche had when he was fifteen years old. He was wandering alone at night in a gloomy wood when a blood-curdling scream from a nearby asylum terrified him. After this he met a wild and uncanny huntsman who blew his whistle with such shrill force that Nietzsche fell unconscious. Jung interprets this dream as an encounter with Odin. It was Odin who in Germanic folklore was said to leave the spirit of the dead on the 'wild hunt' through the forests at night.

In Nietzsche's powerful and poetic philosophy and even in his descent from genius to eventual madness we may recognise the divine imprint of Odin.

Chapter 7

Lost Subterranean Tribes

The democracy to which the most enlightened European politicians look forward as the extreme goal of political advancement, and which still prevailed among the other subterranean races, whom they despised as barbarians, the loftier family of Ana, to which belonged the tribe I was visiting, looked back to as one of the crude and ignorant experiments which belong to the infancy of political science.

It was the age of envy and hate, of fierce passions, of constant social changes more or less violent, of strife between classes, of war between state and state. This phase of society lasted, however, for some ages, and was finally brought to a close, at least among the nobler and more intellectual populations, by the gradual discovery of the latent powers stored in the all-permeating fluid they denominate Vril.

Lord Lytton, *The Coming Race*[1]

Lord Edward George Bulwer-Lytton (1803–73) is one of the more shadowy figures in British occultism and one of the most influential. He coined the phrase 'the pen is mightier than the sword', which everyone knows but few are aware was his. He was a Freemason and an associate of Eliphas Lévi, the most famous French occultist of the nineteenth century. One of Lytton's novels, *The Last Days of Pompeii*, is a fictional account of the ancient cult of the Egyptian goddess Isis. This book was a major influence on the Russian occultist Madame Blavatsky (1831–91), the founder of Theosophy. Her first major literary work was the 1,300-page epic *Isis Unveiled* (1877). The influence of Lytton's novel on her own tome went way beyond simply inspiration and it has been convincingly shown to have extended to downright plagiarism.[2]

Lytton's often rather stodgy prose was well suited to his Victorian audience, but apart from *The Last Days of Pompeii* his present-day readership is mainly limited to occultists seeking hidden truths in his Rosicrucian novel *Zanoni* or alchemical mysteries in *A Strange Story*. Yet the most singular of his works is *The Coming Race*, published in 1871 towards the end of his life.[3] This short novel is difficult to place into a single genre. It has elements of both science fiction and political allegory but it also contains occult psychology and mythology.

Descent into the land of the Vril-ya

The narrator Lytton creates to tell his story explains only a little about himself due to the shocking nature of his discoveries deep underground. He tells us only that he is an American of high social position who, having inherited considerable wealth upon the death of his father, decides to take time out from the pursuit of the almighty dollar to become a wanderer over the face of the earth. During these travels he meets up with an engineer – in a country he refuses to reveal lest he give away the location of his entry into the earth's bowels – who invites him into the interior of a mine. Becoming fascinated by this new world of experience the narrator spends a few weeks exploring the galleries underground.

One day the normally sober mining engineer returns from the solo investigation of a new shaft pale and extremely troubled. After consuming most of the contents of a flask of brandy he then reveals to the narrator the cause of his anxiety. He claims that, deep in the shaft, he saw artificial lights illuminating a wide and level road and heard the distant hum of what seemed like human voices. Although he believes the engineer's tale to derive from hallucinations the narrator agrees to accompany him on another descent. The two go into the depths of a chasm; the narrator descends first and sees that his companion's account was true. He sees 'a diffused atmospheric light, not like that from fire, but soft and silvery, as from a northern star'.

Then, as the engineer climbs down, the rock gives way and he falls, along with the rope and grappling hooks, dead at the feet of the narrator. With no way back to the world above ground the narrator has no choice but to explore the subterranean landscape. The plants and animals that he encounters remind him of prehistoric exhibits he has seen in some museum but such marvels are soon forgotten as he comes across a great building adorned by massive columns like those of ancient temples. Out of its entrance a human form comes towards him. It is as tall as the tallest of men but has a pair of large wings folded over its breast which reach down to its knees. Its face is that

Of the sculpted sphinx – so regular in its calm, intellectual, mysterious beauty. Its colour was peculiar, more like that of the red man than any other variety of our species, and yet different from it . . . a nameless something in the aspect, tranquil though the expression, and beauteous though the features, roused that instinct of danger which the sight of a tiger or serpent arouses. I felt that this manlike image was endowed with forces inimical to man.[4]

Later in the book we learn that the oldest tribes of the sub-terranean world have red skin but that others have fair hair and blue eyes 'though still of complexions warmer or richer in tone than persons in the north of Europe'. Some members of this lost race are described (in the terms of the Victorian science of the times) as having skulls of the Celtic type.

Confronted by this superior-looking being the narrator finds it difficult to overcome his fear. But then the stranger talks to him in an unknown language and, taking him by the hand, leads him into a vast hall. Quiet music and fragrant odours fill the hall and just inside the entrance another figure stands motionless until, touched twice by the stranger's staff, it begins to move noiselessly over the floor. It is then that the narrator realises that this is no living creature but a 'mechanical automaton'. The narrator is led to a bedroom where he soon falls asleep.

On awakening he finds himself in the presence of a number of other strangers, adults and children, seated around him 'in the gravity and quietude of Orientals'. Gradually he learns to communicate with this race and comes to be amazed by their numerous and seemingly supernatural powers. Zee, a female member of their College of Sages, is chosen by his hosts to instruct the narrator and give him some understanding of their world. In exchange he tells them of the world above ground:

> Desiring to represent in the most favourable colours the world from which I came, I touched but slightly, though indulgently, on the antiquated and decaying institutions of Europe, in order to expatiate on the present grandeur and prospective pre-eminence of that glorious American Republic, in which Europe enviously seeks its model and tremblingly foresees its doom . . . I wound up by repeating . . . glowing predictions of the magnificent future that smiled upon mankind – when the flag of freedom should float over an entire continent, and two hundred millions of intelligent citizens, accustomed from infancy to the daily use of revolvers, should supply to a cowering universe the doctrine of the patriot Monroe.[5]

This patriotic speech on the virtues of American democracy does not have the desired affect on his audience. Far from being impressed they are quietly horrified by his account of humanity above ground.

Zee explains to him the hidden force which has transformed their society and made it so dramatically different to his own culture. This force, known as Vril, has no direct equivalent in any surface language. In attempting to explain what he has learned of it to the reader our narrator says it is 'unity of natural energic agencies'. Thus electricity and magnetism are merely aspects of a wider and all-pervasive force. He also explicitly compares Vril to the Odic force of Baron von Reichenbach.

Vril: inner forces

The power of Vril can be both directed and altered by means of a hollow metal staff which can be used to heal or destroy and can affect the body or mind of others. This Vril staff is basically a modernised version of the magic wand. The narrator is told that there are some individuals who can wield it more effectively than others not through practice but through 'hereditarily transmitted organisation'. His hosts have one particular physical attribute that we lack – a visible nerve that starts at the wrist and, skirting the ball of the thumb, forks out at the root of the fore- and middle fingers. This evolutionary mutation has developed among the subterraneans as a result of repeated manipulation of Vril through countless generations. Zee speculates that in one or two thousand years this extra nerve may appear among the higher beings of our own world, should they learn to work with the force of Vril.

The power of Vril is beyond any force known above ground. He is told that its force can be directed over distances of 500–600 miles and instantly reduce to ashes a city twice the size of London. The power of Vril fuels the lamps which illuminate the enormous cavernous spaces within the earth inhabited by his hosts. Vril also makes it possible for them to alter the temperature and weather

conditions in their subterranean world and is also the basis of their
ability to fly with the aid of the artificial wings which they are able to
put on or remove at will. The sight of large numbers of these strangers
flying together through the air brings a demonic image to the
narrator's mind: 'I felt the terror and the wild excitement with which,
in the Gothic ages, a traveller might have persuaded himself that he
witnessed a *sabbat* of fiends and witches.'

By the use of Vril many things which in our world belong to the
realm of the supernatural – such as clairvoyance and telepathic trance
– are routine practices in this mysterious underground society. In fact,
the narrator's own ability to grasp the essentials of their language is
due to the fact that he has been put in a state of trance by his hosts
who have then telepathically transferred this knowledge to him. After
going through numerous further trances the narrator begins to gain a
deeper knowledge and insight into this strange world.

Imaginal ethnography: history of the Vril-ya

He learns of the origin and history of the subterranean peoples (called
the Ana, which means the same as our word, men). According to this
ancient lore their primeval ancestors once lived above ground and
their written records preserve myths which tell of a vaulted dome in
which the 'lamps lit were lighted by no human hand' – clearly a
reference to the heavenly vault, the sun, the moon and the stars. Due
to a great flood, which the narrator calculates probably took place
thousands of years before Noah's flood, many of their ancestors were
wiped out and only a few were fortunate enough to survive. This they
did by entering caves high in the mountains which brought them
eventually to their current homeland deep in the earth, far from the
natural light of both day and night.

Having established themselves in the new world below, the Ana
attained a level of civilisation similar to that of the 'more advanced
nations' of our world today. And, like us, despite their democratic
ideals they lived in a world of conflicting and warring nations. The

narrator is told that many other branches of subterranean humanity still live under such political systems – long surpassed by the loftier tribes of Ana to which his hosts belonged. These backward societies, though 'civilised' by our standards, are contemptuously described as barbarians.

It was the discovery and harnessing of Vril by various tribes of Ana that transformed their societies. Its awesome power, which could be used to destroy and to heal, meant that all war between those tribes who had discovered it had ceased. Since it could cause destruction on such a massive scale, superior numbers, military skill and discipline no longer gave an advantage. With the end of the age of war other dramatic social changes took place. Since each individual member of society – including children – had the power of Vril at their disposal everyone was potentially at the mercy of all other citizens so it was no longer possible to have a government which ruled by force. In this new world there was no need or desire for large states and new communities of moderate size formed. The tribe with which the narrator lives is limited to 12,000 families. When the tribe has surplus population some become voluntary emigrants and colonise new areas of the subterranean world.

The various tribes with knowledge of Vril intermarry, share the same laws and the same language and are collectively known as the Vril-ya – the civilised nations. Since each citizen's basic freedom is guaranteed by his or her mastery of Vril the political system is simple but effective. The motto of their creed is: 'No happiness without order, no order without authority, no authority without unity.' Each tribe is led by an autocrat known as Tur, who nominally takes up the post for life but often retires early at his own request. Despite this autocrat the few do not really dominate over the many as they do in the upper world. As there is no crime and no poverty there is no need for police or lawyers. The drudgery of manual work has also effectively been removed from society as it is performed by robots. It is through the use of Vril and as a result of the lack of strife and stress that so characterises our world that the Vril-ya have increased their life span. Typically they reach a hundred years old.

The status of women among the Vril-ya is much higher than in the world from which the narrator comes. They typically take the lead in making partnerships with the opposite sex, being the wooer rather than the wooed. Their full equality is assured by a number of factors. The females (Gy-ei) are generally taller and physically stronger than the males (Ana) and also have a 'finer nervous organisation' which makes them more perceptive concerning the properties of Vril.

Their religion, in which they all believe and all practise – which as the narrator wryly notes is hardly the case above ground – involves the worship of one divine Creator and Sustainer of the universe. The Vril-ya are also vegetarians, only drink milk and have no alcohol or other intoxicants. During further discussions with Zee the narrator comes to learn much more about the Vril-ya – more, in fact, than he would have liked to know. Having observed that none of the Vril-ya are deformed or in any way misshapen he is told that in the earlier stages of civilisation (to which all cultures above ground belong, according to the Vril-ya) life was about the survival of the fittest. Zee tells him that when life is a struggle 'nature selects for preservation only the strongest specimens'. Their ancient books also preserve a legend that they were driven from the face of the earth and into its bowels in order to perfect their race. Then he is told about the future. Zee prophesies that when this process of perfecting themselves is complete they are destined to return to the upper world to 'supplant all the inferior races' which presently dwell there, in short to exterminate them.

Zee falls in love with the narrator, but, unable to empathise with the ways of the Vril-ya and desiring to return to his own world, he tells her gently that he cannot return her affections. Her father, finding this unacceptable and being generally disturbed by the presence of an outsider in his world, sends his young son out to kill him. Zee, learning of this plan, decides to save her would-be lover. He holds on to her as they fly off and describes how she moves 'swiftly as an angel may soar heavenward with the soul it rescues from the grave'. They find their way to that same chasm through which he first entered her world. She leaves him there, within earshot of the voices of miners above them. She bids him farewell with a kiss, then, blasting the rock to seal up the entrance to their world, returns to her own people.

The narrator finds his way back to the light of day, carefully avoiding his previous lodging and acquaintances whose questions on his prolonged absence would be hard to answer. He returns to America to resume his normal life in his retirement and with illness overwhelming him (echoing Lytton's writing of the book in his twilight years) our narrator decides to put pen to paper so that he may warn his fellow men of the coming race.

The coming race and the master race

Although it is a novel it is a novel with a difference, more like an anthropological study of a lost tribe or more accurately a fictional race. Lytton dedicated the book in 'respect and admiration' to the great German linguist Max Müller (1823–1900). Müller wrote widely on mythology and also was one of the leading orientalists in the nineteenth century. He produced an edition of the complete Sanskrit text of the *Rig Veda*, the earliest holy books of India, published in four volumes between 1849 and 1862. Among his many other enterprises Müller oversaw in the 1870s a series named Sacred Books of the East – essentially translations of the major religious works of ancient India, Iran and the Far East, making many of the major scriptures and sutras of these spiritual traditions available for the first time to the English-speaking world.[6]

In *The Coming Race* Lytton tries to emulate Müller by creating a vocabulary for the language that the Vril-ya speak. It is described as being akin to the Aryan or Indo-Germanic language group. Lytton gives a detailed account of the language, describing elements of its grammar and giving examples of its vocabulary. The book also seems attuned to themes found in ancient myth. The diffuse light which illuminates the inner world of the Ana is described as like that of a 'northern star' – again a reference to the polar myth which appears so often in connection with the hollow earth. The artificially lit inner world of Lytton's lost 'Aryan' tribe echoes the ancient Iranian myths of the lost northern homeland, which, as we have seen, was illuminated by created and uncreated lights.[7]

The description of Vril in the novel as an all-pervading power bears a striking resemblance to the Odic force espoused by Baron von Reichenbach earlier in the nineteenth century, and this is a comparison which Lytton himself makes. Reichenbach said that the understanding and harnessing of Odic force would transform human morality and make us into a higher order of beings.[8] This view is echoed in *The Coming Race*, in which the Vril-ya, through the harnessing of the Vril force, have become a higher order of beings, although their morality does not sit comfortably with our own.

The literary sources for Lytton's idea of a subterranean world remain a mystery. Was he aware of the Hyperborean tradition as found in the writings of Guillaume Postel and Johannes Bureus? We may note in this regard that the works of Postel had an enormous influence on the French occultist Eliphas Lévi, who, as was noted at the beginning of this chapter, was an associate of Lytton. Such connections have never been demonstrated but what is clear is that Verne's book would have been known to Lytton. The central theme of both books is a journey into a subterranean world. Both writers have their heroes deciphering the past through ancient and obscure languages. In Verne the runes discovered by Odin are the basis of the alchemical code which gives the directions to Iceland and from there into the inner world inside the earth (the deeper pagan and prehistoric levels of consciousness), whilst Lytton has a lost Aryan language, spoken by a subterranean race.

The Coming Race is also a political fantasy and in some passages prophetic, predicting both events and inventions that have come to pass since the death of its author. The automatons which perform the chores and other menial tasks for the Vril-ya are obviously robots. The ability of Vril to wipe out an area twice the size of London seems to foreshadow the potential of nuclear energy. But beyond these futuristic visions there are other more remarkable prophecies in the book. That the Ana and their most culturally advanced tribes the Vril-ya are a lost branch of the Aryan race can hardly escape our attention. Are we to see in *The Coming Race* a foreshadowing of the savage rise of the Nazi 'master race'? The author tells us of this superior race of Arys' desire to rise to the surface and overrun the lesser races. The Aryan nature of the people and their physical perfection (no Vril-ya are said to be misshapen or deformed) suggests the science of eugenics. Even the power of Vril-ya children seems to foreshadow that of the Hitler Youth.

At the end of the book the narrator tells of his desire for this subterranean society to remain hidden (remain unconscious) for as long as possible from our own society. But having understood its dormant and brooding power through his journey underground (by his descent into the unconscious through trance) he fears the inevitable return of unconscious forces to the surface. The tribes of the Ana may be ancient in origin but underneath our modern world they are planning their return and our destruction.

Agarthi and Asgard

Lytton's theme of a powerful hidden race residing in a subterranean world continued as an undercurrent in the modern mythologies of French occultists, one of whom, as we shall see, has a direct link to him. With the popularisation of Eastern mysticism and religion, fuelled by the works of Max Müller and others, European fascination with the lost homeland of the Hyperborean myth was transplanted to the Himalayas, which had begun to fascinate Westerners as a centre of esoteric wisdom.

Two subterranean realms named Agarthi and Shambhala appear

in Western occult literature from the late-nineteenth century onwards, but these names have very different origins. Shambhala is a Tibetan word and the present (fourteenth) Dalai Lama has this to say about this mystical realm: 'If you lay out a map and search for Shambhala, it is not findable; rather, it seems to be a pure land which, except for those whose karma and merit have ripened, cannot be immediately seen or visited . . . even though Shambhala is an actual land – an actual pure land – it is not immediately approachable by ordinary persons.'⁹

Thus Shambhala is not a geographical location but a spiritual zone beyond normal levels of cognition. Agarthi, on the other hand, is a recent Western invention. As the name of a lost city or mystical centre, it has been given a number of different spellings – which, as will be shown, gives us a clue to its actual origin. It appears in Western occult literature as Agarthi, Agartha, Agharta, Agarttha and Asgartha, firstly in 1873 in a book by a Frenchman named Louis Jacolliot (1837–90), a magistrate in India. In his book he recounts how certain Brahmins in south India told him the story of Asgartha.¹⁰

According to Jacolliot, Asgartha was a prehistoric city of the sun dating back to 13,300 BC, and was ruled by the Brahmatma, a spiritual leader who was all but invisible and manifested himself to his people only once a year. Around 5000 BC Asgartha was destroyed by a force led by two brothers named Ioda and Skandah who invaded India from the Himalayas. The brothers were then driven back and returned whence they came. They did not stay in the Himalayas but moved north and west, eventually becoming immortalised as Odin and Scandinavia. From this part of the story it becomes clear that Asgartha is none other than Asgard, the Norse home of Odin and the other Aesir. The other spellings of this fabled city do not reveal its etymology as clearly as Jacolliot's version, which being the first is the most transparent. In fact, it seems clear it was Jacolliot himself who created this mythical city.

The myth was however picked up by another French occultist,

Pre-Viking Age picture stone, from the village of Martebo, Gotland, Sweden.

Odin riding his eight-legged horse Sleipnir (detail from a memorial stone, discovered under church floor, Ardre parish, Gotland, Sweden, 8th - 9th Century).

Odin with his two ravens Huginn (thought) and Muninn (memory), from a manuscript copy of Snorri Sturluson's *Edda* in the Royal Library, Copenhagen, Denmark (94 recto: Ny kgl.S.1867 4°).

The house of Snorri Sturluson, Reykholt, Iceland.

Witches' Sabbath
by Hans Baldung Grien,
woodcut, 1510.

Commemorative medallion of Johannes
Bureus (front and back), 1908.

Image from *Azoth* series of alchemical emblems by Basil Valentine,
1613. The Latin inscription reads: 'Visit the interior of the Earth,
by rectifying you discover the hidden stone.'

Members of the *Wandervogel* German youth movement, 1926.

Design by Rudolf Steiner for book jacket of Lord Lytton's *Vril,* or *The Coming Race,* c.1923.

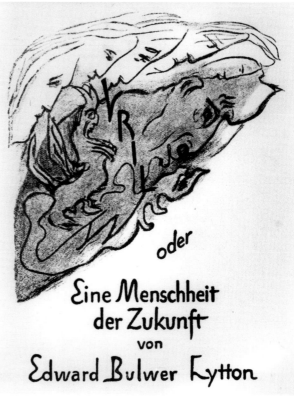

oder

Eine Menschheit der Zukunft

von

Edward Bulwer Lytton

Sexualreligion by the artist Fidus (Hugo Hoppener), 1897.

Nudists worshipping the Sun, 1926.

Ahnenerbe silver bowl (front).

Ahnenerbe silver bowl (back).

Guido von List.

Emblem of the Thule Society.

Death's Head Ring of the SS.

Karl von Wiligut in SS uniform.

Saint-Yves d'Alveydre (1842–1909), who in 1885 began Sanskrit lessons with a teacher named Haji Sharif. Apparently Haji claimed to be of the 'Agarthian School'. Saint-Yves described the subterranean kingdom of the Brahmatma and lavishly embellished the account Jacolliot had published a little over a decade earlier. His Agarttha (to use his spelling) is technologically far more advanced than society above ground – rail and air travel and gas lighting were nothing new to its inhabitants. They have massive archives full of books written in their own 'Vatannian' script. He describes its government as 'Synarchy', which one day will become the universal political system of our own societies. At this time Agarttha will reveal itself to us in all its glory, but until then will remain unknown to the world at large, only occasionally sending one of its messengers forth to the upper world.

As Joscelyn Godwin has pointed out, there are echoes of Lord Lytton's *The Coming Race* in this account – the highly advanced technological society within the earth, the artificially lit world with its voluminous collection of records written in a forgotten arcane script, a benevolent dictatorship ready to take over our societies when the time is ripe. We can be almost certain that Saint-Yves knew the book well as he was a friend of Lytton's son Edward Robert Bulwer-Lytton (1831–91), Earl of Lytton, British diplomat, ambassador to France and Viceroy of India 1876–80.[11] It is thus quite possible that Saint-Yves drew on *The Coming Race* for inspiration.

The realms of Shambhala, Agarthi and the Vril-ya are best understood as mythical inner worlds of the human psyche. The advanced races encountered therein represent higher states of being, archetypal powers which can be contacted through altered states of consciousness. In *The Coming Race* the narrator is only able to understand the Vril-ya through states of trance induced by the female sage Zee. In this regard we should note that a woman is the dominant seer within the lost tribe of the Vril-ya. This can be seen as an echo of the role of

Norse seeresses and other female visionaries in the pagan traditions of northern Europe. In the case of Shambhala and Agarthi their inhabitants – often referred to by Western occultists as hidden masters – are contacted through mediumship and clairvoyance.

Chapter 8

Hollow Earth, Inner Worlds

Like Wotan's oaks . . . the gods were felled and a wholly
incongruous Christianity, born of monotheism on a much
higher level, was grafted onto the stumps. The Germanic
man is still suffering from this mutilation . . . we must dig
down to the primitive in us, for only out of the conflict
between civilized man and the Germanic barbarian will there
come what we need: a new experience of God.[1]

From a letter of Carl Jung to his pupil Oskar Schmitz,
26 May 1923

From his early years Jung was deeply involved in mediumship and
experiments with clairvoyance. This stemmed from his background;
a number of female members of his family were said to have such
psychic capacities. His interest in seances developed into using
techniques of hypnotism to further his psychological researches into
uncharted territories of the mind. For example he hypnotised his
cousin Helly so that she could enter trances which resulted in her
'channelling' various 'spirits' or 'personalities' including Jung's
maternal grandfather.[2] In doing this she was playing a role that
northern European women had been playing for millennia.

In his experiments with trance we can see a practical aspect of

Jung's investigations at the borders of science. In the process of inducing trances in himself and others he delved into the unconscious, experiencing first hand a variety of psychical phenomena, including prophetic dreams. These experiments contributed to practically his geological theory of the mind, as we shall shortly see. The psyches of Jung and Helly, two individual minds belonging to the same family, were connected through the trance which he induced (by hypnosis) and she experienced. Through the trance they then both came into contact with the spirits of dead relatives.

Jung's influence over New Age thinking should be seen in the light of Richard Noll's revealing analysis of his deepest desire – to renew European spirituality by bringing paganism back to the conscious level of experience. Noll points out that Jung's system for gaining access to the deeper levels of the mind has, perhaps, more in common with the practices of occultism than with science. He remarks that the Theosophical technique of accessing ancient memories by means of the Akashic records (a kind of vast immaterial filing cabinet which contains the thoughts and actions of the past) is paralleled by Jung's descent into the collective unconscious and the various levels of the group mind. He also notes that Jung's description of his spirit guide – who took the form of an old man named Philemon – is not dissimilar to Blavatsky's belief in the 'Mahatmas' or hidden masters which she said were her spiritual guides.

Placing Jung in his historical context we find him imbued with a *völkisch* (folkish) idea that pervaded German society in his formative years – the belief that the individuals who make up the *Volk* are linked together by a life force. In Jung's projected pagan revival individuals, by transforming themselves, come to identify the deeper layers of the self with the collective unconscious and, by uniting the conscious and unconscious within their own psyches, become spiritually resurrected. Each individual who achieves this personal transformation increases the likelihood of others being able to do the same, for the transformation of the individual transforms the collective mind. We must concur with Richard Noll when he writes, 'Arguing that Jung undoubtedly considered himself a cell in the body of the *Volk* and wrote from a *völkisch* perspective does not imply that he was a fascist, Nazi, or even an anti-Semite.'[3]

Jung was the primary positive force in the neo-pagan revival in the German-speaking world of his time. He, unlike so many of his period, was not drawn into the maelstrom of unconscious possession which gripped the German people en masse and manifested itself in the collective 'mental epidemy and war' caused by the Third Reich.

Jung, Hesse and the geology of the mind

The mythical geology and geography of the works of Verne, Lytton and others mentioned above have their counterpart in the psychological ideas of Jung. His model of the human mind is couched in geological metaphors. He even talked of the 'geology of the personality' and described the various levels in detail. Jung saw the mind as having eight distinct layers. At the highest level, rather like mountain summits raised above the sea, individuals appear as separate entities, but as we delve down it becomes clear that people are connected at a deeper level. Directly under the individual level is the first of these transpersonal connections, the family. Below that families are linked into a clan and then the clans are themselves united into a nation. Deeper still we find various nations connected into wider divisions of humanity (Jung gives as an example 'European man'). Below that we enter the atavistic levels of our prehuman past – our primate ancestors, our animal ancestors as a whole and finally, at the bottom, the Central Fire. This model of the mind can also be perceived as a series of concentric circles.

The Central Fire equates geologically to the hot core of the earth and mythologically to the 'inner sun' – the light within. The implications of such a view of the mind are enormous. Not only does it allow the individual to access images specific to various levels of a group mind it also suggests that the earth itself is in some way conscious and alive and that we have a line of communication with it. In this respect this Jungian model of the psyche is attuned to the Gaia Hypothesis of modern ecological thinking, which also attributes to the Earth itself some kind of consciousness.

Jung's model allows the individual to mine or uncover his or her own personality and gain access to its deeper levels, work which can be seen as either the geology or the archaeology of the soul.[4] Such 'excavations' were activated by Jung and his fellow analysts during their sessions with patients and others who chose to undertake such a psychic journey. Among these was a man as prominent in his own field as Jung was in his – the Nobel prize-winning novelist Herman Hesse (1877–1962). Hesse underwent analysis with the psychiatrist Josef Lang, who had been trained by Jung. In 1917, with Lang as his guide Hesse descended into his own inner world. During the process Lang said these remarkable words to Hesse:

> You will hear the voice that calls out from the primordial depths of the earth, and I will announce to you the Law of the Magma in whose springs I reign. You shall learn from me the Laws of the Dead which will become the Laws of a New Age . . . I am hammering in your mine shaft, and one day you will understand and read the Runes which I have chiselled into the stones of your soul, the primordial Scripture of men which you must teach them, the tablets of the Law of what is to come.[5]

Here we have direct evidence of a leading Jungian analyst conducting a guided journey into the ancestral Germanic collective memory. Furthermore, the 'Laws of a New Age' are written in the ancient runes and, according to Lang, the decipherment of these symbols will turn Hesse into a spiritual teacher of the New Age which is to arise.[6] The descent into the inner world through a mine shaft and the decipherment of runes as means by which the spiritual journey is made resonate strongly with the plot of *Journey to the Centre of the Earth*. Reading both Verne's novel and Lytton's *The Coming Race* in the light of such a geological model of the mind reveals both their psychological and mythological meanings.

The theme of hidden masters who can be contacted through visionary states is one which occurs in *The Coming Race* before it appeared in the occult doctrines of Madame Blavatsky. The Vril-ya are not only a higher race but are also compared to both angels and demons by the narrator. It is highly significant that the narrator is only able to communicate with the Vril-ya through trance states. It is through trance facilitated by the power of Vril energy – associated with Odin as the god of altered states of consciousness – that he gains understanding of the lost Aryan race. Trance is one of the main ways by which people can consciously access the hidden areas of their mind – the unconscious. Thus modern man (embodied by the narrator) attains knowledge of the racial unconscious (embodied by the Vril-ya) through altered states of consciousness. It is through these trances that he is also able to understand the language of the Vril-ya. The similarities with both Herman Hesse's descent into the unconscious through Jungian analysis and that of the travellers to the earth's core in the books of Verne and Lytton is striking.

In the fictional and mythical accounts the lost continent is sometimes placed in the far north (Hyperborea) and sometimes within the earth, as in *The Coming Race* and the subterranean realm of Agarthi. In Verne's story the two locations are combined in a single narrative – the journey to the far north (Iceland) provides entry to the centre of the earth. Whether the lost continent is in the north (and therefore higher) or in the hollow earth (and therefore deeper) it is a metaphor for an interior world, a psychic and mythological location. This realm exists far away in both space and time from our own mundane world. It is the lost continent of the European mind, submerged in the collective unconscious.

A community on the mountain of truth

Having excavated the elements of this archetypal inner world it is now time to retrace their dramatic journey back to the surface of European consciousness. Like a volcanic eruption a new vision of Europe began to emerge at the epicentre of the continent – on a hill above Ascona in Switzerland. It was here, on land bought by Henri Oedenkoven the son of a Belgian industrialist, that a countercultural movement was born. In 1900 Oedenkoven gave the hill the name Monte Verita – Mount Truth. In doing so he imbued it with a mythological aura which was, bearing in mind the extraordinary role it was to play in the culture of the twentieth century, wholly justified.

The Swiss art critic Harald Szeemann described Ascona around the year 1900 'the southernmost outpost of a far-reaching Nordic lifestyle-reform, that is, alternative movement'.[7] Others have dubbed it the Bermuda Triangle of the mind on account of the heady mixture of occultism, anarchism and pagan experimentalism of the community. Vegetarianism, nudism, 'free love', Eastern mysticism, feminism, natural medicine, drug use and a host of other countercultural theories and practices which were to become commonplace in the social experiments of the 1960s were all foreshadowed by the idealism and radical lifestyles of Monte Verita.

The list of those who passed through this community – part utopia, part sanatorium, part proto-hippy commune – reads like a who's who of creative individuals at the dawn of the twentieth century and practices. Among those who visited Monte Verita in these fruitful years were Lenin and Trotsky, the Russian anarchists Bakunin and Kroptokin, D.H. Lawrence, Paul Klee, the Dadaists Hugo Ball and Hans Arp, the dance master Rudolf Laban and the occultist Aleister Crowley, to name but a few.

As news of the community spread, those seeking an alternative to the social norms of the time flocked to this promised land. In 1907, after seeing a group of long-haired men in sandals on their way to Monte Verita, Herman Hesse decided to follow in their footsteps. His own pilgrimage led to his being successfully treated for alcoholism by a Dr Friedeberg who had rejected the use of medication and devised a natural cure in its place. Others in the community were also to have a profound effect on the future Nobel prize-winner for literature. The most important of these was Gustav Gräser. Having retired from the Austrian army, Gräser put into practice a 'back to nature' ethos, advocating, among other things, the rejection of electricity and indoor plumbing. Hesse not only became a close friend of Gräser but also used him as the model for many of the spiritual masters that appear in his novels.

Ascona continued to be a magnetic centre for revolutionary thinking into the 1930s. An elite group of scholars deeply concerned with the spiritual health of European man met there to give talks and lectures on both Eastern and Western mystical traditions. A major influence on these events, known as the Eranos Conferences, was none other than Jung himself, and in the words of James Webb, a noted historian of the occult, they were 'a compendium of all the elements of the Occult Revival, and an extension of all the elements of Jung's work'.[8]

The German Youth Movement

Beyond the confines of Monte Verita a grass-roots movement was springing up in the German-speaking world. Jung saw the return of the Odinic archetype in the idealistic youth groups which flourished in the Germanic world around the turn of the twentieth century. Before the spectre of Nazism appeared on the social horizon this was a positive force of liberation from the restrictions of rationalism. Young idealists were seeking an alternative lifestyle from that of their parents and formed a loose-knit counterculture of groups dedicated to the love of nature and hiking, folk music, dance and peasant culture, and to encouraging spiritual and intellectual speculation. During its heyday some 50,000 teenagers were wandering the length and breadth of Germany, sharing their money and bathing naked with the opposite sex. Weekend wanderings became more extended and some youngsters went off for weeks at a time. Soon permanent campsites and cabins were built, establishing the basis of the youth hostel association, which began in Germany in 1907.[9]

Like any other idealists they had their role models. Herman Hesse became a patron saint of the movement with his tales of spiritual journeying and enlightenment. Equally influential was the hugely popular artist Fidus (Hugo Hoppener 1868–1948), whose paintings literally embodied the aspirations and ideals of this new generation.

> The new pagans' artistic prophet was . . . Fidus . . . his breathtaking sun-worshipping images seemed to be every-where in the first quarter of the century. Nude, long-haired blond young Aryans – sometimes wearing jewelry made of Runic symbols or swastikas – looked skyward and raised their arms to the sun. The image most often associated with Fidus – the motif of the *Lichtgebet* (Prayer to the light), based on the Norse so-called *Lebensrune* or 'life rune' – depicts a nude man, legs together, arm upraised in a Y-shaped posture.[10]

But behind the human inspiration of Hesse and Fidus lay a deeper influence. According to Jung, the Odinic archetype was the primary driving force behind new cultural movements, stirring new hopes and dreams among the young. Jung makes much of the god's spirit inspiring the German Youth Movement – who, long before Jack Kerouac and the beatniks, took to the road 'armed with rucksack and lute . . . blond youths, and sometimes even girls as well, were to be seen as restless wanderers on every road from the North Cape to Sicily, faithful votaries of the roving god'.[11]

Yet this peaceful, idealistic and optimistic youth movement gradually lost its momentum in the 1920s. What remained of it was, after some dissent, harnessed to a new and sinister purpose – that of the National Socialist Party – and it was reincarnated in demonic form as the Hitler Youth. The wanderers of the earlier movement became the marchers of the new order. This drastic transformation also marked the end of any possibility of a conscious pagan experiment in Germany. The pagan elements were cast back into the unconscious in favour of overt Hitler worship and leading Nazis explicitly denied any links with the cult of Odin. Hitler Youth leader Baldur von Shirach made it clear to the parents of those children he was in charge of that: 'It is my purpose neither to re-erect in the forests of Germany heathen altars and introduce our youth to any kind of Wotan's cult, nor in any other way to hand over young Germany to the magical altars of the herb-apostles.'[12] Alfred Rosenberg, whose Hitler-endorsed book *The Myth of the Twentieth Century* was a best-seller in Nazi Germany, announced, 'Wotan is dead.' Hitler made his own position very clear: 'It seems to me that nothing would be more foolish than to re-establish the worship of Wotan. Our old mythology ceased to be viable when Christianity implanted itself.'[13]

The positive traits of the Odinic archetype manifested themselves in the social experiments of Ascona and the German youth movement – inspired poetry, song and philosophy, freedom of thought, sexuality and expression. These disappeared under the rising tide of Nazism. In this new climate the first Odinic experiment was destined to go disastrously wrong. The negative side of the archetype, epidemy and war, came to the fore, whilst the solar symbol of the swastika, beloved of Fidus and the youth movement, sank back into the unconscious. The sun had turned black and Europe descended into Ragnarok.

Chapter 9

The Chosen People and the Master Race

> While discussing our topic, one involuntarily feels that one is touching something deeper, be they archetypes or simply emotionally charged mythological images. C.G. Jung may well be right with his famous 'Wotan' theory. But this is the point at which serious research and experiments must commence. What affinity is there between the profound symbols of esotericism, religion and mythology, and those of Nazism? Or, put more acutely: Do these politically exploitable symbols necessarily correspond to some structure of the unconscious?
>
> Hans Thomas Hakl, *Unknown Sources*[1]

Many people, by no means all of them fantasists, find the standard historical accounts of the rise of Nazism deeply unsatisfying. The sudden whirlwind of Nazism swept across the cultural landscape of the twentieth century in defiance of the apparently secure rational modern world. Whilst we should not abandon reason in our pursuit of the roots of Nazism we cannot provide a full account of the phenomenon without examining the powerful cultural forces of the irrational. There is no need to throw conventional explanations to the side – economic, political and social factors undoubtedly played a major role – but there is another element which modern myth-makers and fantasists have tried to make their own. They attempt to explain Nazism by occult factors – secret societies, black magic, satanic inspiration and even extraterrestrial intervention.

Jung's explanation of the hidden aspect of the Nazi rise to power – the resurgence of the Odin archetype in the Germanic unconscious – allows us to investigate the missing element without succumbing to fantasy ourselves. I will explore two of the most well-known motifs in Nazi lore – the symbol of the swastika and the idea of the Aryan master race.

The swastika

As we have seen, before the Nazi era Aryan was the generally accepted term for the Indo-European languages, but its usage in the ideology of the Third Reich has meant that, like the swastika (which as we shall shortly see had a widespread and almost completely positive role in the traditional symbolism of many cultures), it cannot be used without conjuring up the spectre of Nazism.[2] In the nineteenth and early-twentieth century Aryan was not just a linguistic and cultural term but was also used to refer to a race. This biological term, again used by the Nazis for their own ends, has become equally unacceptable. Today 'Aryan' has all but been replaced by 'Indo-European'.

In the last few years of the nineteenth century Thomas Wilson, curator of prehistoric anthropology at the US National Museum, amassed a vast amount of information on the ancient symbol of the swastika.[3] The name comes from the ancient Sanskrit language of India and means 'of good fortune'. As such the symbol had a positive value and was thus a sign of benediction. In northern Europe it was known as the fylfot. How it got this name is unclear. One theory is that fylfot comes from 'fill-foot' and was given to the symbol simply because it was used as a design to fill in the foot or base of medieval painted-glass window panels. Others derive it from Old Norse words meaning 'many footed' and Anglo-Saxon 'four-footed' or many-footed.

There is also a three-legged variant of the swastika called the triskelion most famously used as the symbol of the Isle of Man in the British Isles. Cultural traces of the Viking influence on this island are still strong, as is clear from the continuing yearly assembly, or Thing, which celebrates the northern origin of its parliament. The triskelion is often portrayed as three legs extending out from a common centre. Both the swastika itself and its three-legged variant convey an impression of rotating movement. The leg or foot is a way of expressing this apparent motion. Another name by which the swastika has been known is gammadion, occasionally spelt gammation. This name is derived from the Greek letter Γ (gamma), as the symbol can be seen as being constructed from four gammas. It has been used as a decorative motif on the garments of priests of the Byzantine Church.

Despite the various terms for the symbol it is by its Indian name that it has become known across the world. Its origins, however, are to be sought much further back, in an era before the time of Sanskrit or any other written language of antiquity. The fact that the swastika has been discovered among the prehistoric remains of cultures in both North America and Eurasia clearly shows that if a common origin is to be found for this symbol then it must lie in an extremely remote period of time; it would have to be traced back to the Old Stone Age before the peoples of the Old and New Worlds went their separate ways. Whether the symbol developed entirely independently in the two hemispheres or not it is possible to attempt to trace its migration within each land mass but this is a task which need not detain us here.

Earlier generations of Western scholars whose investigations would have been known to Nazi and proto-Nazi ideologists often stressed the widespread Indian use of the symbol. Orientalists from the nineteenth century onwards typically described the swastika as an important Aryan emblem of great religious significance. Although

widely used in the iconography of Hinduism it was its adoption by
Buddhism which seems to have led to its migration into the cultures
of the Far East. Widely used to decorate amulets the swastika has
historically been a popular symbol in India, Tibet, China and Japan.
Swastikas also adorn countless European and Near Eastern artefacts
from the ancient and prehistoric eras – pots from ancient Cyprus,
Greek vases, Egyptian scrolls, spindle-whorls from Troy, ancient
Scandinavian combs and Corinthian coins among them. In the New
World the symbol is also both common and widespread. It appears
among the symbolic repertoire found on artefacts discovered in the
ancient mounds of the Mississippi Valley; it was used among the
Navajo in their sand paintings and other art, and among numerous
cultures in Mexico, Columbia and Peru.

It is integral to the nature of symbols that they should be open to
many interpretations. It is not that one is right and others wrong; the
same symbol can mean different things to people of different times
and different cultures. But one of the very reasons for using a symbol
is that it can simultaneously represent multiple ideas and levels of
meaning even to the same people. It may represent something
concrete and tangible such as fire or the sun and also symbolise an
idea – masculinity or motion, for example. Many scholars have sought
to explain the origin of the swastika and its religious and cultural
meanings. It has often been interpreted as being like a wheel in
motion. To some it is a solar symbol par excellence whilst to others its
four-fold form indicates it is rather a symbol of the earth (representing
the four directions of space – north, south, east and west). The two
crossed lines have been interpreted as two lightning bolts or two fire
sticks – in the latter case thus symbolising the generating or making
of fire by rubbing the two sticks together.

After the atrocities of the Third Reich it is hard to see the swastika
as a positive symbol or use the word Aryan without evoking the shade
of Nazism. Nevertheless, a number of modern groups have sought to
revive the swastika symbol in a modified way. Their reasons for doing

so are based on one of two motives. Neo-Nazis want to keep close to the Nazi use of the emblem whilst avoiding legal and other problems which would occur if they used the conventional swastika. Then there are those, usually pagan in orientation, who are opposed to the doctrines of Nazism and wish to reclaim a symbol which had traditionally been a positive one.

These attempts illustrate the power of modern mythology and its symbols to rewrite the past and to affect the collective psyche. It is not just with the symbol of the swastika that we find this powerful influence from the realm of the imagination. We now turn our attention to a notorious forgery that, though mythical in nature, has had huge consequences in the real world – *The Protocols of the Elders of Zion*.

The *Protocols* and the myth of the Jewish world conspiracy

A clandestine night-time meeting has been arranged to take place in the Jewish cemetery in Prague during the Feast of Tabernacles. At eleven o'clock the creaking gates of the graveyard open and the first of a number of shadowy figures enters. Over the next hour thirteen men approach one of the tombstones. Each in turn kneels and touches the tomb three times, murmuring a prayer. On the stroke of midnight as all the thirteen kneel silently around the tomb a harsh metallic sound emanates from the grave itself and a blue flame ignites to illumine the worshippers. A disembodied voice, belonging to the devil, addresses them: 'I greet you, heads of the twelve tribes of Israel,' to which they reply, 'We greet you, son of the accursed.'[4]

Pure melodrama it may be but this episode from a mid-nineteenth-century novel was to be the inspiration for the world's most widespread and popular work of anti-Semitism the notorious *Protocols of the Elders of Zion,* a book which was required reading in schools under the Third Reich.[5] This colourful account appears in a book entitled *Biarritz* by Hermann Goedsche writing under the pen name Sir John Retcliffe published in Berlin in 1868. Goedsche, a petty official of the Prussian postal service, had already dabbled in forging documents before he penned this anti-Semitic novel. That there are thirteen men gathered to represent twelve tribes is explained by the extra man being present on behalf of 'the unfortunates and exiles'.

The *Protocols,* concocted in Paris in 1897 or 1898 but first published in Russia in 1903, take the form of a series of twenty-four lectures supposedly given during clandestine meetings of the Elders of Zion, allegedly an international Jewish cabal intent on taking control of the world.[6] Each lecture or protocol covers different aspects of the plot – control of the media, destruction of the nation states, international power consolidated by the institution of Freemasonry, control over the banking system, the spreading of alcohol and pornography and other devices designed to destroy morality, the setting up of the king of Israel on a world throne and so on.

The tsarina's final message

Conspiracy theorists have made much of the fact that both swastika and *Protocols* were found at the scene of one of the most famous crimes in history. On 17 July 1918 Tsar Nicholas of Russia and his entire family were murdered by Bolsheviks at Sverdlovsk (formerly Yekaterinburg). A week later their dismembered and partially burnt remains were found nearby at the bottom of a disused mineshaft in the forest. Following the assassination an official investigation of the last imperial residence revealed three books which had belonged to the empress – a Bible, a volume of Tolstoy and a copy of Sergei Nilus' *The Great in the Small,* which contained the *Protocols* as an appendix. Nilus, a Christian mystic and an agent of the imperial Russian secret police, claimed to be drawing on secret Zionist records and traced the international Jewish conspiracy back to Solomon in 929 BC. It was also discovered that the tsarina had drawn a swastika on a window surround in the house. But this was hardly the first time that the empress had made use of this sign. It was a veritable amulet in her mind and she wore a jewelled swastika on her person. She often ordered it to be engraved on gifts she sent to friends. To some anti-Semitic White Russians the presence of the Aryan swastika in conjunction with the *Protocols* in such close proximity to the crime scene was no simple coincidence but a matter of great symbolic significance which could mean only one thing: the Bolsheviks who had disposed of the royal family were working for Jewish forces bent on destroying the power of their beloved Aryan dynasty.

The potency of myth

If ever proof were needed of the power of political fantasy then the *Protocols* is it. The Elders of Zion never existed except in the minds of the enemies of the Jews. That a secret society which never existed could provide the Nazis with what Norman Cohn dubbed 'a warrant for genocide' shows the power of myth in the modern world. The belief that the chosen people had a secret plan to dominate the world did much to create its mirror image – the myth of the Aryan master race who would wage war against the Jewish enemy. With the *Protocols* as its blueprint the greatest conspiracy theory since the European witch hunts of the sixteenth and seventeenth century was set in motion.

The *Protocols* became widely known in the United States. This was largely due to a powerful individual in American industry – the tycoon Henry Ford, the founder of the Ford Motor Company. He vigorously asserted that the *Protocols* were genuine and promoted the economic and political reality of the conspiracy of the Elders of Zion and their supporters. Ford blamed the Jews for causing the First World War and for many years published anti-Semitic diatribes in his own publication *The Dearborn Independent*. Ford's energetic anti-Semitism deeply impressed Hitler and as early as 1922 a photograph of Ford hung on the wall of his office at Nazi headquarters.

The use of the *Protocols* in political propaganda goes way beyond Nazism and its modern adherents. As is well documented, many Nazis fled to the safe haven of Egypt after the war, taking the *Protocols* with them. The Egyptian government was quick to realise their value in the propaganda war with Israel and published an Arabic translation of the book. President Nasser himself endorsed its contents: 'it proves beyond all doubt that three hundred Zionists, each of whom knows all the others, govern the fate of the European continent'.[7] In the 1970s the World Muslim Conference, a Pakistan-based organisation, denied the Holocaust and promoted the *Protocols*. Today the *Protocols* circulate widely in the Middle East and other parts of the Muslim world, even reportedly appearing on school curricula.

Ironically, in view of the fact that some leading Bolsheviks were Jewish, the *Protocols* were also made use of by Russian communist leaders. Under Brezhnev the Soviets revived the use of the *Protocols* as a propaganda tool in their backing of anti-Zionist forces in the Middle East. In the Gorbachev era, with its relaxing of state control, copies of the *Protocols* and similar works became openly available from street vendors. The *Protocols* continue to be published across the globe with editions printed as far afield as Brazil, New Zealand and Romania.

The story of the *Protocols* begins with the rise of anti-Semitism in late-nineteenth-century Russia. During this period about a third of the Jews in the world lived within the borders of the Russian empire, the last absolute monarchy in Europe. Increasing opposition to the regime was blamed on the Jews, a view propagated by both of the last two tsars – Alexander III and his son Nicholas II. Many ideas which would become realities under the Third Reich were foreshadowed in the twilight years of the Russian empire. Anti-Semitic writings were filled with stories of the Jewish ritual murder of Christian boys, secret conspiracies and collusion with the forces of socialism and Freemasonry. The most remarkable individual to write such tracts was a man of various aliases including Osman-Bey and Kibridli-Zade whose real name was Millinger. He was an international con man arrested for his activities in a number of countries. He made much of his income by spreading anti-Semitism through his writings. In these works he claimed to expose an international Jewish conspiracy and wrote in

1886 that it 'can be destroyed only through the complete extermination of the Jewish race'. This augury of the final solution was doubly remarkable as Millinger was himself a Jew.[8]

In August 1921 the London *Times* ran a short series of articles which revealed the literary source of the allegedly Jewish *Protocols*, which had been published in an English translation that year. The book in question was *Dialogue aux enfers entre Montesquieu et Machiavel,* a political satire on the rule of Napoleon III by a French lawyer called Maurice Joly published in Brussels in 1864. Not only was the structure of the *Protocols* lifted directly from Joly's work but also numerous passages in almost all of the twenty-four chapters that make up this notorious forgery. Yet despite the fact that the *Protocols* had been revealed as a transparent literary fraud its use as proof of a powerful Jewish conspiracy among anti-Semites continued unabated.

On completely irrational grounds those who believed in it argued that the attempt to dismiss it as a forgery was yet another deception by the Elders of Zion. As has been pointed out, this is a classic case of a self-sealing premise, 'a premise that is vindicated by proof as well as disproof'.[9] It may also be noted that belief in the *Protocols* is based not on reason but on faith and that Norman Cohn's description of the *Protocols* as an important part of 'Nazi scripture' is very apt. The *Protocols* became the Bible of anti-Semitism, an analogy not as perverse as it may first appear. In the years leading up to the Second World War the *Protocols* was probably the most widely distributed book in the world, bar one – the Bible.[10] It was taken as gospel and the machinations of the Jews as described in the book were believed in as articles of faith. Its adherents saw the Jewish plot as the climax of a conspiracy which has existed throughout the ages. This conspiracy was often represented as a snake making its way through history and across the continent of Europe. At the start of the twentieth century many believed it was on the verge of fulfilling its ancient mission.

The *Protocols* and the Third Reich

The *Protocols* were first published in Germany in 1920 and provided some people with an explanation for their defeat in the First World War and a scapegoat in the form of a Judaeo–Bolshevik–Masonic conspiracy. In 1922 right-wing extremists fuelled by the 'revelations' in the *Protocols* assassinated Walter Rathenau, the German minister for foreign affairs, believing him to be one of the Elders. The following year saw the prominent Nazi Alfred Rosenberg writing a book embellishing the *Protocols* with his own theories concerning the Jewish conspiracy. Exactly when Hitler himself came across the *Protocols* is unclear but by the early 1920s they were fundamental to his anti-Semitic outlook on the world: 'I have read the *Protocols of the Elders of Zion* – it simply appalled me. The stealthiness of the enemy, and his ubiquity! I saw at once that we must copy it – in our own way, of course . . . It is in truth the critical battle for the fate of the world!'[11] Here we have in Hitler's own words not only confirmation of his total faith in the existence of the Elders of Zion but also his plan to mirror their supposed plan for world domination: the German master race was set to do battle with the chosen people.

Like Jung, the historian Norman Cohn notes the remarkable tenacity of myths and their tendency to maintain an independent existence from the individuals and groups who make use of them. 'Myths do not necessarily disappear with the circumstances that first produced them. They sometimes acquire an autonomy, a vitality of their own, that carries them across the continents and down the centuries. This was very much the case with the demonological view of Jewry and Judaism.'[12]

Cohn explains the idea of the Jewish world conspiracy as a case of collective psychopathology on the part of the European peoples. Although Cohn explains this in Freudian terms (the conflict between the father – the Jewish people and the God of the Old Testament – and the son – the Christians and their God) such a psychological explanation resonates with Jung's theory that the unconscious possession of Hitler and the German nation was an episode of mass psychosis. Cohn sees the myth of the Jewish world conspiracy as the resurgence and culmination of the eruptions of anti-Semitism which took place in the Middle Ages. The irrational hatred of Jews has its origins in Christianity and not in paganism. From medieval times onwards the Jews were seen as responsible for the ultimate crime, deicide – the murder of God. The Jews were blamed for the Crucifixion as Christ was killed at their behest. It follows from this, in the peculiar logic of the myth, that they are therefore the enemies of God, and the covenant they once had with God was broken irrevocably by this most heinous crime. Henceforth they are the spiritual enemy and often play the role of demons or satanic agents bent on undermining and destroying Christianity. They are perceived as the enemy within. Such a myth was often employed in the Middle Ages and in later periods of history in order to justify the persecution of Jews and the seizing of their property and wealth.

We can conclude that there is no connection between modern anti-Semitism and ancient paganism. The pagans of the northern world had little or no contact with Jewish people. Among the eastern Vikings there were intrepid traders who travelled as far as the Middle East and it is possible that they had occasional interactions with Jews but there is no reason (and no evidence whatsoever) to believe that any enmity existed between the two. The historical root of the widespread anti-Semitism which exists in the modern world is fundamentally Christian and based on the supposed deicide of the Crucifixion. Thus paganism and anti-Semitism have no historical connection. Historical northern paganism was not anti-Semitic; it was simply non-Semitic.

It is, however, true that some modern racist neo-pagans have espoused a version of the traditional anti-Semitism of Christian European culture. In this variation of the myth it is argued that the conversion of European (or Aryan) civilisation to Christianity was an ideological disaster in which Jehovah, the ethnic god of the Jews, became transformed into the universal God of Christianity. This supposedly resulted in the ideological subordination of the Aryan people to the Semitic race and in some racist writings this is seen as part of the age-old Jewish plot. Thus there are two basic mythologies of anti-Semitism: one originating within Christianity which has been upheld, on occasion, by some Christians, and another, more modern, version which extends its rejection of Jewish influence to Christianity itself.

Not only is there no historical link between northern paganism and anti-Semitic thinking, there is also no fundamental link between modern paganism and hatred of the Jews. There are many anti-Semites in the world today and their religious, ethnic and political allegiances vary widely. A few espouse pagan doctrines but many more call themselves Christians, Muslims or communists. The myth of the Jewish world conspiracy to overthrow the European nations and their traditional hierarchies led to the demonising of the chosen people by a Christian and racist Germany. In Nazi mythology, in which the *Protocols* played such a large role, the Jews became not just political targets and enemies but also came to embody cosmic evil. Whilst most Nazis and their supporters saw themselves as Christian there was nevertheless a stream of pagan which flowed within the Third Reich through the channels of occultism. This stream sprang from the visions of an Austrian mystic named Guido von List.

Chapter 10

The Blind One

Wuotan [Odin] lives in the human body in order to go under; 'he consecrated himself to himself', and he consecrates himself to 'passing away' in order to rise anew. The nearer he feels himself coming to the moment of his 'passing away towards new arising' – his death – the clearer the knowledge grows in him that the secret of life is an eternal 'arising' and 'passing away', an eternal return, a life of continuous birth and death.

Guido von List, *The Secret of the Runes*[1]

Guido von List (1848–1919), a native of Austria, was the founder of the modern runic revival. He was born into a well-to-do merchant family in Vienna, his father being in the leather trade. He was mystically inclined from an early age and was a precocious reader on mythological matters. In 1862, at the age of fourteen, the young Guido accompanied his father and his friends on a visit down into the catacombs of St Stephen's cathedral in Vienna. Whilst exploring the subterranean depths of this Christian edifice his party came across a ruined altar. The excited Guido announced out loud, 'Whenever I get big, I will build a Temple of Wotan!'[2] This turned out to be a prophetic utterance. List was to resurrect the religion of Wotan both through his imaginative reconstruction of the pagan past in one of the most comprehensive occult mythologies of modern times. He also founded the Armanen Order – an esoteric society dedicated to Wotan and the runes.

It was not just the ancient buildings of his native Austria that entranced List, it was also the natural landscape itself which shaped his ideas. Like the god Odin, List loved to wander in search of knowledge and wisdom. As his translator Stephen Flowers has pointed out, two fundamental ideas formed in List's mind as a result of his youthful wanderings. Firstly, he came to believe that nature (the All-Mother as he called her) was sacred and secondly that his own native land was also sacred. These two themes were to pervade all his subsequent work. He was a keen sketcher, hiker, rower and mountaineer, and became secretary of the Austrian Alpine Association. Although he often explored the Austrian landscape with friends he also liked to travel in solitude. He once remarked, 'one must flee those places where life throbs and seek out lonely spots untouched by human hand in order to lift the magic veil of nature'.[3] These mystical solitary reveries on nature seem to be an instinctual echo of the ancient Germanic practice of *útiseta,* or sitting out, the form of pagan meditation described in Chapter 3.

Often List's trips involved rituals of his own devising. On one such occasion in 1875 he and four friends went to the ruins of the Roman town of Carnuntum. List had planned this so he could celebrate a victory of the German tribes over the Romans which he believed had taken place there in AD 375 – exactly 1500 years earlier. As part of his private ritual List buried eight empty wine bottles in the shape of a swastika beneath the Hiedentor (Pagan Gate) of the ancient settlement. List was later to describe the swastika (which he calls the fyrfos, another way of writing fylfot) as an esoteric rune and the 'innermost secret' of the ancient Norse poets. During these formative years List spent as much time as he could in his mystical wanderings whilst fulfilling his obligations to the family business.

After his father's death in 1877 the family business declined and so too did List's economic security. He began a career as a journalist, writing articles about his journeys and his ideas on the meaning of landscape and ancient sites. Such writings appealed to the pan-German nationalism of the time and, encouraged by this favourable reception, he also began to write a historical novel based on his nationalistic reconstruction of events which had taken place at Carnuntum. When it was published in 1888 to wide acclaim List could count many prominent nationalists among his admirers. One of these was an industrialist named Friedrich Wannieck, who became his long-term friend and patron. Not only did Wannieck get his own publishing house to print a number of List's subsequent books he was also to become the financial impetus behind the foundation of the Guido von List Society early in the next century.

The visions of Guido von List

In 1891 List was among the founders of an influential circle of writers known as the Iduna – from the name of the pagan goddess of rejuvenation. The group propagated a neo-romantic stance which was markedly anti-realistic and counted the young Rudolf Steiner among its members. But purely literary interests were soon to be eclipsed by an occult revolution brought about by the rise of Theosophy – a mystical amalgam of modern science, Western occultism and Eastern religion which Madame Blavatsky had founded in New York in 1875. Blavatsky's influence was enormous; she has been described as 'arguably the most influential woman in Europe and America at the time'.[4]

The German translation of Blavatsky's gargantuan magnum opus *The Secret Doctrine* was published at the turn of the twentieth century. In this two-volume work Blavatsky outlines one of the most extensive and detailed modern mythologies to have emerged from the occult underground. Geological time periods are synthesised with mystical ramblings on numerous lost continents and a description of the spiritually advanced 'root races' of humanity.[5] Blavatsky claimed that she was in clairvoyant contact with 'Hidden Masters' who guided her in her occult reveries and allowed her access to numerous ancient mysteries.

Although both List and Steiner were shortly to fall under the spell of Theosophy they used its doctrines in ways not only different to those of Blavatsky but also to each other. Steiner, after becoming a prominent Theosophist, later founded his own movement which he named Anthroposophy. For List the appeal of Theosophy was that it drew heavily on the Hindu tradition which, being 'Aryan' or Indo-European in origin, was highly compatible with the pan-German movement, which sought to cast off Judaeo-Christian influences from Germanic culture. One of List's admirers, the racist gnostic and ex-Cistercian monk Jörg Lanz von Liebenfels, was later to coin the term Ariosophy (wisdom of the Aryans) to describe the occult stream of thought that both he and List worked in.

Whilst proto-Nazi, Nazi and neo-Nazi theorists have all drawn on the discoveries and theories of academic orientalists they gained more inspiration from Theosophy. They found its claims for a supposedly ancient Aryan occultism that was older and more complete than the Judaeo-Christian tradition to be attractive. As Theosophy combined complex mythological themes with an equally developed esoteric theory of the origin of humanity and its various races it was ideally suited to the development of Aryan racial mysticism.[6]

Liebenfels' adaptation of Theosophical ideas provided an occult backdrop to List's literary output which had, up to that time, been largely a combination of his fervent nationalism (with anti-Semitic overtones) and his imaginative reconstruction of the pagan legacy of the Germans. The spiritual turning point for List took place rather late in life, when he was in his mid-fifties. Towards the end of 1902 he underwent a cataract operation and was obliged to wear bandages over his eyes for eleven months. In this state of near-blindness he cultivated his inner vision and claims to have become enlightened concerning the mysteries of the runes and their occult meaning. Without doubt List was aware not only that Odin had been known as 'the blind one' but also that he had sacrificed an eye in order to gain wisdom. List probably also saw parallels between his own revelations concerning the runes and the initiation of Odin when he hung on the tree for nine nights. According to the *Havamal* text in the Eddas, Odin's ordeal ended with his vision of the runes, the powers and uses of which are described as being eighteen in number. The runes that List 'saw' were eighteen in number and from these he developed his idiosyncratic version of the runic alphabet.

The phantom pagan priesthood

List came to believe that his clairvoyant visions into the ancestral past of the Germans had given him unique insights unknown to others. He was convinced that the wisdom of Germanic paganism had existed historically on two levels. The outer or exoteric doctrine he calls Wotanism (or Odinism), whilst the inner, esoteric doctrine of Armanism was concerned with the deeper mysteries. List developed a highly detailed account of this esoteric pagan religion, its teachings and its organisation. In doing so he borrowed heavily from the Rosicrucian and Masonic traditions. According to List, the Armanist priesthood was divided into three grades corresponding to the three degrees of Freemasonry – entered apprentice, fellow craft and master mason. He also claimed that this pagan system continued in the Christian era.

Vestiges of this tradition were said to have been preserved in two ways. Firstly, Armanist initiates within the Church encoded parts of their ancient lore in symbols which List believed he could decipher. Other elements of pagan mysticism were kept alive through folk beliefs and practices. List's way of deciphering the Armanist tradition was based both on his visions and on his own method of revealing the secret meanings of ancient symbols and various German words. Like Blavatsky, List believed that through his visionary activities he could gain access to ancestral memories. He claimed to be able to make contact with the ancient Armanist brotherhood and taught some of his pupils to do the same. Thus his whole reconstruction of the pagan tradition is based on a highly subjective rewriting of the past which bears little resemblance to history.

It is a familiar pattern in occult mythologies that esoteric groups of the past are portrayed as part of a mystical chain in the transmission of secret lore. List wished to recast the European past to fit the mould of his Armanist theory. This included an ideology which required that the Western occult tradition be shown to have not only Germanic roots but, at each stage, to be exclusively Germanic in its manifestations as it sought to survive under the rod of Catholic suppression. The Knights Templar, Renaissance hermeticists, the Rosicrucians and the Freemasons were all portrayed as transmitters of the secret Armanist legacy. That Jewish mysticism in the form of Kabbalism had an enormous influence on European occult thought was something that List could not accept. In order to expunge the role of the Jews he developed tortuous arguments. Nowhere is this more clearly seen than in his interpretation of the historical role of Johann Reuchlin (1455–1522) a leading Renaissance humanist.

Reuchlin had studied Hebrew and became convinced that the writings of Plato were based on the Kabbalistic books of the Jews. At the beginning of the sixteenth century anti-Semitism was rife in Germany and forces within the Catholic Church were calling for the confiscation of the Jewish holy books as part of a campaign to convert the Jews to Christianity. Reuchlin spoke out strongly in defence of the Jews and their right to religious freedom. Despite accusations of heresy from Dominicans, Reuchlin was eventually vindicated. It would be obvious to conclude from this that Reuchlin was clearly not only a student of the Kabbalistic tradition but also the last person to be accused of anti-Semitism. List however had his own explanation for these events.

He claimed that during a period of intense Catholic persecution of the Armanist priesthood which took place in eighth-century Cologne the secret teachings were transmitted to the Jews of that city for temporary safe keeping. The rabbis then wrote the teachings down in the form of Kabbalistic texts which they then claimed to be their own tradition. Thus, like so many other anti-Semites who find much of interest in the Kabbalistic tradition, List created a spurious reconstruction of the past so that he could have his cake and eat it too. The icing on the cake was provided by List's bizarre belief that he was a reincarnation of Reuchlin.[7]

In 1908 the Guido von List Society was founded by Wannieck and other supporters of the 'master'. This was to become the main vehicle for the exoteric dissemination of List's synthesis of racist ideology and occult teachings. Three years later a more esoteric group was founded, the High Armanic Order (HAO), of which List was the grand master. The HAO was set up as a modern counterpart to the old Armanic priesthood. Little is known of the activities of the HAO beyond the fact that its members sometimes made pilgrimages to ancient sites identified by List with the Armanic tradition.

Blueprints for the Holocaust

As has been shown in this book new models for organising the wider society are often foreshadowed by visions and imaginary social worlds. The Vril-ya of Lytton's novel and the phantom Armanist priesthood of List act as visionary blueprints for possible social changes to come. The power of List's vision was not so much that it shed light on the past (as his mythical reconstruction of an Armanist past has little in common with the pagan heritage of history) but that it cast a shadow on the future. Nicholas Goodrick-Clarke in his scholarly work *The Occult Roots of Nazism* makes this clear:

> List's blueprint for a new pan-German empire was detailed and unambiguous. It called for the ruthless subjection of non-Aryans to Aryan masters in a highly structured

hierarchical state. The qualification of candidates for education or positions in public service, the professions and commerce rested solely on their racial purity. The heroic Ario-Germanic race was to be relieved of all wage-labour and demeaning tasks, in order to rule as an exalted elite over the slave castes of non-Aryan peoples. List codified a set of political principles for the new order: strict racial and marital laws were to be observed; a patriarchal society was to be fostered in which only the male head of the house had full majority and only Ario-Germans enjoyed the privileges of freedom and citizenship; each family was to keep a genealogical record attesting its racial purity; a new feudalism was to develop through the creation of large estates which could not be broken up but inherited only by the first-born male in a family. These ideas, published as early as 1911, bear an uncanny resemblance to the Nuremberg racial laws of the 1930s and the Nazi vision of the future.[8]

We have already seen how politically charged mythologies and fantasies like *The Protocols of the Elders of Zion* affect the real world and List's vision of a new order is a blueprint for the Nazi regime. List's visions had much more to do with forming the ideology of totalitarianism than with any genuine revival of pagan traditions. There can be no doubt that List understood the power of myth and its effects on concrete social realities. He made this clear when discussing the myth of the revival of Odin: 'The reborn Wuotan [Odin], i.e., the renewed Wuotan who has climbed down from the world-tree after his self-sacrifice . . . is personified in the young sun- and sword-god, Tyr. According to the rule of mysticism, every magical belief moves parallel to mythology, in that the mythic pattern is adopted in analogies to human-earthly processes, in order to reach results similar to those given in the myths.'[9] The 'mythic pattern' (blueprint) that List

created and desired to become a social reality was not based on real
pagan roots but was rather a modern mythology which had its
analogy to 'human-earthly processes' in the Nazi state which sought
to reach results similar to those given in his myth – in word and in
action a modern totalitarian nightmare.

List's life and work were clearly driven by the Odinic archetype.
His temporary blindness and his vision of the runes present us with a
human parallel to the archetypal myth. List's overall mythology was
created out of altered states of consciousness – his clairvoyant and
visionary journeys into the streams of supposedly ancestral memory.
List exhorted his followers to 'read with our souls the landscape which
archaeology reconquers with the spade'.[10] 'Psychic archaeology' was
set up in opposition to the findings of the spade; the tangible evidence
of the archaeologist was of little interest to List and his followers.

How are we to explain List's interaction with the Odinic
archetype? It seems he was possessed by the archetype. As a
consequence of this he created a series of fantasies not only about the
pagan past but also the supposed continuity of this ancient lore within
the Christian, and even Jewish, religious traditions. His visions led
him to believe that his modern mythology was a genuine revival of
the primordial 'Aryan' tradition.

Chapter 11

Rune Yoga

Runes are not just letters or verbal symbols but primal symbols of a living magical nature which whisper to us. These may be experienced through Runic postures and dances and are useful for your own well-being and even for the blessing of all mankind.

Siegfried Adolf Kummer, *Rune Magic*[1]

Guido von List believed that the Germanic peoples (Teutons as he calls them) had maintained a balance between the spiritual and physical aspects of life that the other Aryan peoples had lost. In his opinion the 'Aryo-Indian' Buddhists had cultivated the spiritual at the expense of the physical and as a result had preserved their ethnic individuality but lost their political freedom. The Mediterranean Aryans (the Greeks and the Romans) had done the reverse. By concentrating on the physical and material they had become world powers but damaged their moral vitality in the process and so lost any distinctive culture they had possessed and so they disappeared. The Germanic peoples, by cultivating the physical and spiritual as two inseparable parts of a whole, had preserved both their ethnic identity and political autonomy.[2]

In the wake of the modern runic revival initiated by List a number of individuals drew on Indo-European cultural traditions in order to balance the physical and spiritual poles. They attempted to develop a European version of Indian yoga using the runes as the starting point for both bodily postures and related spiritual techniques. They did so more in the belief that Indian yoga derived ultimately from some lost Atlantean tradition of spiritual exercises rather than on the basis of the striking archaeological evidence gathered together here in Chapter 3. A close look at the runic physical exercises developed by these modern pagan experimenters shows them to be based on theories closely akin to the kundalini of yogic philosophy and a field of energies which can be tapped into by a system of inner technology. The two key figures in the runic revival who outlined a physical basis for the runes were Friedrich Marby and Siegfried Kummer.

The life of Friedrich Marby

Friedrich Bernhard Marby (1882–1966), born in Friesland in the northern Netherlands, was of mixed Frisian and Swedish extraction. As a young man he moved to Hanover, where he became a printer's apprentice in 1896. During his time there he began his studies of the runes mainly through reading the works of Guido von List, although he claimed that his initial esoteric study of the runes took place in 1907, a year before List published his *Secrets of the Runes*. Later, after Marby had moved to Stuttgart in 1917 to take up a post as a newspaper editor, he began to combine his interest in the runes with astrology. In 1922 he published the first of a number of books on his own system of esoteric rune studies. In order to make contact with his Scandinavian roots he made journeys to both Sweden and Denmark before founding the International Central Association of Germanic Runic Researchers on 1 July 1931. This association still operates – now run by Rudolf Arnold Spieth, who has also reprinted Marby's works.[3]

In 1933 he returned to Germany, hoping to find it congenial to his mystical study of the runes. Yet even though he had been an open supporter of the Nazi party and had espoused anti-Semitism in print he was to become a victim of the Third Reich in 1936 when he was arrested by the Gestapo. What exactly led to his arrest is unclear but he was deemed an anti-Nazi occultist. It has been suggested that it might have been due to a letter sent to Heinrich Himmler in 1934 by a rival occultist named Karl von Wiligut (the subject of Chapter 13) which denounced not only Marby but also another important rune occultist, Siegfried Kummer. Whatever the cause of Marby's arrest it led to his imprisonment, firstly at Welzheim concentration camp and subsequently at Flossenbürg and Dachau. He was freed from Dachau by American troops on 29 April 1945. Although he claimed that as a journalist he had spoken out against the Nazi regime he received no compensation, due to the pro-Nazi and anti-Semitic statements that had appeared in his pre-war publications. After liberation he continued to write and pursue his rune studies until his death in Stuttgart.

Marby in Atland

A key influence on Marby's ideas was the *Oera Linda Book.* The legend concerning the supposedly ancient origin of this text states that Cornelius Over de Linden, from whom the book gets its name, inherited a very ancient manuscript which had been in his family for untold generations. The text was translated into Dutch and published in 1871. An English edition appeared a few years later (William R. Sandbach, *The Oera Linda Book: From a Manuscript of the Thirteenth Century,* Trubner, London, 1876) containing a translation by Sandbach from the Dutch version by Dr J.O. Ottema along with the original Frisian text. Ottema describes 'Atland' as a land stretching far out from the west of Jutland of which Heligoland and the islands of North Frisia are the last remnants. In 2193 BC Atland was said to have been destroyed by a natural catastrophe but some of its inhabitants survived and later founded many of the world's ancient civilisations. There are even hints that one of its 'sea-kings' may have founded the Inca empire in Peru. Along with this pseudo-history the book contains a number of runic diagrams using the thirty-three runes of the Anglo-Frisian tradition.[4]

As the *Oera Linda Book* purported to be an account of the remote prehistoric civilisation of his native Friesland it naturally appealed to Marby. Following the *Oera Linda Book,* Marby believed that this runic system had its origins in an ancient tradition once practised in the lost world of Atland, the Frisian version of Atlantis, said to have sunk beneath the waves of the North Sea. This lost motherland provided the mythological backdrop to Marby's ideas and practices.

Rune gymnastics

Marby was the first modern occultist to understand the runes not just as signs and sounds but as bodily postures, developing a mystical system of physical exercise which he called Runengymnastik, runic gymnastics. Unlike List, who used his own Armanic version of the futhark, Marby drew on his heritage, using the ancient Anglo-Frisian futhorc – a runic script that, as we have seen, he believed had originated in Atland. Marby thought that rune gymnastics were once practised widely across the Germanic world in Scandinavia, in Britain and on the continent. He saw vestiges of this practice in the fact that in Scandinavia children learned the alphabet by imitating the shape of the letters with their bodies.[5] Marby developed a number of body postures based on the shape of the Anglo-Frisian runes. He believed that this mystical form of gymnastics allowed the practitioner access to hidden energies coursing through the universe.

In Marby's cosmology there are five zones of space, depicted as a series of concentric circles (see Figure 7). At the centre is the zone he calls Inner Earth Space, echoing the mythology of a hollow earth which appears in Lytton's *The Coming Race,* Verne's *Journey to the Centre of the Earth,* and in Herman Hesse's Jungian journey into the psychological interior. Marby describes this zone as a vast and tranquil repository of energies which can be accessed by the practice of runic gymnastics. The second zone is Material Earth Space – the

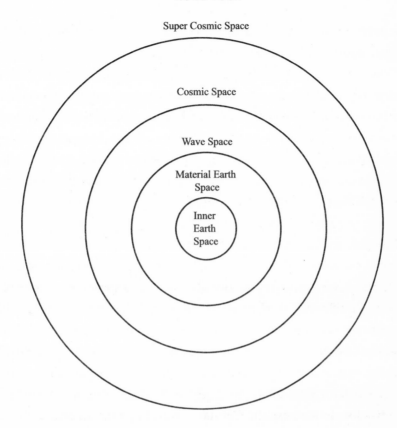

Figure 7: Diagram of Marby's cosmology

physical body of our planet pervaded by various ancient forms of energy. Wave Space lies just above the surface of the earth. Being the third of the five zones it is in this region that the streams of energy from both above and below are exchanged. The fourth zone he calls Cosmic Space, and this is filled with the energies of the planets and stars. Beyond this is the fifth and final zone, Super Cosmic Space, which, like Inner Earth Space, is tranquil yet filled with subtle forms of energy.

The third zone, where the energies from above and below meet, is also the region in which our physical bodies exist. It is for this reason that the body itself and the runic gymnastics which it can perform are so significant for Marby. He likens the rune magician to an antenna which can receive, store and transmit numerous subtle energies like radio waves through his mystical system of gymnastics. These energies can be recognised and worked with through the runes themselves. Marby believed that by working with these energies the individual can be spiritually and physically healed. He also believed that if a group or even a nation were to practise his system in unison the body of society itself would also benefit by being spiritually purified by these higher energies (a notion clearly inspired by Völkisch ideas).

Like List and countless other occultists Marby believed that certain places were repositories of energy. As we have seen, such places of power could be simply natural or sites of ancient cultural importance. Different kinds of energies pervade different kinds of site. If the magician wants to perform operations concerned with the everyday sphere of existence then he or she should go to a level piece of land where the zones of Wave Space and Earth Space interface and allow the practitioner to draw on these twin sources of energy. For the development of new ideas and visions of the future the magician should tap into the energy field of Wave Space by placing him- or herself on a tower or raised platform in order not only to be more fully attuned to the third zone but also to decrease contact with the energies of Earth Space. We have already seen that the pagan practice of *seidr* took place on platforms raised above the ground and it was from such elevated positions that the seeress would go into trance and see visions of what was to come to pass. The raised position that Marby describes can also be compared to Norse myths which tell of the elevated seat of Odin from where he was able to see all the worlds.

Marby also identified mountains and hilltops as places which combined access to the energies of Wave Space whilst maintaining contact with the Earth Space energies that are especially strong in such places, spiralling upwards in a cone of power. These locations are to be used for turning spiritual visions into concrete realities. Marby claimed to have discovered the remains of anciently fashioned 'funnels' – artificial structures dug into the ground in the shape of descending spiral terraces. If practices were performed at the bottom of such places then the earth energies would be paramount and the energies of Wave Space concentrated at the base of an inverted spiral of power. In such workings the magician would be able to tap into old ideas and memories and bring them to fruition. As such these kinds of operation are opposite (but also complementary) to those performed on hilltops or mountain peaks. Marby also mentions another kind of location – an enclosed subterranean place such as a natural cave, an ancient passage grave or an underground room. It is in such places that the magician is able to use the Inner Earth energies to tap into the ancient ancestral memories which can most strongly be felt in these chthonic realms.

The actual practice of Marby's runic gymnastics system is based on the I-rune exercise. This may be performed whilst standing, walking or sitting and is a form of meditation. When standing upright and still the practitioner should look directly ahead with the chin facing down, chest out and with the feet making a right angle with the heels touching. When walking the feet should face forward with the elbows slightly bent and the palms facing forward in a cupped position. When sitting in a chair the knees should be together and the palms placed on them with the arms close to the body. All of these three variations of the I-rune exercise have the same aim – to concentrate the mind on the single and simple thought: 'I am here.' In Marby's system of runic gymnastics the I-rune plays a role similar to the lotus position of yoga: it is the core posture of the system and the most conducive to meditation.

The I-rune exercise and the other exercises he describes are not simply postures; the breathing must be regulated and the sound of the particular rune chanted and modulated. It is through runic gymnastics and their accompanying chants that the various subtle and hidden energies of the cosmos can be worked with by the magician. Steve Anthonijsz, a writer on runic exercises, explains how

Marby's system works on the whole nexus of the mind, body and spirit of the human organism. The practitioner:

> Is able to send and receive energy patterns to/from all five of these zones not unlike transmissions sent and received through a short-wave radio antenna. By controlling the body (via runic postures/dances), controlling the thoughts (by visualizing the stave, usually in its assigned colour), by controlling the breath (through breathing patterns and by intoning the rune), and control of the emotions one is able to secure the rune. Attuning to a particular rune might be compared to tuning to a certain frequency on a radio; the antenna still receives all the various signals, but only the selected frequency is being manifested and manipulated by the system.[6]

The benefits and powers of these exercises include an increased psycho-physical vitality (a direct result of tapping into the energies), control over the emotions and a tranquil state of mind. Marby claimed that success with his exercises also had an effect on the magician's relationship with other people. Charisma or personal magnetism would be increased and the combined effects of greater vitality and tranquillity would emanate to those around the magician, thus quelling strife and social discord. Despite his numerous writings over a long period, Marby never developed a complete system of runic postures for all thirty-three runes of the Anglo-Frisian futhorc.

The rune yoga of Siegfried Kummer

Whilst Marby was developing his idiosyncratic set of runic exercises another occultist named Siegfried Adolf Kummer was developing List's eighteen Armanen runes into a form of Germanic yoga he called Runenyoga, setting up Runa, his own rune school, near Dresden in 1927. According to followers of Marby, Kummer's claim to have originated his system was untrue; they maintain he was a wayward student of Marby who falsely claimed to have first developed the practice of rune postures in the modern era. Kummer seems to have taken the practical aspect of Marby's ideas and combined them with theories derived from Armanic thinking. Little is known about the life of Kummer and even less concerning his death. He disappeared from history when Karl von Wiligut apparently denounced both Marby and him in a letter to Himmler in 1934. Unsubstantiated rumours claim that he fled to South America, although it is more likely that he perished in one of the camps that Marby was to survive or died during the Allied blanket bombing of Dresden.

Although there are a number of similarities between Kummer and Marby there are also marked differences. Unlike Marby's exercises those developed by Kummer were inspired by Indian yoga. The basis of his system can be found in his *Runen-Magie* (*Rune Magic*) published in Dresden in 1933 and translated by the scholar and rune magician Edred Thorsson (the pen name of Stephen Flowers).[7] At the beginning of this book Kummer defines rune magic as knowledge of cosmic energies and the hidden energies of nature.

Through this magic contact can be made with energy streams, subtle wave-forms and otherwise unknown entities and powers. Drawing on the modern mythology of the Ariosophists, he describes the runes as the original (and Aryan) language from which all others derive. For him the earliest futhark was the Armanen rune row of eighteen which List 'recovered' from the primordial past through his visionary access to ancestral memories.

Kummer's apparent debt to Marby seems to surface when he describes the wider nature of the runes and the energies to which they may give access. The runes are not just letters and sounds but can also be experienced physically through runic postures and dances. They can be used to benefit not only oneself but also humanity as a whole. The runes can reveal great secrets if one learns how to perform the exercises and dances in the radio waves and other subtle energies which pervade the universe. Clairvoyance, prophetic visions and other psychic powers can be developed with their aid. The ultimate aim of his system is to develop the higher powers so that the magician can overcome his lower nature and become a 'god-man'.

In addition to drawing on the Indian yoga tradition Kummer was also inspired by the grimoires, magical manuals associated with the notorious Dr Faustus and other sorcerers. Almost all grimoires describe the use of a Kabbalistic circle adorned with the names of God and various spirits. It is within such protective circles that the magician must conduct his spells and conjurations. Taking inspiration from the writings of Guido von List, Kummer's magical circle has the eighteen Armanic runes drawn around its circumference and the names of various Germanic deities within this outer circle. The circle must be drawn on the ground with green chalk and the names of the runes and gods must be written with red chalk (traditionally, carved runes were coloured red). Whilst inscribing the circle (beginning in the north with the first rune Fe) the rune magician must meditate and pray in order to banish evil spirits and malign forces. If he is working at night the magician can also use a candlestick, a censer and holy water to aid him in his operations. Once the circle has been completed along with the inscribing of all the runes and god-names the magician can begin his runic postures within the spiritually purified zone.

Kummer outlined a magical training programme consisting of a series of thirteen 'sacred' exercises each connected directly to a particular rune and its shape. Why he did not expand this to the full eighteen runes of the Armanen futhark is not clear. The practitioner is instructed to concentrate for a fortnight on the first rune in the series before moving on to the next, which also should be practised for a further fourteen days before continuing. Whilst each runic posture is performed it must be accompanied by the appropriate runic chant – comparable to the *mantras* used in yoga. Each exercise causes particular spiritual results and working with all of the Sacred Thirteen was said to be the key to unlocking the secrets of the runes.

As Marby described the body as an antenna for receiving, collecting and transmitting radio waves so Kummer exhorted his magicians to intone, 'I am a staff for beams and waves of rune might!'[8] He also gave detailed descriptions of the movements of energy through the body which accompany the performing of the various runic exercises. For example, the exercise of the Man rune involves energy from the all-power streaming like radio waves into the back of the magician's head and flowing through the back and sympathetic nerves until it gathers in the solar plexus region. Other waves of power also flow through the body at the same time stimulating the thymus gland in the chest and activating the spleen before boosting the energies in the solar plexus region and then dissipating from there out into the aura that surrounds the physical body.

Kummer notes that the heart and kidneys play a major role in the developing of spiritual and magical powers. He also details a subtle anatomy of the human organism which highlights the other important glands and higher centres of the body. These key regions of the body play an important role in receiving and discharging subtle energies. The pineal gland, navel and sexual organs are among the centres for the reception of energies, whilst the feet and the sexual organs (again) are centres for the discharge of energies. Beyond the direct confines of the physical body is the aura or psychic cloak – a personal sphere of energy which we may describe as analogous to the atmosphere of a planetary body.

The *mudras*, the ritualistic and symbolic hand signs used in yoga, are also echoed in Kummer's description of the hand positions which correspond with the Armanen runes. These hand positions are to be performed whilst in the appropriate runic posture and their use is said to cause some unusual supra-sensory phenomena or hallucinations – affecting not only vision but also hearing and the sense of smell. The hand signs in conjunction with the rune postures cause the appearance of various 'astral' colours, images and dis-embodied voices. Some even cause the practitioner to experience strange smells such as that of ozone, sulphur, burnt electrical wires or gunpowder.

Baron von Reichenbach's notion of an Odic force is taken up by Kummer, who describes how the advanced rune magician is able to construct around himself a 'very strong Odic mist' which he equates with the 'cape of invisibility', one of the magical treasures obtained by the hero Siegfried in the German epic the *Nibelungenleid*.

Chapter 12

Thule: Island of Darkness

Thule in the Tyrian tongue was 'a shadow,' whence it is commonly used to signify 'darkness', and the island Thule is as much as to say, an 'island of darkness' . . .

R.F. Burton, *Ultima Thule*[1]

We have seen how the lost continent of the European imagination has surfaced in many forms – in the mythical geography of Hyperborea, in the works of Verne and Lytton and in the pseudo-history of the *Oera Linda Book*. This theme became a source of inspiration for the growing anti-Semitic and proto-Nazi organisation called the Thule Society. Thule is a word which means little to anyone except those interested in ancient history or familiar with that branch of modern history which concerns itself with the darker side of occultism and political extremism.

Textbooks on the history of polar research invariably start with an intrepid Greek voyager named Pytheas. Around 2300 years ago he set out from the trading port of Massalia (modern Marseille) and journeyed further north than any of his compatriots had ever gone, travelling beyond Britain to a location that he named Thule. He recorded these travels in his *On the Ocean*, the original of which has unfortunately been lost. However, Pytheas was quoted by various other ancient writers such as the geographer Strabo, who mocked his apparently wild assertions about this undiscovered northern land.

Debate still rages as to the actual geographical location of Pytheas' Thule. Trondheim in Norway, the Shetland Islands and the Faroes have all been put forward as possible candidates but most scholars agree that he was probably referring to Iceland.[2] The fact that Pytheas' account of his voyage was not widely believed in the ancient world meant that whilst Thule did sometimes appear on maps of the earth it had another existence, namely in the realm of the imagination. Ultima Thule became an evocative symbol for a fabulous land in the far north in the works of Roman poets. The word Thule itself has many variants both in how it is written (Thula, Thyle, Tyle, Tula, Tila among them) and in its suggested meaning.[3] It is variously interpreted as denoting a resting place (of the sun), most remote land, the furthest place and in some instances Thule was equated with Hyperborea.

The mystical Thule or Ultima Thule continued to play a minor role in European thinking. Johann Wolfgang von Goethe wrote a short poem entitled *The King of Thule* (1774) and it began to become a more common theme in German occultism around the turn of the twentieth century. Whilst living in Paris MacGregor Mathers, the leader of the Hermetic Order of the Golden Dawn, Britain's leading occult order in its day, struck up a close friendship with a German named Max Danthendey (1857–1918) who wrote a number of occult novels including one entitled *Die Frau von Thule* (1898).[4]

The Thule Society

But this trickle of interest in the old myth was soon to turn into a politically charged torrent. In 1918 the Germanenorden, a secretive quasi-Masonic lodge of anti-Semites, decided to change its name to the Thule Society. This new incarnation took as its emblem a swastika adorned with a dagger (see Plate 1, page 8). Entry was subject to strict racial guidelines and questions about skin, eye and hair colour appeared on the forms to be filled in by prospective members, whilst the physically handicapped were barred. A prominent member was Ernst Haeckel (1834–1919), one of the leading German biologists of his day. Haeckel had shown that humans were descended from apes a few years before Darwin proposed the same (as Darwin himself acknowledged). He was also interested in applying Darwinist thinking to human society and even set up Monism, a religion designed to replace Christianity, which drew its inspiration from the findings of modern science.

The clandestine meetings of the Thule Society in Munich were rudely interrupted when, in November 1918, Bavaria was suddenly but peacefully taken over by socialist revolutionaries led by a Jewish journalist named Kurt Eisner. The Wittelsbach royal family was deposed and it seemed that the Thule Society's worst nightmare was coming true. The society's leader, the occultist and political activist Rudolf von Sebottendorff, addressed the assembled brethren the day after this revolution and reportedly said,

> Yesterday we experienced the collapse of everything which was familiar, dear and valuable to us. In the place of our princes of Germanic blood rules our deadly enemy: Judah. What will come of this chaos, we do not know yet. But we can guess. A time will come of struggle . . . I am determined to pledge the Thule to this struggle. Our Order is a Germanic Order . . . our god is Walvater, his rune is the Ar-rune. And the trinity: Wotan, Wili, We is the unity of the trinity. The Ar-rune signifies Aryan, primal fire, the sun and the eagle.[5]

Nicholas Goodrick-Clarke a leading authority on the history of Nazi and neo-Nazi mysticism, points out that Sebottendorff's words reveal the influence of Guido von List. The trinity of pagan gods was one of List's innovations and the multiple meanings given to the Ar-rune in the speech are taken directly from List's work. Goodrick-Clarke also suspects that the name of the Thule Society owes much to List's indirect inspiration. According to List, Iceland had been the refuge of Armanist sages fleeing the persecution of the Catholic Church. Sebottendorff identified Iceland with Thule, making the Thule Society a symbolic stronghold of the Armanist faith. The Thule Society soon became a powerhouse of the political right. Weapons training, counter-revolutionary activity and the infiltration of communist groups were all high on their agenda.

The Thule Society also played host to a number of individuals who were to become prominent Nazis, including Alfred Rosenberg and Rudolf Hess, and it is possible to trace other, more symbolic, links with the Nazi party. A member of the Thule Society named Friedrich Krohn advocated in 1919 the use of the swastika as the symbol of the National Socialists – the forerunner of the Nazi party. Hitler approved a modified version of Krohn's design for use on the Nazi flag. Although the pagan influences of Guido von List began to wane when the Thule Society was suppressed under the Third Reich there were a few individuals associated with the Nazi movement for whom northern paganism and the Odinic archetype played an important role and it is to them that we now turn our attention.

The lost Arctic homeland

Hermann Wirth (1885–1981) was born in Utrecht in the Netherlands; his father was German and his mother Dutch. He attended the universities of Utrecht and Leipzig before completing a dissertation on the folk music of the northern Netherlands at the University of Basel. In 1909 he began to teach the language and literature of the Netherlands at the University of Berlin. After the end of the First World War he moved back to his home country, settling in Friesland and working as a high-school teacher. He also became a leader of the youth movement which swept through the Netherlands as it had through Germany. Whilst investigating the folk architecture of his country, he came to believe that ancient traditions dating back to a lost northern homeland had been preserved by Frisian craftsmen. This provided the inspiration for his magnum opus, a huge volume entitled *The Rise of Mankind*, published in 1928. Joscelyn Godwin has brought this long-forgotten work back to life by summarising it for the English-speaking world. Godwin sees rare qualities in his writing:

> Wirth inhabited that borderland that lies between scholarship and the world of the imagination. Such people, and they are rare, serve an invaluable purpose on both sides of the frontier. They bring to the dry bones of academic research an infusion from the mythic imagination, while at the same time they exercise objectivity, reason and control in dealing with subjects that often induce delusions, paranoia and inflation . . . it was important to him that his version of the 'Rise of Mankind' . . . should become a true image in the collective mind, that is, a myth. His whole motivation for this . . . was a concern for the spiritual state of Western man. A similar concern prompts me to study and write about him.[6]

Wirth believed that the technological and scientific progress made in the West had been achieved at the expense of spiritual health. Meditation, without which one can have no meaningful inner life, was actively discouraged by the social environment of the modern world. This spiritual crisis affected different people in different ways. Some sought solace in the revival of Catholic mysticism or fundamentalism, others in Theosophy or Anthroposophy, still others in their pre-Christian roots. As Godwin remarks, this spiritual crisis continues in America with Protestant fundamentalism and the New Age vying for peoples' souls.

Wirth sought spiritual understanding by delving into the ancient and prehistoric northern world. He believed that inscriptions on rocks and on bone and wooden artefacts across the northern hemisphere were examples of a system of symbolic language which he was able to decipher. He claimed that before the last Ice Age Europeans were anything but primitive. He also believed that the earliest human script came from a Stone Age civilisation in the Atlantic–European region and this itself stemmed from an even earlier culture with its now lost homeland within the Arctic Circle.

This Arctic homeland had to be abandoned with the coming of the Ice Age and its inhabitants (whom he calls the Arctic-Nordic race) migrated southwards to North America, to the northern Atlantis which then still existed and to northernmost Asia. It was to the remnants of this race that the subsequent civilisations of ancient Egypt, Sumeria and other ancient cultures were ultimately indebted. In propounding this theory Wirth was turning what had become received wisdom on its head: it was not the east but the north which was the origin of true religion and civilisation; the northern peoples were not barbarians civilised by the more advanced Mediterranean cultures but the heralds of high culture themselves. His version of European prehistory also failed to align itself with the prevailing patriarchy of his day, for the primordial culture he evoked was not simply a male-dominated warrior society but a culture in which peace and the wisdom of women played a major role. Despite his going against so many prevailing dogmas in 1933 he was offered a pro-fessorship in Berlin and commissioned to open a museum dedicated to the old German religion. But in the same year he also published an edition of the *Oera Linda Book*, which he believed, like Marby, contained a core of truth, although it was almost universally rejected as a transparent nineteenth-century forgery.

Wirth felt that because the *Oera Linda Book* included elements of matriarchy and an ancient civilising force from a lost northern homeland its publication in Germany would support his theory. Exactly the opposite happened and his attempt to bolster his own work by means of a book which was condemned as a forgery backfired, bringing him not praise but derision. Nevertheless his reputation was strong enough to survive this setback and in 1935 he became a co-founder of the Ahnenerbe, the research bureau set up by Himmler to investigate the ancestral heritage of the Germans. In 1938 Wirth was dismissed from his post, cast out into the wilderness like many other thinkers and occultists who believed that the Third Reich was the vehicle by which Western spirituality was to be transformed. How wrong they were.

Chapter 13

The Dark Lord of the Rings

I bestow upon you the death's head ring of the SS . . . The death's head is an admonition to be prepared at any time to risk our own individual lives for the life of the collective whole. The runes opposite the death's head are holy signs from our past, with which we have been newly reconnected through the philosophy of National Socialism . . . The swastika and Hagall-rune are to keep our attention on our unshakeable faith in the victory of our philosophy . . .

Wear the ring with honour!

Heinrich Himmler, from the ring presentation ceremony of the SS[1]

From the start we can leave aside spurious and unsubstantiated claims about the practice of satanic rites and other occult goings-on among the Nazi elite. Such stories have grown into a modern mythology and have a cultural importance in that they influence people's perceptions of Nazism. However, we are on much firmer historical ground when we turn to the case of one particular man who emerged from the occult scene to reach a position of power and influence within the Third Reich. Without doubt the occultist who had the most marked influence on the Nazi elite was Karl Maria Wiligut (1866–1946). Like

Guido von List before him, many aspects of his career and personality seem to reflect aspects of the Odinic archetype, as will become clear. Wiligut has been called Himmler's Rasputin on account of his close relationship with the head of the SS. Himmler was, of all the leading Nazis, the one most interested in occult and mystical matters. A vegetarian like Hitler and Hess, he was also a believer in reincarnation and fascinated with legends of the Holy Grail and other ancient mysteries.

Wiligut was born in Vienna in 1866 into a family with a strong military tradition. Both his father and grandfather had been officers in the Austrian army and he followed suit. His military career was successful and he eventually attained the rank of colonel in 1917, before retiring to Salzburg in 1919. He wrote poetry imbued with nature mysticism, myth and nationalistic themes, his first collection, entitled *Seyfried's Runes*, being published in 1903. His interests also extended into the occult, something he claimed was a family tradition. From his own account of his formative years, it was his grandfather Karl Wiligut (1794–1883) who first taught him about the runes and his father initiated him into this secret family tradition in 1890.

In 1889 he had joined the Schlarraffia, a quasi-Masonic lodge. As in his military life Wiligut rose through the ranks of the order reaching the grade of knight and becoming its chancellor until he left the lodge in 1909. His name in the lodge was Lobesam (praiseworthy), the same pseudonym he had used when his first collection of poems was published. Here we can see the elements of a personality which shows connections with the Odinic archetype, for Wiligut was simultaneously warrior, poet and occultist, reflecting Odin as patron of war, poetic inspiration, the runes and the realm of magic. As we shall see shortly, there were other aspects of the god's power that also came out later during his life.

By 1908 Wiligut's claims to belong to a secret Germanic royal bloodline had become known in occult circles in Vienna. That summer he wrote the *Nine Commandments of Gôt*, a series of nine pagan pronouncements designed to replace the Ten Commandments of the Old Testament, the number nine being one of the most important in the mythology of the northern tradition, as we have already seen. Later he published his own version of the Lord's Prayer which he called the Original Our Father.[2]

The ancestral memory

Wiligut claimed to have access to the remote past by means of his highly developed ancestral memory. He portrayed himself as the last in a line of Germanic wise men which he called the Uiligotis of the Asa-Uana-Sippe, maintaining that his clairvoyant powers allowed him to tap into the memories of members of his Germanic tribe right back into prehistoric times. As with his connections with war, poetry, the runes and his membership of an occult lodge, the clairvoyant trances he undertook also relate to Odin as the god of altered states of consciousness.

From such visionary journeys into the memory of his forefathers Wiligut developed his own mythological version of Germanic history and prehistory – which whilst highly idiosyncratic also echoed the visions of Guido von List. Like Blavatsky before him, Wiligut created a new mythology that stretched back to a fantastically remote era. According to one of his most ardent followers, an Austrian named Ernst Rüdiger, Wiligut's mythical prehistory began some 230,000 years ago when the earth was warmed by not one but three suns. The earth was populated at this time by the dwarves, giants and other familiar beings of northern mythology. Some 80,000 years ago a city named Arual-Jöruvallas was founded on the site of the Austrian city of Goslar, supposedly by Wiligut's own ancestors. After numerous inter-tribal wars and migrations to now-lost continents the Irminist religion arose about 12,500 BC and the primordial city of Arual-Jöruvallas became a centre of their faith.

The Irminist religion, to which Wiligut gave his spiritual

allegiance, worshipped a Germanic god named Krist. It was from these roots that the later religion of Christianity would arise, having distorted the original message of the faith. This strange rendition of the religious history of the Germanic peoples was made more complicated by the rival faith of Wotanism, a breakaway religion from Irminism. In 9600 BC Wotanists crucified the Irminist prophet Baldur-Chrestos.[3] After further millennia-long struggles between the opposing faiths the Wotanists laid waste the city of Arual-Jöruvallas in 1200 BC. The Irminists then founded a temple at the Extersteine – the ancient site which plays a similar symbolic role in Germany to that of Stonehenge in Britain. This too was eventually overrun by Wotanists in AD 460 who lost it in turn when the Christian Charlemagne destroyed the pagan Saxon stronghold in the ninth century.

The ancient Wiligut line fled before the forces of Charlemagne, taking a tortuous route in their exile. Escaping first to the Faroe Islands, they then moved on to Russia and subsequently to Hungary in 1242. Throughout this whole period, during which they were threatened by both their old enemies the Wotanists and the Catholic Church, the Wiliguts managed to preserve their Irminist faith intact. Wiligut felt that this persecution had continued to his day and that he was being conspired against by various forces, most notably Catholics, Freemasons and Jews, all of whom were enemies of Irminism.

Like many other Ariosophists Wiligut found it hard to reject his Christian tradition and preferred to deny its foreign and Semitic origins and claim it as Germanic in origin. Thus he also claimed that the Bible was first written in Germany. How literally Wiligut's mythological scheme was meant to be taken is unclear. It is perhaps to be read more as a symbolic journey into the past rather than as an attempt at an alternative literal history. Wiligut sought to preserve Christianity by re-creating its history and, removing its obvious Old Testament origins, placing it far back in Germanic history.

However, it was not just the supposed machinations of Jews, Freemasons and the Catholic Church which threatened the survival of Irminism. Events in his own private life also worked against the continuity of his line. He had married in 1907 and his wife had borne him two daughters and a son. The boy had died whilst still an infant. Wiligut's grief was compounded by his fear that without a male heir to continue his line the future of Irminism could not be assured. He blamed his wife for the death of his son and became increasingly disturbed. An unsound investment in a sawmill, a business venture of an old army comrade, added serious financial difficulties to his problems.

Mental epidemy

Late in 1924, as a result of violence and death threats directed at his wife and increasingly irrational behaviour, he was put in a straitjacket and forcibly committed to a mental asylum in Salzburg, where he remained until he was released early in 1927. His psychiatric report noted that he been certified insane on the basis of his behaviour and had been diagnosed as a schizophrenic suffering from megalomania and paranoia. Certainly his comments to his doctors suggest a polarised attitude to the Odinic archetype. At one stage he told them that his family could ultimately be traced back to Wotan, whom he explained was not a god but a man with remarkable characteristics. On another occasion he dismissed any such relationship claiming to have 'nothing to do with Wotan'.[4] No doubt these contradictory statements were seen as further evidence of his mental disturbance by the medical authorities.

It seems he could not reconcile the Christian and pagan traditions in his mind, and that this led, at least in part, to his breakdown. Odin, the frenzied one, had now caused Wiligut's own personal Ragnarok, the mental epidemy that Jung saw as a symptom of unconscious possession by the Odinic archetype. We should recall also the views of the academic expert on Norse mythology Hilda Davidson, who describes the Ragnarok myth as a metaphor for mental breakdown (see Chapter l).

Throughout the period he spent in the asylum Wiligut kept in regular contact with his devoted group of disciples, some of whom were prominent members of racist occult groups such as the Order of the New Templars and the Edda Society. He also met Frieda Dorenberg in 1932. She was a member of the Edda Society and one of the very first members of the Nazi party, and it was with her help that Wiligut was able to move across the border into Germany with a false identity. On his release Wiligut wished to start a new life and leave both his family and the Salzburg which had incarcerated him behind. He moved to Munich and soon became revered among occultists dedicated to the esoteric study of runes. Wiligut would lecture on his family's secret lineage and the doctrines of Irminism to groups such as the Free Sons of the North and Baltic Seas.

The esoteric meaning of Wiligut's family seal was explained in terms of his personal mythology in an article published in the journal of the Edda Society in 1933. This article made his claims of ancestral wisdom more widely known. The following year saw the Edda Society publish a number of obscure texts by Wiligut, who had by now assumed a new alter ego, writing under the pseudonym Jarl Widar. Jarl is an Old Norse title from which comes the English word earl. Widar (or Vidar) is the son of Odin who the Norse myths tell us is set to rule the new world arising out of the cataclysmic events of the Ragnarok. Wiligut's use of the pseudonym suggests that perhaps, after his years in the asylum, he felt reborn after his personal Ragnarok and wished to renew his personal expression of his ancestral noble status.

Wiligut's new institution

Wiligut's profile was raised by these publications and he had already made links with the new Reich. An old friend of his named Richard Anders had joined the SS and arranged a meeting between Wiligut and Himmler. Heinrich Himmler is said to have believed himself to be the reincarnation of more than one hero from Germanic history and found Wiligut and his ideas fascinating. As a result Wiligut was put on his staff in September 1933, taking yet another pseudonym, now styling himself Karl Maria Weisthor. Himmler was aware of his new recruit's psychiatric history but chose to keep it hidden. He was also soon to become aware of Wiligut's bouts of heavy drinking.[5] Under Himmler's wing, Wiligut was promoted from SS captain to the rank of brigadier and he was officially employed to undertake 'prehistoric research' within the SS until 1939.

Surviving correspondence between Wiligut and Himmler shows that the two were quite close, even sending each other birthday cards.[6] Wiligut continued to produce a stream of writings on his ancestors, on mythology and on the religion of Irminism. That Himmler initialled the copies of these writings sent to him and kept them amongst his private papers indicates that he not only read them but valued their contents. To those unfamiliar with the strange mythologies of the ancient Gnostics and the modern Theosophists the kind of material Wiligut supplied to the eager Himmler may seem bizarre indeed.

Although the status of Darwinism and social evolutionism within the Third Reich is undeniable there were also other influences including occult notions of the origins of humanity which present a very different picture of our past. Whilst the evolutionary model has humanity emerging from the ape, many occultists held the opposite view. In the theosophical works of Blavatsky and those of the Arisophists who followed in her wake (Wiligut among them) mankind gradually descended into matter from more spiritual and ethereal states of being. During fantastically remote periods humanity had many powers which it has subsequently lost. The occult tradition has the idea of ancient wisdom at its heart. Thus the primordial golden age marks the spiritual high point to which humanity must find some way back. Wiligut's work must be seen in the light of this kind of belief system.

One of Wiligut's mythological texts was *Description of the Evolution of Humanity from the Secret Tradition of our Asa-Uana-Clan of Uiligotis,* an SS document dated 17 June 1936 and marked as read by Himmler.[7] In this text, echoing many themes clearly derived from Theosophy, humankind is said to pass through seven epochs, the current era being in the midst of the fifth epoch, with two yet to come. Each change of epoch has been the result of some major global catastrophe which has led to intermittent ice ages. At the beginning of each epoch the remnants of humanity which survived the cataclysm had to begin again. Beings from the heavens (the stars) then interbred with these survivors, and through this process new races and types of humanity came into being.

Wiligut claims that his account of these seven epochs is drawn from the secret tradition of his family line. This saga, as he calls it, was written in the 'ancient Aryan linear script' on seven 'Runo-wooden' tablets made of oak handed down to his grandfather. These ancient tablets along with others of a similar kind were destroyed when his grandfather's three houses were burned down during an uprising in Hungary. Since that time the saga of the seven epochs has been transmitted orally – via his father to Wiligut himself.

In the first human epoch there were two kinds of creatures, Aithar beings and water-beings, both sexless and self-propagating. This epoch was brought to a dramatic end when a moon (at this time the earth had a number of moons) crashed into the earth. In the second epoch the air and water entities came together and transformed into more solid beings. These new beings were angelic hermaphrodites that lived part of the time in water and part on dry land but were also able to fly. The saga tells us that they attained 'to the level of Got' (God) – that is to say they had creative consciousness. This epoch also ended abruptly when another heavenly body collided with the earth.

Those who survived to live on into the third epoch called themselves the first humans and evolved out of their hermaphroditic form to become single-sex beings, but they still differed from modern humans and had three eyes, the third one said to be in the middle of the forehead. Here we can see the influence of Indian ideas of a third

eye which probably reached Wiligut through the distorting lens of
Theosophy. Yet another 'fiery ball from heaven' came to put an end
to this epoch.

In the fourth epoch mankind (the Uana-culture) gained great
knowledge of astrology and the Runo-script was invented by two
races – the red-skins and an albino strain of humans who had white
hair and red eyes. They fought against other races known as the beast-
men. As this epoch faded away so too did the third eye of humanity.
With their advanced state of knowledge the Uana were able to prepare
for the next catastrophe (yet another falling moon) and built giant
cave and tunnel systems to protect themselves. As the Uana emerged
from their caves at the beginning of the fifth and present epoch they
were confronted by the Asa, a race which had previously lived
separately on the newly fallen moon. The Asa established their society
in Eden whilst the Uana lived in Asgard (home of the Norse gods) and
the two peoples merged. The children of the Asa-Uana carried the
wisdom of Got with them on their subsequent migrations. With this
the saga of the seven epochs ends. That Himmler took such stories
seriously is a remarkable historical fact in itself.

In 1935 Himmler was instrumental in setting up a mainly
academic institute within the SS named the Ahnenerbe (ancestral
heritage). Its brief was to conduct research into the past of the
Germanic peoples. It is important to note that these activities were
driven by Himmler's own enthusiasm; his explorations into German
ancestry did not have the support of Hitler. In fact, Hitler found the
desire to concentrate on the glories of prehistoric Germany rather
absurd. He was dismissive about Himmler's obsession:

> Why do we call the whole world's attention to the fact that
> we have no past? It's bad enough that the Romans were
> erecting great buildings when our forefathers were still living
> in mud huts; now Himmler is starting to dig up these villages
> of mud huts and enthusing over every potsherd and stone

axe he finds. All we prove by that is that we were still throwing stone hatchets and crouching around open fires when Greece and Rome had already reached the highest stage of culture. We really should do our best to keep quiet about this past. Instead Himmler makes a great fuss about it all. The present-day Romans must be having a laugh at these revelations.[8]

However, we can be sure that Himmler's 'discoveries' when suitable for use in propaganda were appreciated by Hitler, and such research was well funded by the Third Reich. The staff of the Ahnenerbe consisted of a strange mixture of, on the one hand, trained academic specialists and, on the other, a motley crew of mystics, amateur theorists and eccentrics. One of Wiligut's fellow mystics was Günter Kirchhoff, who also had his own eccentric vision of prehistory. Together the two undertook excursions into the Black Forest and elsewhere 'reading' the landscape and its ancient ruins according to 'ancestral wisdom'.

Kirchhoff submitted his work to the Ahnenerbe but his field studies were unintelligible to the more rational elements, who reported it as 'rubbish' and dismissed him as 'a fantasist of the worst kind.'[9] Nevertheless, both he and Wiligut continued to be endorsed by Himmler, who urged the Ahnenerbe to look more deeply into Kirchhoff's work. In 1939 Himmler even ordered them to undertake an archaeological excavation of a phantom site that Kirchhoff had 'discovered' in the countryside. As it turned out the project was permanently suspended when war broke out. As Nicholas Goodrick-Clarke has made clear, what is important about this conflict between Kirchhoff and the archaeologists in the Ahnenerbe is the fact that Himmler sided with the amateur and occultist against the academics of his own organisation.[10] This in itself indicates that occultists did have some influence over the Nazi elite.

Wiligut's influence over Himmler extended beyond the sharing of his mystical ancestral memories. When in November 1933 Himmler selected the seventeenth-century Wewelsburg castle in Westphalia as the ceremonial headquarters of the SS he was accompanied by Wiligut, who gave his clairvoyant prediction that the castle would become a magical stronghold for the Germans against an invading army from Asia. This prophecy was similar in spirit to Himmler's own belief that for the next 200 years the SS were destined to defend Europe against military attacks from the east.

Wiligut was also instrumental in the organisation of ceremonial life at the castle. He managed to convert Manfred von Knobelsdorff, the castle commandant, to the Irminist religion. They worked together to integrate Irminist ceremonies into the lives of SS officers. Wiligut, carrying an ivory-handled rune staff tied with blue ribbon, would oversee the marriage of SS officers and their brides in a quasi-pagan wedding ceremony. When interviewed in 1997 by Manfred Lenz, Gabriele Winckler-Dechend remembers that Wiligut carried a carved wooden cane (*Gotenstock*) which he told her had been passed down from his grandfather to his father and finally to him. She thought that it had a golden pommel in the form of a head. Wiligut used it in an obscure way on a number of occasions and in what seemed to be his own private rituals. She recalled how when they first went to Goslar together he had tapped his cane three times on a fountain as they passed it.[11]

In the cause of racial purity and to promote the Nazi eugenics programme higher-ranking SS men and their wives-to-be would have to demonstrate they could trace their Aryan heritage back to at least 1750. Wiligut also designed a ceremonial wooden bowl inscribed with runes which was used in SS wedding rites. Seasonal festivals of his devising were also celebrated at the castle, attended by both the SS and the local villagers.

Himmler also gave Wiligut the task of designing the death's head ring worn by members of the SS (see plate 1, page 8). The symbols which Wiligut selected were a border of oak-leaf designs, the death's head itself, a swastika, a hagall rune, a double sig rune and three further runes – the last of these were runes directly associated with the personal tradition of Wiligut. Himmler himself gave out these rings with which SS members also received a certificate explaining the meaning of its designs. It is from this document that we learn that the death's head symbolised the commitment to give up one's life for the cause; the swastika and the hagall rune were reminders to have faith in the victory of the Nazi philosophy; the two sig runes symbolised the *Schutzstaffel* or SS, which had grown out of Hitler's personal bodyguard; and the oak leaves were emblems of the tree of German tradition. The three runes particularly associated with Wiligut are simply glossed over as holy signs from the German past.

The rings of dead SS men were ordered to be returned to the Wewelsburg, where they would be kept in a chest to symbolise their ties with the castle and the order. It is said that this chest was stored in the vault of the northern tower of the castle, which became known as Walhalla. Valhalla, the hall of the slain, as has been said, was, in Norse mythology, Odin's heavenly hall and the destination of warriors slain on the battlefield.

Wiligut's status continued to rise. He developed ideas for an Irminist renaissance which included a plan to seize Church property, which he believed had been stolen from the ancient Irminists. He hoped and believed that one day Irminism would become the national religion of Germany. Wiligut's relationship with both the Odinic archetype and with the mythology of the pagan north was by no means straightforward. For Guido von List, Armanism – basically the same as Irminism – was the esoteric basis out of which the exoteric religion of Wotanism (Odinism) had developed. The two were not in conflict but were aspects of the same spiritual force at work in history.

Wiligut, as we have seen, saw Irminism and Wotanism as contrary forces. As Stephen Flowers has shown, Wiligut's bizarre ideas owe little to any genuine historical pagan traditions: 'For Wiligut "Wotanism" embodied all those heathen theological and mythological aspects from the *Edda* and other old Norse sources which seemed "foreign" or "disgusting" to him . . . the effort to re-mythologize Christianity as an "Aryan religion" enjoyed a good reception among many National Socialists of Wiligut's day.'[12]

Wiligut's reputation since the fall of the Third Reich has suffered an equally dramatic collapse. Aside from a few disciples his work has been dismissed by many rune occultists even within Ariosophical circles and by rune occultists. Hermann Wirth (see the previous chapter) was singularly unimpressed by Wiligut. He wrote a letter to Wiligut's biographer, a former Waffen-SS man named Rudolf Mund, in which he dismissed Wiligut as a plagiarist of Guido von List's works, a notorious swindler and con man who should be ignored and forgotten.[13]

Modern Wotanists are also scathing of Wiligut and his doctrines. Adolf Schleipfer, a recent grand master of the revived Armanen Order originally founded by Guido von List, has been particularly vocal in this respect. He points out that if the ancient Irminist faith had been preserved by the male line of Wiligut's own family then his father's choice of names for his son – Karl Maria – was bizarre. Wiligut claimed that one of the main enemies of the Irminists in historical times had been the Roman Catholic Church. Schleipfer says that it would be hard to imagine a more Catholic choice of Christian names than Karl Maria. According to Wiligut's own account fifteen of his own ancestors were killed by Karl the Saxon-slayer (Charlemagne) so why would his father, a supposed Irminist, choose to name his son after an enemy of the faith? Schleipfer dismisses Wiligut's Irminism as 'a Trojan Horse within the enclosed walls of the Wotanic religion'.[14] This is a telling analogy. Wiligut was essentially smuggling Christianity back into his mythic reconstruction of the pagan Germanic past.

His closeness to Himmler meant that Wiligut was often consulted on the works of other occultists. Julius Evola (1898–1974) was the most prominent occult thinker in Italy in the 1930s. Although many of his ideas were far from incompatible with aspects of Nazi ideology,

Wiligut was of the opinion that Evola's lack of knowledge concerning the true nature of Germanic prehistory (as, of course, perceived by him) meant that his ideas were antipathetic to the Third Reich. An occultist whose ideas and ancestral memories were perhaps too close to his own for Wiligut's comfort was Ernst Lauterer, also known as Tarnhari, who was an 'Aryan' mystic and a member of the Guido von List Society.[15]

By 1938, Wiligut, who had now reached his seventies, was an alcoholic and a heavy smoker. SS doctors were prescribing him undisclosed drugs in an effort to help him keep up with the hectic routine demanded by his post. Himmler's respect for Wiligut was by no means shared by all of the officers on his staff and he was not without his enemies. Wiligut's time in the asylum was a well-kept secret but Chief of Staff Karl Wolff decided to do some delving into his past and met Wiligut's estranged wife, who told him about her husband's years in the Salzburg mental institution.

Wiligut's past had come back to haunt him and once confronted he was left with little choice but to retire immediately on grounds of ill health. He did so in August 1939 and spent his last years living off a modest SS pension. His twilight years found him wandering, not like Odin in search of wisdom, but in search of a resting place. During the war he moved from place to place, first in Germany and then later in Austria. On one last trip back to Germany in December 1945 he collapsed, and died in hospital on 3 January the following year.

It is clear from Wiligut's tortuous attempts to preserve Christianity in his semi-pagan personal mythology that he was torn in two directions. His anti-Semitism could not accommodate a Christianity with its roots in the Old Testament of the Jews. The Christian culture in which he had been brought up did not satisfy his desire for a religion drawn from direct Germanic roots. Was his schizophrenia the result of his being torn between the ways of the two different archetypes, Christ and Odin?

*

The first Odinic experiment that Jung saw gripping the collective psyche of the Germanic peoples began positively. From the mid-nineteenth century spiritual seekers began to look for alternatives to a Christianity which could no longer provide answers to their innermost questions. The influence of the Odinic archetype first manifested itself in a number of seemingly unconnected ways. In his experiments to identify a hitherto unrecognised source of energy coursing through the universe the scientist Baron von Reichenbach took inspiration from Odin, naming this energy Odic force. In Jules Verne, Odin's runes encode the route by which the journey to the centre of the earth can be made. Nietszche's theory of the overman owes much to the frenzied inspiration of the Odinic archetype, as Jung makes clear. These three themes – a hidden energy, a subterranean world and a higher kind of being – came together in the prophetic science fiction of Lord Lytton's *The Coming Race*.

Jung himself, along with the novelist Herman Hesse, made psychic journeys deep into the unconscious, where the runes were symbolically carved on the soul of European man. At Ascona the community of Monte Verita began to experiment with new ways of living, drawing on pagan roots. This new spirit invigorated and informed a grass-roots movement among an idealistic German youth. But a rising tide of nationalist fervour gripped the German-speaking world accompanied by virulent anti-Semitism. The *Protocols* became the basis of a powerful and perverse modern mythology arising from a phantom enemy – the secret society of the Elders of Zion, who were supposed to have been plotting the fall of European society for millennia. The pagan spirit was evoked by Guido von List who created an equally nebulous society – the Armanen priesthood said to have been the guardians of Aryan knowledge throughout the Christian era. The spiritual pole of Hyperborea was replaced by the political cabal of the Thule Society whose doctrines and actions foreshadowed the Third Reich.

As Nazism grew the influence of paganism diminished, surviving only within the SS in the schizophrenic ideas of Karl von Wiligut, whose mythology was a hopeless amalgam of Christian and pagan beliefs. The theory and practice of Nazism had a number of sources. Its totalitarian politics were inspired by aspirations derived ultimately from the model of the Roman Empire. Nazi anti-Semitism took its immediate inspiration from the *Protocols*, which itself was an outgrowth of the dark side of the Christian heritage of Europe. The concept of the master race was a mirror image of the Jewish notion of the chosen people reworked by drawing on Darwinist biology. As a part of their rewriting of history Nazi ideologues inevitably drew on the rich lore of the Germanic past. Much of this past was Christian but some of it was pagan. Their manipulation of the pagan past of Europe was no more authentic than their abuse of its Christian heritage – both were simply grist to the satanic mills of the Holocaust.

Part Two

THE SECOND ODINIC EXPERIMENT: THE ANGLO-AMERICAN WORLD

Chapter 14

An English Mythology

Myth is alive at once and in all its parts, and dies before it can
be dissected. It is possible, I think, to be moved by the power
of myth and yet to misunderstand the sensation, to ascribe it
wholly to something else that is also present: to metrical art,
style, or verbal skill. Correct and sober taste may refuse to
admit that there can be an interest for *us* – the proud *we* that
includes all intelligent living people – in ogres and dragons;
we then perceive its puzzlement in face of the odd fact that it
has derived great pleasure from a poem that is actually about
these unfashionable creatures.

J.R.R. Tolkien, *Beowulf: The Monsters and the Critics* (1936)[1]

The psychological and political arena for the first Odinic experiment
was the German-speaking world. As this experiment came to a close
with the defeat of Nazism a new cycle began with the second taking
place in the cultural laboratories of the English-speaking world – most
notably in the United States. The second experiment commenced as
benignly as the first – tranquilly, with the creation of a new English
mythology by a quiet Oxford don – before it too, like the first, started
its descent into violence and madness.

Middle-earth/Midgard

J.R.R. Tolkien (1892–1973), best known for *The Hobbit* (1937) and *The Lord of the Rings* (1954–5), was also Merton Professor of English Language and Literature at Oxford University and renowned for his writings on the Old English masterpiece *Beowulf* and other works from Anglo-Saxon times. He had always been fascinated by language and in his teens began to make up his own elvish tongue. His academic career as a philologist (his early training included two years working on the *Oxford English Dictionary*, a book in which the word hobbit would one day appear) meant that he was eminently able to take his youthful experiments in language creation to a new level. The language seemed incomplete without characters to bring it to life so Tolkien created them. Then they too needed animating through a plot and so his much-loved stories came into being.

From his deep knowledge of the ancient literature and cultures of northern Europe, Tolkien realised that unlike, for example, the Celtic, Finnish and Icelandic worlds, England did not have anything that could truly be called a mythology. To fill this gap in the English psychological landscape was his life's work. He explicitly stated that it was both his desire and intention to create such a mythology. From this seed Middle-earth and the Undying Lands grew in his mind, and the many tales including *The Lord of the Rings* became parts of a whole which was never completed but developed in such detail that few 'fantasy worlds' can match it either for breadth or depth. Tolkien was anxious to point out that the world he created was not to be seen as a fairy land; the name Middle-earth has its roots in Midgard, the central world of the Norse myths – the world of men.

Tolkien drew heavily on the tales, gods and supernatural creatures of northern myths and many of the names of his characters, including Gandalf, Gimli, Thorin and Dwalin, are taken directly from the Eddas. Here is not the place for a detailed study of his sources and influences, but it is notable that one of his most famous characters, the wizard Gandalf, is largely inspired by the Norse tradition. Whilst the legendary figure of Merlin seems also to have influenced Tolkien's development of this character, Norse myths seem to be the central inspiration. The name Gandalf appears in the *Prose Edda,* a treasure house of Icelandic mythic lore written down by the great Icelandic storyteller Snorri Sturluson (1179–1241), and translates as magic-working elf or sorcerer-elf.

Gandalf possesses many of the traits of Odin: both are masters of magic, cunning and wise wanderers known by a number of names, and both ride the swiftest of steeds – Odin's eight-legged horse Sleipnir, Gandalf's Shadowfax. Gandalf the Grey is an old man with a long beard who wears a wide-brimmed hat and a long dark cloak. He is also, when events require it, a prodigious fighter. These features he shares with Odin but there are also differences. Gandalf does not have the ambivalent nature of the old Norse god; much of Odin's darker side may be seen in the character of Saruman, the wise wizard turned bad.

Tolkien's epic *The Lord of the Rings* is often cited as the most popular work of fiction of the twentieth century in the English-speaking world. In 1997 Waterstone's, Britain's leading chain of bookstores, polled its customers asking them to nominate their favourite book of the century. More than 20 per cent of the 25,000 people who voted nominated *The Lord of the Rings*; it was top of every poll in all but one of 105 branches. Subsequently the broadsheet newspaper the *Daily Telegraph* polled its readers on their favourite book, followed shortly by the Folio Society. Tolkien's epic came out top in both surveys.

The author's aim had been to create an English mythology and bearing in mind the endorsement of his vast readership (recently swelled enormously by the trilogy of films which brought countless new visitors to the imaginary landscape of Middle-earth) he can be counted as having succeeded, no doubt beyond his own wildest expectations. Any mythology must appeal to many people in its culture; it cannot remain the preserve of an elite. Tolkien's works have revived the mythological and pagan traditions of northern Europe in the minds of countless readers and as such his influence has had a major cultural effect far beyond the enjoyment of the books and films.

Despite being the people's choice Tolkien's reception among the critics and literary intelligentsia has been more mixed and usually hostile. His work has been praised for its imagination but damned as escapism, thus limiting its value – in the eyes of some – as a work of 'higher' fiction. Politically the work does not sit well with modern liberalism and the ideology of eternal progress. Its message is overtly anti-modern and anti-globalisation. According to his son Christopher, Tolkien 'disliked the modern world'. Middle-earth provides a mythical alternative to a modern, secular and soulless world.

Decentralisation and pluralism characterised the opposition of the various races of men, hobbits, elves and dwarfs to the new world envisioned by the dark powers. Tolkien saw – before many others – that technological progress and industrialisation were ecologically damaging. He admired and savoured craftsmanship and loathed the age of the machine. *The Lord of the Rings* evokes a war between the various and disparate forces of good – the traditional – and the modernising and totalitarian forces of evil under the leadership of Sauron, Lord of the Rings. Sauron is aided by the corrupt magician Saruman, embodying the soulless scientist, whose pursuit of technological innovation is fuelled by war mongering. Despite the mythological aura of *The Lord of the Rings* there is very little description anywhere of religious activities; prayers, ceremonies and rituals are conspicuously absent. Magic plays a much bigger role in his imaginary world than religion and imbues even the commonplace with a supernatural air.

When probed by inquisitive journalists Tolkien willingly discussed the geographical setting for *The Lord of the Rings*: 'The action of the story takes place in the north-west of Middle-earth, equivalent in latitude to the coastline of Europe and the north shore of the Mediterranean . . . if Hobbiton and Rivendell are taken (as intended) to be about the latitude of Oxford, then Minas Tirith, 600 miles to the south, is about the latitude of Florence.'[2] On other occasions he expanded on these remarks. The hobbits were English, most of them simple country folk or yokels; Mordor was 'around the Balkans'; and Rhûn, the elvish word for east, approximated to Asia (the Far East); south of Harad was Africa. Númenor Tolkien described as being in the midst of the Atlantic Ocean, which was the location, according to many, of the lost continent of Atlantis. In fact, Tolkien even told a journalist working for the *Daily Telegraph* that in his creation of Middle-earth his aim was to rewrite the old Atlantis myth.[3]

We can see an echo of Lord Lytton's *The Coming Race* in *The Lord of the Rings* when Gandalf has to solve a riddle written in elf letters on the dwarf gate of Moria so that the fellowship can enter the subterranean realm of the ancient mines. In *The Coming Race* Lytton goes into considerable detail in his creation of a lost branch of the Indo-European language tree with a grammar and vocabulary. Such works translate ancient myths for the modern world. Verne, Lytton, the *Oera Linda* book and the works of Tolkien all use invented or modified languages derived from Indo-European sources.

Tolkien's admission that the geography of Middle-earth was a variant of our own world inevitably led to speculation that the whole story was a complex allegory of political and cultural events in Europe rather than simply a mythical prehistory. Tolkien was particularly irritated by questions in this vein and routinely denied any such allegorising. Nevertheless, it is impossible for many readers to resist interpreting his work as an allegory, perhaps of the First or Second World War.

Tolkien was certainly very patriotic and saw his mythology as a gift to his beloved nation. He also believed Germany to be a great nation but was contemptuous of the Nazis' appropriation of the northern imagination which had spawned the myths he loved so much and taught throughout his working life. He personally encountered their obsession with racial origins in 1938 when George Allen & Unwin, who had published his *The Hobbit* the previous year, forwarded to him a letter from German publishers interested in bringing out a German edition of the book. The letter more or less asked Tolkien to inform them whether or not he was of Aryan blood. Tolkien was disgusted and had this to say in one of his own letters written in 1941 to his second son Michael:

> I have spent most of my life . . . studying Germanic matters . . . there is a great deal more force (and truth) than ignorant people imagine in the 'Germanic' ideal . . . you have to understand the good in things, to detect the real evil . . . I have in this War a burning private grudge . . . against that ruddy little ignoramus Adolf Hitler (for the odd thing about demonic inspiration and impetus is that it in no way enhances the purely intellectual stature: it chiefly affects the mere will). Ruining, perverting, misapplying, and making for ever accursed, that noble northern spirit, a supreme contribution to Europe, which I have ever loved, and tried to present in its true light.[4]

Ironically, interest in Tolkien's work has extended to the far right. If he were still alive he would be horrified to discover that neo-fascists in Italy have appropriated his mythology, even naming one of their summer youth resorts Camp Hobbit.[5]

The notion of the return of the pagan god Odin to Western consciousness sits awkwardly with the scientific, religious and political status quo of modern Europe and America. The emphasis on the Germanic god and the northern mythology of which he is a part present a problem to the Western world; they have been rejected because they are fundamentally incompatible with the dominant intellectual culture of our day. Both Jung and Tolkien have huge grass-roots followings despite their being rejected by the intellectual powers that be. Richard Noll, the most perceptive and critical of Jung's numerous biographers, despite his great misgivings about Jung had to admit: 'Freud may still be the genius of choice for the learned elite of the late twentieth century, but it is clear that, in sheer numbers alone, it is Jung who has won the cultural war and whose works are more widely read and discussed in the popular culture of our age.'[6]

The popular success of both Jung and Tolkien gives weight to the idea pursued in this book – that the ancient blueprints of the European mind embodied in northern mythology are returning to the surface of the modern cultural landscape. Paganism is a growing popular movement and its success is also to be explained by the workings of these forces.

Gandalf's Garden

Tolkien's epic was an icon of the flower power era, and this was exemplified in 1968 with the founding of *Gandalf's Garden*, both a countercultural magazine and a hippy cafe which doubled up as a meditation centre in World's End, Chelsea, London. The cafe served the typical countercultural fare of the times, vegetarian food and herbal tea; incense filled the air and the table talk was of yoga, Zen and magic. The magazine, with its articles on Tolkien, Atlantis and the Age of Aquarius, was sold not only at the cafe but at other outlets including the Middle-earth rock club.[7]

The hippy scene was characterised by long hair, loose clothes and nudism, vegetarianism, rejection of alcohol in favour of psychedelic drugs, pacifism, ecological awareness, music and dance. It was, like the German youth movement it so resembled, a brief golden age of idealism, creativity and hope. Yet the hippies were to suffer a similar fate as the violence epitomised by the Vietnam War became embodied in one who was ostensibly one of their own – a drifter named Charles Manson.

Chapter 15

The Possessed

Odin 'the horseman' or 'the attacker' is also the god of dangerous marauders . . . Helmeted like a Hell's Angel . . . he wanders his path in search of people to cast spells on, animals to hunt, misfortunes to inflict on others, wars to wage, or women to abduct. Odin . . . is also the god of the secret paths that lead to hell. Route I-35 is such a path, and, since Toole and Lucas travelled it, it could be renamed *Helvegr*, 'the road to hell' in the Ancient Germanic language.

Denis Duclos, *The Werewolf Complex*[1]

Charles Manson was born in Cincinnati, Ohio in 1934. After spending the first half of the 1960s in jail for car theft, Manson emerged in 1966 as a guitar-playing wanderer whose charisma led to a growing cult of followers, many of them young women, who became collectively known as the Family. Obsessed with apocalyptic fantasies, he set up the Family headquarters at the Spahn Ranch, an abandoned movie set outside Los Angeles.

In 1969 he sent out some of his entourage to commit murder in Beverley Hills, counting a heavily pregnant Sharon Tate – the wife of film director Roman Polanski – and four others at her house among the victims. According to the chief prosecutor, District Attorney

Vincent Bugliosi, Manson ordered these murders because he hoped they would be blamed on the black population and this would precipitate an apocalyptic race war. Race war, as we shall see, is one of the key themes among radical white separatists in America. The apocalyptic war Manson envisioned derived from what he saw as prophetic insights which 'came to him on his frequent acid binges, orgies and manic trips into Death Valley, in search of the entrance to a mystical city that existed beneath the sands'.[2]

Manson described this entrance as the Hole. He believed that if it were found it would provide him and the members of the Family with a refuge when the predicted apocalypse began.[3] This obsessive search for a subterranean world echoes the theme of the inner earth which has surfaced at various points in this book. Manson embodies many of the traits of the Odinic archetype: he plunged himself and his followers into frenzied altered states of consciousness; his complex personality combined a self-image of an inspired poet and prophet with the realities of a psychopathic murderer and violent mystic.

The sources for Manson's mysticism were diverse. It is known that he had made contact with a number of cults, among them splinter groups and breakaway sects of the Church of Scientology. He also drew heavily on the mythical languages of both Christianity and Eastern religions. Herman Hesse's *Siddhartha* was one of the few books Manson permitted Family members to read.[4] Interestingly, another Hesse novel popular in the 1960s was *Steppenwolf*, the name of which was adopted by a rock band. Steppenwolf's most famous song, 'Born To Be Wild', was an anthem extolling the Hell's Angels lifestyle. At the Altamont rock festival on 6 December 1969, headlined by the Rolling Stones, the Hell's Angels were employed to provide security. The atmosphere soured during the day and reached its nadir during the Stones' set when a teenager was stabbed to death by Hell's Angels and several other members of the audience were wounded. Like Manson, the Angels seem to manifest the Odinic archetype: a wandering band of road warriors inducing frenzy through drink, drugs, sex and violence. They also incorporate Nazi symbols into their iconography including the swastika, a symbol that Manson had tattoed on his forehead.

Manson is not the only killer to have evoked the Nazis and used their symbols. The British child-killer Ian Brady was an avid reader of books about the Nazis and James Oliver Huberty, who shot dead twenty-one people in a McDonald's restaurant in California in 1984, was described by his wife as a Nazi. In 1999 Dylan Klebold and Eric Harris, the two nihilistic youths responsible for the Columbine High School massacre, chose 20 April, Hitler's birthday, for their murderous spree in which they killed twelve students and a teacher before turning their weapons on themselves.[5]

American werewolf in Paris

In the early 1990s a prominent French sociologist named Denis Duclos set himself the task of trying to explain why modern society – particularly in the United States – had been experiencing a rapid and dramatic increase in violent crime. In his book *The Werewolf Complex: America's Fascination with Violence* (1998) he makes an explicit connection between 'the collapse of an alternative ideal to post-modern liberalism' at the end of the 1980s and the subsequent explosion of crime rates in the following few years. In his search for answers Duclos concerns himself not only with real-life murderers, especially serial killers, but also looks at fantasies and portrayals of violence in popular culture – on TV, in movies and in the books of horror writers like Stephen King. He is seeking the modern counter-parts to the heroes and monsters of the Anglo-Saxon world of *Beowulf* within the myths of the media.

Duclos's psychopaths and other violent criminals are portrayed as modern versions of the mythical figure of the werewolf. They, like the wolf-men of old, are divided within themselves. One part, the human side, dominates by day and complies with the rules of orderly society. The other side, bent on destruction and at the mercy of its own murderous impulses, takes over at night. Both the fantasies of popular American culture and the criminal acts of real killers play out this deadly interplay of Jekyll and Hyde. In order to find the cultural origins of this dangerous social pathology which is threatening to spin out of control Duclos believes we need to look to ancient models of behaviour. He finds the mythological background which fuels the American culture of violence in the figure of the wild Germanic warrior of Nordic and Anglo-Saxon lore; the mythic mad warrior has returned to haunt the United States.

Rambo, about an out-of-control serial killer, and the endless flow of slasher movies, DC comic book heroes and shoot-'em-up video games all share this lore as a common source. Fantasy has a horrible way of becoming reality. America has become subject to a wave of random and seemingly motiveless mass killings since the 1980s. In one incident a Texas man dressed in camouflage killed six people; his nickname was Rambo. In 1986 an Oklahoma postal worker killed fourteen of his workmates. In the same year a crazed ex-employee of the University of Kentucky, dressed as a ninja and armed with a samurai sword and a rifle, was overpowered before he could go on a killing spree. The first of a wave of school massacres took place in Stockton, California in 1989 when a man named Patrick Purdy armed with an AK-47 and dressed in army gear killed five children and wounded another twenty-nine before committing suicide.

Since then there have been numerous other crimes in which the killers have acted out the role of the crazed soldier. Duclos would argue that in both real and fantasy violence the inspiration comes from the frenzy and ecstatic fury of the northern warrior.

Readers who have followed me thus far will have noted that the psychological profile built up by Duclos for the mythological perpetrator of these countless acts and images of violence is none other than Odin, the northern god of battle frenzy. The apparent continuity of this cult of Odin into modern times is called the werewolf complex by Duclos. Both the serial killers and other modern 'mad warriors' that Duclos makes the object of his study clearly combine the violence and the mental epidemy that Jung says characterise the Odinic experiments.

America's most notorious serial killers: Odin and Loki?

The star witnesses Duclos brings to the stand to demonstrate his case against Odin are probably America's most notorious serial killers, Henry Lee Lucas and Ottis Toole, who went on killing sprees separately and then later together. The total number of their victims remains unknown but, if their confessions are to be believed, it may run into the hundreds. Arson, murder, rape, incest, necrophilia, mutilation, dismemberment, transvestism, bestiality and cannibalism are all said to be elements in the duo's orgy of violence.

Henry Lee Lucas was born in a two-room log cabin in the Appalachian mountains of Virginia in 1936. His parents were both alcoholics and had their own still for making moonshine. The family was dominated by his violent mother Viola who, having given up custody of some of Henry's eight brothers and sisters to relatives, foster care and state institutions, concentrated her malice on Henry and his father Anderson.

Anderson had been nicknamed 'No Legs' since he lost both his lower limbs in a drunken accident involving a freight train. Apart from the pittance he earned selling pencils on street corners Anderson didn't bring in any money, and Viola supplemented their income from the moonshine by casual prostitution, often making Henry and his father watch her having sex with clients. One night, humiliated beyond endurance, Anderson dragged himself out of the cabin to sleep outside. Shortly afterwards he died of pneumonia.

When Henry was a young boy his deranged and sadistic mother would sometimes send him off to school dressed as a girl and without shoes. One day a teacher took pity on him and sent him home with a pair of shoes. Viola beat him for accepting charity, a punishment that would have come as no shock to the boy. During his trial in 1960 for the murder of his mother he told the court that beatings were meted out to him every day. By his teenage years his violence and sexual predilections were already out of hand. He confessed to having sex with his half-brother and also with animals that the two of them killed first by cutting their throats. When Henry was seventeen he lost an eye after one of his brothers accidentally injured him with a knife. Despite the seriousness of the wound Henry was not taken to hospital for some days by which time it was too late for the doctors to save his eye and he was fitted with a glass one.

By this time Lucas had inevitably drifted into crime and first went to jail for burglary at the age of eighteen. After escaping and being recaptured twice he was eventually released in 1959 and went to live with his sister. His mother contacted him and demanded he come back to live with her, which he refused to do. Viola insisted they talk about it so in January 1960 they met up in a bar. They got very drunk and began to argue. On returning to his sister's house later that night they had a fight which resulted in Lucas stabbing Viola fatally in the neck. On his arrest he confessed that he had also raped her dead body. He was found guilty of second-degree murder and imprisoned. After he had attempted suicide on more than one occasion he was moved to a mental hospital. After his release in 1970 he was soon in trouble again, ending up in jail for the attempted kidnap of two teenage girls.

Out again in 1975 he continued his drifting existence and in 1979 met Ottis Toole and, according to the latter, they became lovers. Toole's rather simple-minded niece Becky Powell, who was at that time not even a teenager, took an instant liking to Lucas and she was subsequently to go off alone with him. This unlikely pair then moved in with Kate Rich, a woman in her eighties, until her family kicked them out. Rich became a missing person and Lucas was the prime suspect. When he was arrested he told police that he was giving Rich a lift to church one day when he was overtaken with the desire to kill her and have sex with her corpse, which he did. He then chopped up her body and disposed of the pieces by burning them in a stove in his yard. He then surprised police by telling them he had also killed Powell and then dismembered her in an attempt to conceal her death. Lucas told them he had loved her and that the killing was a consequence of the problems that had plagued his whole life. He had also had sexual intercourse with her dead body. He gave his liking for necrophilia as the reason for the other killings to which his name has been attached.

In June 1983, after admitting to the judge that he was guilty of the Rich murder, Lucas staggered everyone in the courtroom by announcing that he had murdered a hundred women. He initially compiled a list of seventy-seven women from locations across nineteen states, but by the time he had finished, including the many hitchhikers that he and Toole had picked up and killed together, the total exceeded 600. How many of these supposed slayings were really committed by them and how many simply confessed to by the attention-seeking Lucas, who revelled in the media attention and constant communication with police investigating scores of unsolved murders, is impossible to say.

A few sceptics believe that Lucas was only responsible for three murders – those of his mother, Kate Rich and Becky Powell – and that all the others are fabrications. Lucas's knowledge of numerous other murder scenes and victims is explained away by the eagerness of the various police forces, who fed him, intentionally or otherwise, details of the cases in order to get unsolved murders off their books. However, it is generally believed that Lucas and his accomplice were genuine serial killers even if they were not responsible for as many murders as they claimed to have committed.

One crime to which Lucas confessed and for which he faced the death penalty in Texas was the 1979 rape and murder of an unidentified woman whose body was found naked apart from a pair of orange socks. It was subsequently proven beyond all reasonable doubt that Lucas, despite his confession, could not have killed Orange Socks, as the victim had become known. As a result of the investigation of the Attorney General of Texas into the case Lucas's death sentence was commuted to life imprisonment in 1998 by the then Texas governor, George W. Bush. Lucas was the only prisoner on death row to be thus treated by the soon-to-be president of the United States.

Some of Lucas and Toole's more outlandish statements indicate that their accounts are a mixture of fact and fiction – most of the fantasy originating with Lucas but corroborated by his partner in crime. Lucas claimed that the motive for many of the murders they committed together was that they were working for a satanic cult named the Hands of Death, which required young female human sacrifices whose slain corpses would then be cooked or sometimes simply buried or cremated. In another perverse twist Toole said to his interrogators that Lucas and he both ate human flesh with barbecue sauce.

Toole told the authorities that Lucas had introduced him to cannibalism: 'Lucas gave me bits to eat but I never believed him until I saw him cut someone's throat, collect the blood that was spilling out in a jar and drink it. Then he said how good it was . . . that it was much better than drinking champagne or wine.'[6] This grisly anecdote Duclos connects with the Norse myth of Kvasir, who, after being murdered by two dwarfs, has his blood mixed with honey. The mixture then becomes the sacred mead which gives poetic inspiration to all who drink it. Even allowing for poetic licence it is hard to see exactly how this ancient myth is connected with the blood-sharing of two psychopaths.

Conversing with the dead was one of Odin's means of obtaining wisdom and knowledge. Toole's own experience of dealing with the dead started very early in his life. From the age of five he claims his grandmother took him along on many of her nocturnal visits to graveyards in Florida, where he witnessed her digging up bodies and then using them in necromantic rites. After his mother's death Toole lay on her grave and thought he heard her calling him to join her by killing himself. What relationship these experiences had to his necrophiliac desires one can only speculate.

The facts about modern serial killers and their crimes are almost impossible to separate from the folklore, media sensationalism and the murderer's own bragging. It is impossible, in this case at least, to separate entirely the strands of fantasy from the brutal facts of the crimes themselves. Duclos, despite being a serious academic investigator, contributes to the aura of mystery surrounding the two killers. He cannot resist noting the 'uncanny resemblance' between the names Ottis Toole and Odin and between Henry Lee Lucas and Loki, Odin's treacherous brother in Norse mythology. He pushes the point even further:

> Comparing Ottis with Othon, 'son of Odin', is, of course, far-fetched, but, if one adds the patronym Toole, the full name can be read as 'instrument of Odin's son'. Did these imaginary connections escape Toole's grandmother, a necrophagous witch who was well-versed in the ways of satanic cults? Whatever the case may be, she called Toole a 'son of the devil', which reminds us that Odin's grandfather, who leaves a trail of suffering behind him wherever he goes, is named 'Horn of misfortune' (Bölthorn).[7]

That Henry Lee Lucas shared two of Odin's physical attributes, namely that he was very tall and had only one eye, is also described by Duclos as 'too provocative to resist'.[8]

In one of his many guises Odin, on his journey to Hel, the realm of the dead, assumes the pseudonym Vegtamr, meaning 'one used to journeys or road-wise. Duclos sees this aspect of Odin as a kind of patron god of the serial killers who haunt the highways of America. Odin is also a trickster or, as we are more likely to put it today, a con man. This penchant for deception is also shared with the cold-blooded killer, who uses lies and deceit as aids to murder.

Duclos is quite right to point out that Toole's life has already been mythologised. The extreme actions of serial killers, as well as the sheer number of their crimes, make them difficult to place into normal categories of human behaviour. There are many things which can result in a person becoming mythologised – the tragic shortened lives of Marilyn Monroe and James Dean, the belief that Elvis Presley and Jim Morrison did not actually die are among the many examples in modern American culture. Mythologised figures become more than human; they seem to embody archetypal forces and so come to be perceived almost as gods or goddesses. But the mythologising of serial killers turns them into something *less* than human – they become demonised, embodiments of evil, devils or, according to the sociologist Duclos, the dark side of the pagan gods of the north.

Ottis Toole is compared to Loki not just on the basis of their shared villainy but also because they both have a confused and confusing sexual life. Toole was essentially pansexual. He claimed to have had sex with a number of animals – cows, dogs and goats among them. The age or sex of his human sexual partners was highly variable. When he was a boy his twelve-year-old sister Drusilla dressed him up as a girl and encouraged him to prostitute himself on the streets. His transvestism remained a part of his sexual persona throughout his adult life. Loki is a master of transformation and is able to turn himself into a mare. In this form he is mounted by the stallion Svadilfari and the offspring of this union is Sleipnir, the eight-legged steed of Odin.

The frenzied one

Although Duclos alerts us to the violent nature of many of the northern myths which still influence film and TV, popular fiction, comics and computer games, of the many serial killers he cites as resembling Odin *not one* mentions the god by name. Many psychopaths ascribe no religious or spiritual significance to their murders and those who do more often describe their actions as the work of

Satan or God, but not Odin. If the resurgence of Odin is an explanation for the proliferation of serial killers then the perpetrators themselves are unconscious of the fact. In the case of Lucas and Toole it was Satan who featured openly in their own accounts of their deeds, and Manson mentions both God and Satan in his apocalyptic rantings.

Nevertheless, it is Duclos's belief that the violence in American culture has its roots in paganism rather than the Judaeo-Christian tradition. Whether we accept his thesis or not it must be said that his work in itself adds to the modern mythology of Odin. Whether the god speaks through serial killers themselves or just through Duclos is for the reader to decide. What is certain is that in Old Norse literature the cult of Odin was sometimes associated with bloody murder. Written in the thirteenth century, *Egil's Saga* is one of the most famous works of Norse literature. Egil, a follower of Odin, displays many of the character traits of his patron god – he is an ambitious and wily wanderer, a poet and magician, and a prodigious warrior as well as a drinker. Although Egil is a serial killer he is no psychopath for he murders simply for worldly gain and revenge.

Jung saw archetypes or mythical figures as having the power to influence events. Entire civilisations could have their destinies altered by the inexplicable and irresistible power of an archetype – as he argued was the case with the rise of Nazism in Germany and the return of Odin, or Wotan, as he was known to the Germans. Duclos sees the old pagan god reappearing in another part of the northern cultural world, the United States. He perceives Odin as being responsible for destructive social forces – as the key factor in the modern explosion of violence within America and beyond – but makes it crystal clear that he does not follow Jung's theories and, oddly enough, makes no mention of Jung or his Wotan essay despite its obvious bearing on his subject. Duclos writes, 'Although I absolutely do not believe in symbolic archetypes, I do think that the solidity of certain myths, conceived in very different circumstances, can be almost blindly affirmed, in other places and periods, provided that certain resources are available for them to be reused or even elaborated on.'⁹

He goes on to suggest that the 'cultural ecology' of the medieval Nordic world and that of (post)modern America actually have much more in common than might at first appear. Firstly, he compares the Germania's struggle for autonomy from ancient Rome with America's, freedom from the more centralised order of Europe. Secondly he notes that much of North America beyond its sprawling cities, like the northern Europe of old, has vast wilderness with many remote and often isolated communities. Thirdly, and for him, most importantly there is a large Nordic population in North America of Anglo-Saxon, German and Scandinavian in origin. These factors make modern America an ideal place for the northern myths to revive: 'Medieval Nordic society's culture-nature myth, which is characterized by an oscillation between discipline and energy, mechanical flow and savagery, "put itself on hold", storing up its potential over time until it could release it into the more receptive environment of American culture.'¹⁰ The key phrase here is 'put itself on hold'. However you read this the implication is that, in some way, the myth has a life of its own, and, like a biological organism, has its own preservation at heart.

There is, then, a consensus between Jung and Duclos – namely that Odin has returned to exert a dramatic effect on the northern peoples in a violent and catastrophic fashion, in Germany in the earlier part of the twentieth century and in America in the final stages of the twentieth and the beginning of the twenty-first century. And, for all their differences, the two agree that Odin is a force which cannot be suppressed and that he has his own agenda.

Odin has been identified as the prototype of Father Christmas and the inspiration for Tolkien's wizard Gandalf, yet his sinister presence is implicated in the rise of Nazism and Adolf Hitler as well as in the depravities of modern American serial killers. Is the pagan legacy to be found in the demonic ravings of the Führer or in the gentle yet hypnotic attraction of the *Lord of the Rings*, or do both tell part of the tale? How are we to explain the appearance of a single pagan god in modern culture under so many different and contradictory guises? Bearing in mind what we know of Odin's complex character and moral ambiguity, that the archetype could actually be manifesting in all these ways simultaneously cannot be ruled out and in fact obeys its own peculiar logic. One thing at least is clear: Tolkien the novelist and philologist, Jung the psychologist, and Duclos the sociologist all claim that myths are alive and affect us today. All three see the power of northern myths at work in different ways in our culture.

Duclos predicts that the continuing dominance of Nordic mythology – inherently pessimistic in his opinion – will lead to inevitable disaster. The only solution he sees is for America to 'develop a mythological tradition in which reversal of the hoped-for catastrophe and an acceptance of the shortcomings of civilization were possible'. In short, both Odin and the northern mythology of which he is an integral part must be exorcised from the cultural landscape of America and the rest of the northern world. However, it must be said that not only is Duclos guilty of some pretty tortuous comparisons between the Norse gods and American serial killers, he also presents northern mythology in a very dark way. His theory that serial killers, horror fiction and random violence in the United States may be due in large part to a rebirth of northern mythology may be compelling but it nevertheless remains a theory difficult to prove. But, looking beyond the largely apolitical crimes of serial killers and random shootings, there are groups in America with political agendas in which Nazism and its ideas are more than just posturing or the rantings of perverse individuals.

Chapter 16

American Armageddon

The takeover came in a great, Europe-wide rush in the summer and fall of 1999, as a cleansing hurricane of change swept over the continent, clearing away in a few months the refuse of a millennium or more of alien ideology and a century or more of profound moral and material decadence. The blood flowed ankle-deep in the streets of many of Europe's great cities momentarily, as the race traitors, the offspring of generations of dysgenic breeding, and hordes of *Gastarbeiter* met a common fate.

The great dawn of the New Era broke over the Western world.

Andrew MacDonald (William Pierce), *The Turner Diaries*[1]

The FBI and the Armageddon report
In 1999 the FBI published a report entitled *Project Megiddo* which focused on their concern about the potential for extremist violence on the eve of the third millennium, particularly in the year 2000.[2] The name of the report derives from Megiddo, a hill in northern Israel which has seen many battles over the millennia. Armageddon means 'hill of Megiddo', and refers to the place where the final battle

between the forces of good and evil will begin (see Revelation 16: 16). To understand the need for such a report, and the motivations of those likely to be involved in sedition and the other revolutionary activities the FBI were worried might occur, it is important to consider the fears inspired by globalisation, the increasingly multiracial make-up of American society and the thinking of racists on the far right of the political spectrum.

The rapid advance of globalisation presents challenges and questions. Is it a good or bad thing? Is it a dangerous runaway train taking us in a direction no one can predict? Is it an inevitable historical process which we should simply accept and get on with the rest of our lives? Is it the result of an agenda driven and designed by certain nations, groups or factions to benefit themselves and realise their own goals and future aims? Outside North America many see globalisation as a US-led attempt to Americanise the world, yet for many inside America globalisation is a threat to the integrity of the country, a corrosive force undermining national sovereignty. Alongside the fear of being absorbed into a totalitarian global society many Americans and also Europeans fear they are being over-whelmed by mass immigration, which undermines their cultural values and even their very survival. Globalisation and the influx of other ethnic and religious groups into the Western nations challenge the identity of both individuals and the groups to which they belong.

Conspiracy theorists were once a small minority seen by society at large as either cranks or sinister religious or political extremists. Today for an individual to believe in one or more conspiracies is commonplace. Since *The X-Files* was broadcast into millions of homes with its weekly diet of FBI cover-ups, alien liaisons, secret tech-nologies and a host of other mysterious goings-on, no one has batted an eyelid at the mention of conspiracy. The proliferation of tech-nologies of satellite surveillance and other means of social control has been accompanied by an understandable paranoia among citizens of the United States and other Western nations. Many people want to know who is watching who and why.

Along with the widespread acceptance of conspiracy as a major factor in national and international events there has been an increase in apathy and cynicism towards political leaders and their party machines. The result has been lower turnouts on voting days. Many people no longer believe in the system and see elections as media circuses masking control by multinational corporations or other more shadowy forces. To white separatist groups in the United States the Jews and the federal 'puppet' government which is believed to do their bidding are the enemy within America. Many on the far right refer to 'ZOG', the Zionist Occupation Government, whilst others see a new world order at work behind the scenes. To the political mainstream such extremist groups are themselves the enemy within as they are seen to threaten sedition and violent non-compliance with the prevailing attitudes of multiculturalism and liberalism.

Christian Identity and Aryan Nations

In both theory and practice American white racism has changed dramatically since the Ku Klux Klan was formed in Tennessee in 1865. The heyday of the Klan was in the 1920s when it was estimated to have had between four and six million members and was less a fringe organisation than an integral part of the Protestant ideological landscape. It was and still is not only anti-black but also virulently opposed to Catholicism, Judaism, communism and feminism. Its decline has been steady and the once-monolithic organisation has disintegrated into more than thirty factions. Today other groups dominate the far right – most notably Christian Identity and Aryan Nations.

Christian Identity, although it has its roots are in the 1930s, is very much a movement of recent times, growing in prominence during the 1970s with its powerful mix of Christian beliefs and racism. It is loosely organised, having neither a single figurehead nor a theology shared by all its preachers and their congregations, although certain fundamental beliefs are held in common. The northern European peoples also referred to as the Anglo-Saxon or Nordic peoples (or by some Christian Identity believers as Aryans) are believed to be the lost tribes of Israel and as such the chosen people. To outsiders the choice of Old Testament names for their children and even the taking of Jewish surnames is difficult to understand alongside their virulent anti-Semitism.

Members are scattered across the USA but are linked not only by churches and home Bible study groups but also by publications, mail-order cassettes and videos, radio stations and the internet. The number of Identity Christians has been estimated at less than 100,000 nationwide. Despite its numerical insignificance when compared to the numerous other Christian denominations and sects in America, Christian Identity is notorious for its association with armed insurrection and the veneration of Hitler alongside Jesus. Its hard-core membership believes that the Jews are not only false Israelites but also the offspring of Satan, while non-white races are not the descendants of Adam but belong to an earlier and inferior creation. It is from these beliefs that their separatist ideology and their resistance to interracial marriage spring.

Most members of Aryan Nations (AN) are also Identity Christians; AN was founded by Richard Butler, a Christian Identity pastor. Based in Idaho since the 1970s, the ultimate aim of AN is the separation from the rest of the United States of the five north-western states of Washington, Oregon, Idaho, Montana and Wyoming. This idea, the so-called Northwest Territorial Imperative, was first proposed by AN ideologue Robert Miles in his book *Birth of a Nation* (1980). It was to be achieved by encouraging white people with separatist ideals to leave the multicultural life of the cities behind them and relocate to rural areas. By buying land next to others similarly inclined white enclaves could be set up. Such groups were also encouraged to have large families and to home-school their children in order to inculcate

AN ideology rather than that of the mainstream. By breeding in large numbers it was hoped they could counteract their greatest fear – the extinction of the white race through interracial marriage and general population decline in the face of the perceived population explosion among other ethnic groups. AN not only espouses anti-Semitism but is also hostile to other ethnic groups and the federal government. Many of its ideas have their roots in the ideology of the American neo-Nazi movement which began soon after the Second World War.

The emergence of neo-Nazism in America

The neo-Nazi movement in the United States was founded by George Lincoln Rockwell (1918–67). Rockwell was a born showman whose parents were both popular entertainers. His father was a famous vaudeville comedian and his mother a dancer, while after his parents divorced frequent guests at his father's house included figures such as Groucho Marx and Benny Goodman. On leaving university in 1938 Rockwell was already opposed to the liberal politics that had underpinned his teaching there. In the spring of 1941 he joined the Naval Air Corps and was involved in active service throughout the rest of the war, receiving a number of decorations. His involvement in the Korean War and the anti-communist witch hunts instigated by Joseph McCarthy led him to probe deeper into the identity of America's enemies. He soon found himself mixing in anti-Semitic circles and began to believe that there was a secret Jewish–communist plot to take over the world. He described his first reading of *Mein Kampf* in 1951 as like a ray of 'mental sunshine' and National Socialism as a 'new religion'.[3]

The following year he was sent by the navy to a base in Iceland, and there he met his second wife, the daughter of the Icelandic ambassador to the United States. They honeymooned in Germany, paying homage to Rockwell's hero by visiting Hitler's retreat, the Eagle's Nest. In the late 1950s, with the financial backing of a rich anti-Semite, he began a political campaign against what he perceived to be Jewish control over the US government. Things turned ugly in October 1958 when a synagogue in Atlanta was bombed. Rockwell was implicated and his face appeared in national and international newspapers. The upshot of this notoriety was that his backer severed their links and, following attacks on his house, Rockwell's wife and children packed their bags and returned to Iceland.

Rockwell's isolation did not deter him from his chosen path. His conviction that Nazism was his destiny was strengthened by dreams and visions he had which almost invariably involved Hitler. In 1959 in Arlington, Virginia he founded the American Party, which later became known as the American Nazi Party. Rockwell and his small entourage of uniformed storm troopers staged stunts which made sure they stayed in the public eye, gaining much more attention than a group which never exceeded 200 would normally expect. He openly espoused the gassing of Jews and the mass repatriation of the American black population to Africa. The most unlikely venue for one of his inflammatory tirades was a 1962 convention of more than 12,000 black Muslims where, as a guest speaker, he described Elijah Muhammad, the leader of the separatist organisation the Nation of Islam, as the black man's Adolf Hitler.

In the summer of the same year Rockwell travelled to Britain to attend a meeting of neo-Nazis from various countries organised by his English counterpart Colin Jordan. At this conference it was decided to found the World Union of National Socialists (WUNS). This could count on a membership drawn not only from Britain and the United States but also France, Denmark, Australia, Argentina and Chile. Affiliates in Germany, Belgium and Switzerland would join soon after. Although Jordan was to be its leader he was almost immediately imprisoned for his activities and the leadership passed to Rockwell.

By 1966 the WUNS journal *National Socialist World* was being published by Rockwell and his editor William Luther Pierce (1933–2002). Pierce, who was to have a huge impact on the direction the far right was to take in America, was a physicist who, after receiving his doctorate, had taught for three years as an assistant professor at Oregon State University in the early 1960s. He shared Rockwell's hatred of the Jews and his apocalyptic visions of race war between whites and blacks in America. The journal was filled with eulogies of Nazi and neo-Nazi thinkers and detailed expositions on the role of America in the race war to come.

On New Year's Day 1967 the American Nazi Party was reincarnated as the National Socialist White People's Party (NSWPP) with Rockwell as its leader, but he was not to see out that summer. He was assassinated in Arlington, Virginia by John Patler, a dissident member of the ANP. Rockwell's right-hand man Matt Koehl inherited the Arlington headquarters and the name of the NSWPP. Like his predecessor, Koehl's Nazism was imbued with religious fervour. Despite vehemently rejecting Christianity as a Semitic religion, his eulogies to Hitler leaned heavily on Christian themes. Hitler was described as the way to redemption and salvation, and comparisons were made between the small numbers and persecution of the early Christians and the NSWPP.

Other neo-Nazi factions also arose during this era, fighting among themselves for dominance, although William Pierce was to consolidate his position as the major voice of American neo-Nazism. In 1974 Pierce founded the National Alliance (NA) to propagate his radical views. For Pierce the Nazi final solution had been interrupted by their defeat and it was the destiny of Aryan Americans to complete the master plan and dominate the world in the process.

A modern *Mein Kampf*

Of all his various activities and writings it is probably for two works of fiction that Pierce will be best remembered. In 1978 he published under the pseudonym Andrew Macdonald *The Turner Diaries*,[4] a novel which has become an international underground best-seller having sold hundreds of thousands of copies. In the words of Nicholas Goodrick-Clarke, *The Turner Diaries* 'circulates widely among

American and European neo-Nazi groups as a kind of modern *Mein Kampf'*.[5] It led to Pierce being described as 'the most dangerous man in America' and the compilers of the FBI report *Project Megiddo* to predict that not only in 2000 but also in years to come that *The Turner Diaries* would inspire far-right terrorist actions both with its prophecy of a successful revolution against the American government and its propagation of a race war. In this respect it echoes Charles Manson's apocalyptic fantasies of 'Helter Skelter' and the frenzied murders he instigated in an attempt to manifest his prophecies.

The novel is the story of Earl Turner, a white warrior in a race war which engulfs America at the end of the 1990s. His diary is unearthed from the ruins of Washington DC after an apocalyptic conflict has resulted in victory for the Aryans over the 'System'. The crisis is set in motion when the authorities ban the private ownership of firearms under a piece of legislation entitled the Cohen Act – a clear reference to Jewish influence. After being arrested for possessing a firearm Turner decides to resist this infringement on his liberty and joins the underground resistance known as the Organization controlled by an inner Aryan elite named the Order. Large-scale robberies provide the financing of the revolutionaries and Turner is given the mission of blowing up the FBI headquarters. In this section of the book detailed instructions on how to build a truck bomb using ammonium nitrate fertiliser are given. Hundreds die when the bomb goes off and whilst Turner has some regrets at having killed many who belonged to his own Aryan race he nevertheless believes that the ends justify the means.

As the Organisation grows in strength it causes havoc across America by targeting power plants and transportation systems, interfering with food supplies and counterfeiting on a large scale to destabilise the economy. The first state to be seized by the Organization is California and the persecution of tens of thousands of 'race traitors' begins on the Day of the Rope – lynched lawyers, teachers, actors, politicians and priests hang from the trees and lamp posts of Los Angeles. White women in mixed marriages are forced to hold placards reading 'I defiled my race' and are hung in their thousands. The legacy of the Ku Klux Klan is all too clear but the sheer scale of the killings catalogued by the author also echoes the atrocities of the Nazi era. The book is filled with blatant anti-Semitism and racial abuse of blacks and other ethnic groups. Among the more lurid passages is the description of the discovery of a basement containing the dismembered remains of some thirty white children eaten by black cannibals during the height of the race war.

California is then purged of all non-Aryans by mass deportation to the south and by mass murder. The Order takes part in a three-way nuclear exchange with the System and the Soviet Union. Among the places hit are New York, Detroit, Miami and other American cities plus Tel Aviv and other targets in Israel. With the collapse of the Jewish state vengeful Arabs wipe out every last Jew. The death toll in America alone reaches sixty million. Having successfully taken control of North America the Aryans then continue their crusade.

Cells in Europe first become active in 1993, and six years later, as economic collapse strikes across the continent in the wake of the Organization's victory over the System in North America, Europe falls to the harbingers of the New Era. The streets of Europe's great cities are ankle-deep in the blood of millions as Jews, race-traitors and other undesirables are slaughtered by members of the Organization. By 1999 the major power centres of the world are all under the control of the Organization with the single exception of China. The Chinese authorities precipitate the final conflict with the Organization by invading the Soviet Union, which is unable to resist as its nuclear capability has been destroyed. The Chinese send a vast army through the Urals to take over Europe. With no time to muster and train a sufficiently large number of troops to resist, the Organization deploys nuclear, chemical and biological weapons successfully against the enemy.

This massive attack results in the defeat of China and the creation of the Great Eastern Waste, a post-nuclear wasteland of some sixteen million square miles stretching from the Urals to the Pacific and from the Arctic to the Indian Ocean. For those who share Pierce's ideals the book has a happy ending as the Organization and its inner core the Order achieve their final goals – the annihilation of all other races across the globe and 'wise and benevolent rule over the earth for all time to come'.

It should not surprise any reader of this potted account of *The Turner Diaries* that Pierce has been described as so dangerous. If he had not written his apocalyptic ideas down in the form of a novel he would undoubtedly have been prosecuted for inciting racial hatred and encouraging sedition. Pierce published a second work, *Hunter*, in 1989, also using the pseudonym Andrew Macdonald. The book is dedicated to the serial killer and racist Joseph Paul Franklin (born James Clayton Vaughn), who went on a three-year killing spree from 1977 to 1980. He began his one-man race war by bombing a synagogue and then went on to shoot numerous strangers in a number of states including Wisconsin, Georgia, Oklahoma and Utah. His victims were blacks, Jews and mixed-race couples.

Whilst *The Turner Diaries* is a full-scale apocalyptic fantasy about a highly organised and nationwide Aryan guerrilla army fighting an epic war, *Hunter* is a very different story although it shares the same ideology – the propagation of racial hatred and violence. *Hunter* concerns the actions of a single man, its hero is Oscar Yeager, modelled on Joseph Paul Franklin, who returns from serving in the Vietnam War to a multicultural America little to his liking. Working essentially as a solo operator he hones his military skills until he is a trained assassin who targets mixed-race couples and other race traitors, Jews and homosexuals. During the unfolding of the story he receives instruction on Aryan politics and related subjects from members of a group called the National League, a thinly disguised fictional version of Pierce's own National Alliance.

In 1997 a Swedish professor of the history of religions, Mattias Gardell, interviewed Pierce who told him,

This is the way to teach people. Write novels, write plays, write film scripts, because a person not only experiences the actions of the protagonist, but if you have the protagonist in decision-making situations, when he has some sort of a conflict that he has to resolve, the reader, or the viewer, undergoes the same thought processes, and then you can carry the audience along, to educate them, to get them to change their minds, to get them to see things the way the protagonist learns to see things.[6]

The Turner Diaries and *Hunter* are not just dangerous fantasies but also – as the words of Pierce make all too clear – manuals to be used. It was not long before someone sought to make his dreams a reality.

Chapter 17

Armed Insurrection in Aryan America

We say: 'Rise and join us! . . . The Aryan yeomanry is awakening. A long forgotten wind is starting to blow. Do you hear the approaching thunder? It is that of the awakened Saxon. War is upon the land. The tyrant's blood will flow.

> Bob Mathews, from an open letter sent to
> the American press[1]

The Order – fantasy becomes reality

Only a few years after the publication of *The Turner Diaries* the fictional Order, the core group of the Organization representing the Aryan revolutionary force, became a reality. In September 1983 the Brüder Schweigen (Silent Brotherhood, originally called the Aryan Resistance Movement) was founded by Robert Jay Mathews (1953–84) and soon became known simply as the Order. Pierce openly acknowledged that his novel had been inspirational to Mathews and congratulated the latter on his activism.

Bob Mathews brought together a group of nine white supremacists eager to put their ideals into militant action. At his home in Metaline Falls, Washington Mathews led the initiation ceremony which brought the Order into being. The members linked hands within a circle of burning candles, and with a six-week-old baby girl on a blanket in their midst and a portrait of Hitler overseeing the rite swore the following oath, which Mathews intoned: 'I, as a free Aryan man, hereby swear an unrelenting oath upon the green graves of our sires, upon the children in the wombs of our wives . . . to do whatever is necessary to deliver our people from the Jew and bring total victory to the Aryan race.'[2]

Mathews was both a member of Pierce's National Alliance and an Odinist. Despite the fact that fellow Order members were a mixture of pagan and Christian Aryan supremacists the oath and accompanying ritual were definitely based on pagan models. The number nine is, as we have seen, an important sacred number in northern lore. An oath was also the standard means by which any serious contract between man and man or man and god was sealed in the pagan north. There were also references to past ancestors – 'the green graves of our sires' – and the generations to come – 'the children in the wombs of our wives' and the presence of the infant child in the ceremonial circle.

Within the Order there were marked differences of opinion concerning *The Turner Diaries*. When interviewed by Mattias Gardell two members, David Tate and Gary Yarbrough, dismissed it as mere pulp fiction whilst Randy Duey described it as a 'blueprint for action'. Another member, Richard Kemp, made his view of the novel even more explicit: 'Not so much the science-fiction part, but the underlying message of how to set up an organization and what to do with it, how to assassinate, and things like that. Although I am embarrassed to say that that was what we patterned ourselves after . . . I think that as far as *Turner Diaries* being a guide, I think that it was more than a guide, all our criminal activities were patterned after that.'[3]

The Order began an ambitious campaign to raise money through counterfeiting – using a printing press belonging to Aryan Nations – and armed robbery. They amassed millions of dollars through robbing banks and armoured cars, their most spectacular success being the theft of over three and a half million dollars from a Brink's armoured car in Ukiah, California in the summer of 1984. Some of the haul was used to buy arms, vehicles and other equipment required to continue their campaign. Donations were made to Aryan churches and other organisations. The Order also bankrolled safe houses and a paramilitary training facility for Aryan militia men.

The group carried out two murders. One was of suspected informer and Aryan Nations member Walter West, who was said to have revealed the Order's activities during drinking bouts. The other victim was Jewish radio talk-show host Alan Berg, a well-known and very vocal critic of right-wing extremism. The escalation of its activities and the recruiting of more members – who had to take a lie detector test before being admitted – meant that the Order was more vulnerable to infiltration by the authorities. Utilising its informants within Aryan Nations and penetrating the Order itself the FBI were by the end of 1984 in a position to break up the group. Escaping after a shoot-out Mathews found the motivations of his pursuers hard to understand.

> Why are so many men so eager to destroy their own kind for the benefit of the Jews and the mongrels? I see three FBI agents hiding behind some trees . . . I could have easily killed them . . . they look like good racial stock yet all their talents are given to a government which is openly trying to mongrelise the very race these agents are part of . . . I have been a good soldier, a fearless warrior. I will die with honor and join my brothers in heaven.[4]

Mathews was finally hunted down and trapped in his isolated hideaway on Whidbey Island, Washington state, in December 1984. Surrounded, he refused to lay down his weapons unless the government allowed a separatist Aryan republic to be set up in the north-western states of America. Failing to convince Mathews to surrender the FBI sought to drive him out by setting fire to his house. He decided to stay put and died in the flames. To sympathisers Mathews had died as an Aryan warrior, a martyr who had resisted the Zionist Occupation Government to the end. David Lane, one of his inner circle, on hearing on the radio of his death went out to a Confederate soldiers' graveyard and wrote a poem entitled 'Ode to Bob Mathews'. One verse reads:

> They knew they'd met their match,
> So they set the house on fire.
> And soon the flames touched the sky,
> A Viking funeral pyre.

The anniversary of Mathews' death, 8 December, is commemorated as a day of martyrdom and Whidbey Island has become a site of pilgrimage for some Aryan supremacists. Over the next two years the rest of the core membership were caught; those not imprisoned turned informer. Despite the brief existence of the Order it continues to be a source of inspiration to the Aryan revolutionary movement.

FBI hunters and lone wolves

Not long after Pierce published *Hunter* in 1989 relations between fringe groups in America and the FBI took a drastic turn for the worse. The turning point was an FBI raid on an isolated twenty-acre property in the Ruby Ridge area of northern Idaho, the home of ex-Green Beret Randy Weaver and his family.[5] As members of Christian Identity the Weavers had visited Aryan Nations at its headquarters in Hayden Lake, not far from Ruby Ridge. When Randy Weaver attended an Aryan Nations convention at Hayden Lake in 1989 Kenneth Fadeley, an undercover federal informer, eventually persuaded Weaver to sell him two sawn-off shotguns despite the latter's concerns about committing a crime. Subsequently Weaver was approached by Bureau of Alcohol, Tobacco and Firearms (BATF) agents, who had recorded the exchange with Fadeley. They offered not to prosecute him if he agreed to inform on Aryan Nations. He refused and was charged with the firearms offence. He failed to appear in court because his parole officer had given him the wrong date, although the indications were that he would not have gone anyway. Weaver was now deemed a fugitive and he sent a number of inflammatory letters to the authorities, in one of them quoting an apocalyptic passage from Bob Mathews.

The US Marshals Service had been keeping him under surveillance and on 21 August 1992 a group of six heavily armed, hooded and camouflaged SWAT-trained marshals entered the Weavers' land. Three of them went ahead (Deputy Marshals Degan, Roderick and Cooper) and observed Randy Weaver, his thirteen-year-old son Sammy and a close family friend named Kevin Harris in the yard. The boy's dog, a Labrador named Striker, started barking at the marshals and ran into the woods after them. Believing the dog had come across a deer, Harris and Sammy grabbed their rifles and set off together in the direction the dog had taken. Weaver went by another route but was close by. Harris and the boy then ran into the marshals. According to the testimony of the two surviving marshals, when they identified themselves Harris shot their colleague dead. They returned fire and Harris was injured and the dog killed. Neither agent subsequently confessed to the fatal shooting of the boy.

The account given by Harris placed the blame firmly on the marshals. He reported that when he and Sammy met the three men they failed to identify themselves. Their masks and camouflage made Harris and Sammy fear their intentions. When the dog was shot Sammy fired back and was himself shot in the arm. Harris fired to cover the boy and told him to run back to the cabin. Randy Weaver, who by now had realised what was going on, fired his gun in the air and also yelled to his son to get back to the family cabin. As the wounded Sammy tried to make it home he was fatally shot in the back. Weaver and the wounded Harris made a successful retreat to the cabin and the marshals withdrew from the mountain. Randy and his wife Vicki placed the body of their son in a shed near the cabin.

That night the FBI, having cordoned off the area, sent in snipers to surround the Weavers' home. At six the next morning Randy, his sixteen-year-old daughter Sara and Harris cautiously left the cabin to see to Sammy's body. Without warning an FBI sniper named Lou Horiuchi opened fire, wounding Randy in the arm. Hearing the shot, Vicki, with her ten-month-old daughter Elisheba in her arms, flung open the kitchen door and shouted to her family to get back indoors. Again without warning the same sniper fired another shot, this time with deadly accuracy. Vicki was hit in the head and died within a few minutes still clutching her baby in her arms. It was left to Sara and her younger sister Rachel to look after the baby during the following nine days until the stand-off finally ended.

During this time not only did the FBI presence increase but the media also arrived en masse. Friends and other local protestors against the gung-ho attitude of the FBI were joined by a mixed group of Identity Christians, neo-Nazi skinheads and Aryan revolutionaries. The combined efforts of Vicki's best friend and a far-right Christian politician, James 'Bo' Gritz, finally led to Randy Weaver being persuaded to surrender. In July 1993 Weaver was acquitted on all counts except his failure to attend court for the firearms offence which had precipitated the whole affair. Harris was also exonerated. Just over two years later, in August 1995, the US Justice Department paid out $3.1 million to the Weaver family and accepted that federal actions at Ruby Ridge had been contrary to both the law and FBI policy.

To right-wing separatists, who already believed that the federal government was the puppet of Jewish financiers and that Aryan people were being persecuted, the events at Ruby Ridge merely confirmed their fears. They interpreted the shooting of the Weaver family as an escalation of their conflict with the agents of the New World Order, a shadowy and clandestine group who in popular conspiracy theory planned to takeover the whole world. So much concern was voiced by various elements of the white separatist movement that two large-scale meetings were organised in October 1992, the first in Naples, Idaho, the second at Estes Park, Colorado. The effect of these two meetings was, temporarily at least, to unite the movement against the common enemy – the federal government and the shadowy forces believed to be behind it. A new strategy of countering the New World Order was put forward.

The 'leaderless resistance' campaign was proposed by Louis Beam, a Vietnam veteran, Klansman and Identity Christian. Due to the infiltration of larger hierarchically organised groups by the authorities it was becoming increasingly difficult for armed opposition to be effective; detection and subsequent arrest were becoming almost inevitable. Beam proposed that whilst ideological unity should be maintained, organisational unity should be reassessed. Those on the radical right already known to the authorities should henceforth concentrate on propaganda and stay on the right side of the law. Direct action should be undertaken either by small units, 'phantom cells' or lone wolves acting independently. These small-scale operators would have no direct links with the separatist establishment and, as such, would be particularly difficult for the authorities to detect. Predicting and preventing acts of terrorism would be more difficult. Other extremist organisations round the world have also adopted such operational strategies, most notably al Qaeda.

The notion of leaderless resistance was not entirely the invention of Louis Beam. The reclusive eco-terrorist Theodore Kaczynski (the Unabomber) had conducted an intermittent bombing campaign beginning in the late 1970s until his arrest in 1995. The fact that he had no links with any organisation and operated alone had undoubtedly made him extremely hard to track down. Such terrorists can be seen as the political version of Duclos's serial killers who, with very few exceptions, murder alone. No doubt if Duclos investigated such political killers he would make the point that the wolf is one of Odin's totem animals. Beam's strategy was expounded in an article in the right-wing *The Seditionist* has been widely influential. In *Project Megiddo* the FBI acknowledged that domestic extremists have largely rejected more traditional forms of organisation and that fragmentation and autonomy has taken the place of structure and hierarchy.

19 April: day of infamy

Leaderless resistance has also influenced terrorists beyond America. In London the one-man bombing campaign of David Copeland in 1999 bears all the hallmarks of a lone wolf operation. Copeland saw himself as 'the spark, that's all I plan to be. The spark that would set fire to this country.'[6] In 1996, at the age of twenty, Copeland already harboured fantasies about starting a race war through bombing ethnic minorities. He joined the far-right British National Party in 1997 and then the more extreme National-Socialist Movement. NSM included many members of Combat 18, a militant neo-Nazi group with its roots in football hooliganism and ethnic violence. Combat 18 derives its name from Adolf Hitler, A being the first letter of the alphabet and H the eighth. Despite his links with these extremist groups Copeland seems to have decided to pursue a solo mission.

On 19 April 1999 he planted a nail bomb in the largely black area of Brixton in south London, wounding nearly forty people. A few days later another bomb went off in Brick Lane, home to a large Asian community, causing a further six injuries. On 30 April the third and last bomb caused even more mayhem, exploding in a pub which was a favourite of the gay community. Three died and another sixty-five were wounded in the blast. Copeland was quickly apprehended by police and the NSM leadership, fearing the group would be implicated, promptly folded. Like a number of other far-right activists, Copeland openly admitted to having been influenced by *The Turner Diaries*.

That Copeland began his bombing campaign on 19 April seems extremely unlikely to have been a coincidence. The selection of this particular date was most likely symbolic, to connect his attack with something which had occurred exactly four years before – the bombing of the Alfred P. Murrah Federal Building in Oklahoma City by Timothy McVeigh and Terry Nichols.[7] In the strange world of modern Aryan separatism a calendar has begun to develop in which certain dates have assumed a symbolic significance. It has already been noted that 8 December, the day Bob Mathews burnt to death when he refused to surrender to the FBI, has become a day of remembrance for Aryan supremacists in America.

However, 19 April has assumed, if anything, a greater significance, and its importance did not begin with the Oklahoma bombing but with the FBI siege of the headquarters of the Christian cult of David Koresh, the Branch Davidian Students of the Seven Seals, just outside Waco in Texas. This reached its bloody climax on 19 April 1993. Seventy-four members of the sect, including its leader and seventeen children, died along with four federal agents.

The Branch Davidians had no connection either politically or ideologically with Aryan separatists and white supremacists – they were a multicultural group with no overt political agenda – yet FBI actions at Waco, described as a holocaust by their critics, coming so soon after the killings at Ruby Ridge, seemed to those on the far right to foretell a clampdown on all dissenters. Since 1993 Aryan radicals have commemorated this day, which allows remembrance services to be held alongside the most important day of the year for many of them, the birthday of Adolf Hitler, which falls on 20 April.

Timothy McVeigh was among those who saw Waco as a confirmation of their worst fears about the federal government. He chose the date for his bombing to commemorate not only the second anniversary of Waco, but also the 220th since the battles of Lexington and Concord in 1775 in which American colonists fought the British. McVeigh saw himself, like the patriots of old, as rising against an alien government. Before the bombing conspiracy theorists had already marked down Oklahoma City and the Murrah building in particular as significant in government plots. Among the more outrageous claims was that radical political opponents of the government were taken to the city and then put in concentration camps or disposed of in one of a number of gigantic crematoria.

Whether this particular echo of the Holocaust was ringing in McVeigh's ears is not clear but the evidence indicates that these ideas were known to him. Fully expecting to be killed or arrested after the bombing McVeigh deliberately left a bundle of papers inside an envelope in his car. These documents were selected as expressions of his political position and rationale for the bombing. Among them was a pamphlet which compared the modern militias with the American revolutionaries of old. Another equated the FBI's actions at Waco with Nazi attacks on the Jews. What is clear from the reports of his family and friends and from his own admissions is that McVeigh was obsessed with *The Turner Diaries*, which he read and reread. The bombing itself was clearly inspired by the episode in which Earl Turner blows up the FBI headquarters with a bomb made of ammonium nitrate fertiliser – the exact method used by McVeigh. Despite the fact that he had belonged briefly to the Ku Klux Klan McVeigh claimed that what attracted him to the book was not its overt racism but its stand against gun control.

McVeigh was obsessed with his guns and the idea that the government might take away the right to bear arms was anathema to him. It was at gun shows that he began peddling *The Turner Diaries*. In the envelope of documents in his car was a quote from the book about the psychological effects of terrorist acts: the aim is not just to cause actual casualties but also to send out a message to bureaucrats and politicians that they too are not safe. However many tanks they bring on to the streets of America and however much barbed wire they put up even their fortified country estates are not beyond the reach of terrorists.

Whilst he was awaiting trial McVeigh read another anti-government book, *Unintended Consequences* (1996). Written by John

Ross, a champion of American gun culture, its hero is a hunter who, after many examples of government attacks – Ruby Ridge among them – turns assassin, targeting agents and officials in revenge. McVeigh said that he thought it was a much better book than *The Turner Diaries* and that had it come to his attention first he may have made that his battle plan instead of the bombing. He also remarked that if people thought *The Turner Diaries* was his Bible then Ross's book would be his New Testament. No clearer testimony exists of how fantasy can turn into reality. When McVeigh's bomb exploded just after nine o'clock that morning 168 people, including many children, were to die and hundreds more were injured, making it the biggest ever terrorist atrocity on American soil at that time.

Aryan supremacists also remember another activist, an Identity Christian named Richard Snell who was racially motivated to kill two men – one black and the other who Snell mistakenly believed to be Jewish. Snell's fate is linked to that of McVeigh in a strange way. Both had dealings with Elohim City, a separatist Christian Identity enclave in eastern Oklahoma, and Snell had been implicated in a plot to attack the Murrah Building in the 1980s. In another strange twist Snell was executed in Arkansas approximately twelve hours after the Oklahoma bomb exploded that morning on 19 April 1995.

McVeigh's connections with Elohim City were investigated and a BATF informant named Carol Howe supplied information suggesting that the bombing may have been a more widespread conspiracy. She reported that several months before the bombing she overheard militants talking about blowing up a government building. Among the discussed targets was the Murrah Building. She informed BATF that the lynchpins of this purported plot were Dennis Mahon, an American white supremacist, and a German citizen, Andreas Strassmeir ('Andy the German'), who was director of security at Elohim City. Both men denied involvement and McVeigh also told the authorities that neither had anything to do with the bombing. That Strassmeir and McVeigh had met at a gun show, talked politics and even exchanged addresses was not disputed by either party. McVeigh also tried to telephone Strassmeir at Elohim City about a week before the explosion, apparently to find out if he could hide out there after he had planted the bomb. He could not get through to him.

Strassmeir's grandfather was an early member of the Nazi party and his father Günter a close friend and top aide of former Chancellor of Germany Helmut Kohl. His introduction to the world of American white extremism was organised by Kirk Lyons, an American attorney who has defended numerous neo-Nazis and other supremacists. Martin Lee, an investigator into right-wing extremism, interviewed Lyons, who told him that he not only helped to arrange for Strassmeir to come to the States in the first place, he even visited his parents in Berlin to let them know in person that their son was flourishing in America. Lyons also introduced him to the community at Elohim City.[8]

Carol Howe claimed that the prime mover in the Oklahoma bombing was Strassmeir and that he had a powerful influence over McVeigh. Martin Lee has speculated on the possible reasons why Howe's evidence of a conspiracy was ultimately discounted. Was it that what she took to be serious plotting was in fact nothing more than drunken talk? Was the government unwilling to admit that it had failed to heed Howe's warning that the Oklahoma attack was imminent? Was Strassmeir's alleged involvement played down because of his powerful family connections? Or was it that the prosecutors simply wanted to be sure that they would get their man and feared that a complex and shadowy conspiracy at Elohim City might stymie their chances of convicting McVeigh? Which if any of these factors played a part remains unclear and despite Howe's information Strassmeir was not formally implicated and subsequently returned to Berlin.

The Oklahoma atrocity was undertaken by a man who had repeatedly read *The Turner Diaries* and turned its fictional account of a bombing into reality. Drawing on the actions of real-life killer Joseph

Paul Franklin, William Pierce's other novel *Hunter* became, in turn, an inspiration to others to perpetrate actual crimes. In this sequence we see the symbiotic relationship between fantasy and actuality. The two go hand in hand to inspire action, for fantasy is far more than empty daydreaming; it is a modern, and often debased, version of traditional mythology and as such often the blueprint for action. Fantasy may become prophecy which may become concrete reality. The Order, which first appeared as an imaginary group of Aryan elitists, soon became a real neo-Nazi terrorist cell. This was not the first fictional secret society to have dramatic repercussions in the real world – the Elders of Zion never existed outside the pages of the *Protocols* yet this phantom cabal was used to justify the Holocaust.

So far the seemingly independent reports of Odin's return by the psychologist Carl Jung and the sociologist Denis Duclos have been followed and found to be inextricably linked. Jung's identification of Odin as the hidden unconscious force behind the Nazi movement and Duclos's notion that the mad warrior of northern myth embodied by Odin is the shadowy inspiration for an epidemic of violence seem to meet on the common ground of right-wing extremism in the United States.

There is a growing pagan movement in the New World which includes a number of Odinic cults. Many individuals on the far right have cast off their Christian identity and turned back towards the heathen gods. The Latin *paganus*, from which we get our word pagan, means country dweller. Likewise heathen, a word which exists in numerous Germanic languages, means people of the heaths. Pagans or heathens were perceived to be backward rural people who clung to their traditional ways and resisted the new religion of Christianity. Mattias Gardell, who has made a detailed study of American white separatists and their pagan beliefs, notes that the equivalent in modern urban American speech are the words hick or hillbilly; in Britain bumpkin or yokel.

It is interesting to note that many of those people who make up these growing pagan communities come from what urban Americans see as hick towns or rural backwaters. We would do well to recall Denis Duclos's remarks on the similarities between medieval northern Europe and the modern state of America, for it is in the vast hinterlands beyond fast-moving city life that paganism is regaining ancient ground. It is the lesser-known America of Idaho, Washington State and West Virginia – far from the metropolitan centres of California and the eastern seaboard – which is home to the growing communities of both pagans and white separatists.

Chapter 18

Wotansvolk

In light of these . . . innumerable crimes against the collective White race, as well as the self-evident policy of genocide, we hereby forswear allegiance or support for our executioners' institutions. In obedience to nature's laws and recognizing that nature and her laws are the work of God, whatever a man's understanding of what the Creator might be, and that the highest law is the preservation of one's own kind, we further demand the formation of exclusive White homelands on the North American continent and in Europe. If denied, then we will seek redress by whatever measures are necessary.

David Lane, *White Genocide Manifesto* (1994)[1]

A Silent Brother is sentenced to 190 years in jail

Bob Mathews and some other members of the Order (Silent Brotherhood) have described themselves as followers of Odin and undoubtedly the most prominent of these is David Lane, one of the original circle. He was captured by the FBI on 30 March 1985 in North Carolina and convicted for racketeering by a court in Seattle on 30 December the same year. Before he was sentenced – to forty years –

Lane addressed the court at length, denying the right of the government to charge him since its 'single aim is to exterminate my race'. He was subsequently also found guilty of violating the civil rights of the murdered Alan Berg – Lane was the getaway driver – and given a further 150-year sentence in November 1987. In 1989 Lane unsuccessfully appealed against this second sentence. He will not be eligible for parole until around 2035, by which time, were he still to be alive, he would be almost a hundred years old. Lane is now in a maximum-security prison in Florence, Colorado.

The extraordinarily long sentences he was given along with his numerous published prison writings have made Lane the most high-profile white supremacist revolutionary in the American prison system. Seen by some as a prisoner of war he has become something of a legendary figure alongside the deceased Bob Mathews. Originally an Identity Christian, Lane later came to the conclusion that Christianity in whatever form was an alien faith. He rejected it in favour of the pagan tradition of Odinism (which he prefers to call Wotanism for reasons given below).

What is significant in our quest to trace the influence of the Odinic archetype is that because of Lane's high profile and the fact that his writings are widely circulated and read by those in the separatist underground the Odinism he espouses has been spread along with his racist ideology. Lane embodies a significant and conscious move among extremists away from Christianity and towards Odinism.

The small town of Woden in Hancock County, Iowa was founded at the turn of the twentieth century. Originally this small community was called Bingham and then Ripley, but both names were rejected by the post office as too similar to those of other towns in the region. According to local history it was subsequently renamed Woden on account of the frequent dynamiting that accompanied the construction of the Klondike railroad which passed through the town. The noise was likened to Woden in his role as a god of war. It was into this community of just over 200 people that David Lane was born on Wednesday, 2 November 1938, one of four children of an itinerant farmer.

According to Jung, the law of synchronicity is a fundamental principle, linking the subjective world of the human mind with the objective, outside world. Jung describes it as follows: 'Synchronicity takes the coincidence of events in space and time as meaning something more than mere chance, namely, a peculiar interdependence of objective events among themselves as well as with the subjective (psychic) states of the observer or observers.'[2]

What this suggests is that a synchronicity is a coincidence with *meaning*, with a direct link to the thoughts and actions of the observer. We have already seen how aspects of the lives of Guido von List and Karl von Wiligut display weird synchronicities with the Odin archetype. Lane himself sees such synchronicities in his own life, noting that not only was he born in a place called Woden but also that he was born on a Wednesday (Woden's day). As a result he adopted the pen name Wodensson.

Lane says he always felt like a stranger in this world and that his earliest memories revealed to him that there was something wrong with it.

I remember two emotions from earliest childhood. The first was fear. My father was a drunk who often beat his wife and children, causing severe injuries. Then at about the age of five I went to an orphanage. From there I was soon adopted by an equally scary fundamentalist Lutheran minister and his wife. So fear was the first and most enduring emotion. However, in the first grade at a little country school near Morehead, Iowa, I saw a little blond goddess named Mary. I was bewitched, enthralled, enchanted and in love. That love has never died although several 'goddesses' have passed through my life since then.[3]

This brief account is expanded on elsewhere in Lane's auto-biographical writings. He recounts that his brother was made permanently deaf by the beatings meted out by his drunken father while his mother was prostituted to provide her husband's 'booze money'. Lane's adoptive father the Lutheran minister was not only scary but interminably boring, subjecting the young Lane to endless services, prayers, Bible studies and sermons until he equated the very name of Jesus with 'pure boredom'. He also says that he heard the pagan gods Thor and Odin spoken of early in his life as the vanquished and instantly identified with them. Childhood play with his brother revealed his nascent Nazi leanings. When they played at soldiers Lane would always be the Germans in the Second World War and enjoyed chanting '*Sieg Heil*' and '*Heil Hitler*'. Lane also recalls disbelieving his mother when she told him that the Nazis had killed millions of Jews.

Graduating from high school in Aurora, Colorado Lane began working for a power company. Soon after starting this job he married his first wife. It was not a happy union and the couple soon split up. In the 1960s he became more politically aware and began to investigate conspiracy theories in the wake of the Kennedy assassination and the Vietnam War. By 1978 he had reached a watershed in his thinking and was convinced there was a Zionist conspiracy to destroy the Aryan race. He wrote a pamphlet entitled 'The Death of the White Race' and made thousands of copies of it on a photocopier belonging to the insurance company for which he worked, distributing the pamphlet during his time off work. In 1979 he joined a Klan organisation and two years later began to work for Aryan Nations. His activism continued when shortly afterwards he began to run the Colorado office of the White American Political Association (WAPA), a California-based supremacist group founded by a contemporary of Lane's named Tom Metzger, an organisation which still exists today as White Aryan Resistance (WAR). Such was the prelude to his joining Bob Mathews's Order, and to his subsequent imprisonment.

No longer having the capacity for direct action to further his cause Lane has turned to writing from his prison cell as his main weapon. He has been a prolific contributor of articles to numerous white separatist and anti-Semitic publications and has also produced a number of works including *White Genocide Manifesto* and *The 88 Precepts* which have become key texts in far-right circles. Lane is philosophical about spending the rest of his life behind bars. Whilst obviously preferring to be free he acknowledges that without his incarceration his message would not have achieved the prominence that it has. As he puts it, 'Death or imprisonment is the best way for a revolutionary to gain credibility. In a strange way I must thank the tyrants, liars and devils incarnate who put me here.'

Wotansvolk, the creed of iron

Lane makes a distinction between Odinism and his own brand of Wotanism. Odinism he associates with other neo-pagans who do not espouse the racism and separatism integral to his beliefs. Although Wotanism is the name he prefers for his creed, it should be noted that this is very much his definition and not a division in general use in pagan circles. Not all those groups and individuals who describe their activities and beliefs as Wotanism are racist; not all those who profess Odinism are non-racist. Lane finds the name Wotan particularly useful not just because it gives him the opportunity to distinguish his creed from the mainstream but also because as an acronym WOTAN can signify Will of the Aryan Nation. Also Wotan, being the name by which the god was known on the continental mainland of Europe, also makes it more likely to appeal 'to the genetic memory of more of our ancestors' than Odin, as the god was known in Scandinavia. In 1995 Lane named his organisation Wotansvolk (Wotan's folk or people). Wotan was also the name Lane gave to a paramilitary organisation he envisaged which would follow the strategy of leaderless resistance.

Wotansvolk is highly militant and openly inspired by the exploits of the Vikings. The warrior creed is underpinned by a Wotanist philosophy of both life and the afterlife. Lane believes that everything in the universe is made up of electromagnetic patterns and forces – including biological life forms, thoughts and ideas. The soul is defined as the patterns of energy which produce thought and is considered capable of existing outside biological life forms. Lane's view of the afterlife is that when the physical body dies its soul chooses either to return to Asgard, the realm of the gods, in order to merge with the cosmic mind – symbolised as Wotan (Odin) – or to go to Valhalla. The souls who go to Valhalla will, according to Lane, be reincarnated to struggle again in Midgard, the world of men. The souls belonging to those who have an easy, ineffectual or indifferent earthly existence (known as slaves or thralls) will go to the shadowy realm of Hel, the Norse underworld, where their soul patterns 'dissolve into an energy chaos without form or thought'. Such slaves are of little use to the cause and he exhorts Aryans to attain a more noble death.

Lane's main slogan or battle cry, known as the Fourteen Words – 'We must secure the existence of our people and a future for White children' – has become something of a mantra among the white separatist movement. It is complemented by another fourteen-word slogan, Lane's own private counterpart: 'Because the beauty of the White Aryan woman must not perish from the earth'. Both of these key phrases came to him in his sleep, and, on scrutinising them more closely, Lane discovered that not only did both slogans have fourteen words, twenty syllables and sixty-one letters, but they also shared a numerical value of 741 (A = 1, B = 2, etc.). The full significance of these connections and particularly the meaning of the number 741 only became clear to Lane a few years later when he was reading a weighty tome on occult symbolism.[4]

With the coming of Christianity to northern Europe the pagan religion of Wotanism gave way to the new faith. Faced with persecution, torture and murder at the hands of the new order pagan adepts are said to have taken refuge within the Church, disguising themselves and their teachings in a number of ways. Lane's idiosyncratic readings of the Book of Revelation have led him to conclude that it can be interpreted as referring to his own life. Many of his otherwise staunch followers have distanced themselves from these messianic musings. Numerology plays a role in a number of Lane's writings and many of these have 14/88 printed at the end – shorthand for the Fourteen Words followed by the dual meaning of the number 88: Heil Hitler, H being the eighth letter of the alphabet, or *the 88 Precepts* of Lane's own philosophy.

The preservation of the white race is the primary concern of his philosophy. This aim follows directly from the laws of nature: 'Nature and nature's laws are the work of the Creator. Therefore nature's laws are God's laws, and nature's first and highest law is the preservation of one's own kind.'5 'One's own kind' means one's own race. Lane defines a racist as 'one who loves and preserves his race'. To him 'racist' is not an insult and he would also argue that being a racist (using his definition) does not mean hating other races. To make his point he draws an analogy from nature. Wolves, coyotes and foxes whilst able to interbreed do not because in their natural state God gave them the instinct to preserve their own kind. He applies this analogy to his three main or root races of humankind – Caucasoid (white), Mongoloid (oriental) and Negroid (black) – and argues that each, if it follows nature's course, should remain separate.

He calculates that the white race is doomed, under present circumstances, to die out. He quotes statistics to make his point. According to these, 8 per cent of the human population is white and only a quarter of them are females of child-bearing age. Due to outside propaganda and programming many of these younger women are persuaded to mate outside their race, thus reducing the white population even further. Homosexuality and abortion among Aryans are similarly condemned because they counter white population growth. The institutions and ideologies which dominate today are either directly under the control of enemy races, particularly the

Jews, or are ineffectual at dealing with the danger. Lane believes the Jews have a deliberate plan to wipe the white population off the face of the globe. America and the other 'once white countries' have denied the white race: 'Not only White nations, but White schools, White Organizations, White neighbourhoods and everything necessary for our survival as a biological and cultural entity. It is deliberate, malicious genocide. An example of their deceitful words is the term "minorities" for the colored world, while we approach extinction.'[6]

Lane also contrasts white resistance movements and those of other peoples. He argues that those Aryans who resist this genocide are persecuted economically, socially and politically. Further resistance results in imprisonment or assassination by government agents. He compares the treatment of whites and non-whites – the latter, if they resist the genocide of their own people, are praised as heroes.

He cites the 101st Airborne Division of the US Army using bayonets to force young white girls to integrate in southern schools and mounted police beating the white mothers of south Boston when they resisted the integration of their neighbourhood schools. He compares the ideology behind this exercise of American police and military power at home with the Allied forces' war against the Germans. German aggression towards the Jews and others under the Third Reich is seen by Lane as simply another example of the traditional role of the Germanic peoples as defenders of the race. The Jews, like the Mongol hordes of Genghis Khan and the Moors of North Africa before them, are seen as threats to the survival of the white race and its civilisation. However, despite his virulent anti-Semitism and racial slurs he writes: 'Hatred of all Jews because a few Zionists have sentenced the white race to death is absurd. Hatred of Negroes for protecting their territorial imperatives or for not fitting into White society is absurd. The same with Hispanics.'[7]

Lane calls Zionist Jews and those whom he believes serve their goals the Sons of Muspell or Muspellheimers. In Norse mythology Muspell is a giant from the south who, along with his followers causes the conflict with the gods at the Ragnarok, or end of the world. Non-whites are also referred to by Lane as skraelings, a word used by the Vikings who first came to America to describe Native Americans. He gives his anti-Semitism a historical justification by arguing that the present problems of the world have their roots in ancient history. In the ancient world the eastern Mediterranean was the trade crossroads of Europe, Asia and Africa. In order to make alliances, white, oriental and black merchants and bankers married off their sons and daughters to each other. In doing so they created a mixed race, carrying the genes of all three root races. This Lane identifies as the Semites – the Jews and the Arabs.

Lane sees evidence for Jewish control over the American government even in the Great Seal of the United States. The two symbols which he sees as hidden proof of the Zionist Occupation Government are the Star of David above the eagle's head and the 'All Seeing Eye of Judah' on top of the pyramid. Other conspiracy theorists have seen the symbolism of the Great Seal as proof of a Masonic, rather than Jewish, plot to control America. In this regard it should be noted that much of the symbolism of Freemasonry is derived from Jewish tradition.

It is because of his particular brand of anti-Semitism that Lane, unlike many more traditional white supremacists, does not see himself as a patriot. His allegiance is to the Aryan race and not to the Stars and Stripes. As he sees it, America is run by Zionist forces bent on destroying the white race and therefore if a white person supports the government they are an enemy unto themselves. He dismisses the United States and its foreign policy in no uncertain terms: 'the red, white and blue travelling mass murder machine has been an engine of holocaust, genocide and death unmatched in human history'. He cites many wars and conflicts, from the American Civil War – which, needless to say, he believes to have been won by the wrong side – to

Afghanistan,, as support for his argument and castigates the United States for making war on Nazi Germany.

Lane asserts that the basic pattern of old Nordic society – which was divided into leaders, freemen and slaves – is the model most suitable for modern white society. He believes individuals fit naturally into one of these three classes. Most people are slaves: 'they never have an original thought in their entire lives. You see them today watching multiracial sports on TV or debating the latest propaganda from the establishment media.' Scientists, inventors, craftsmen and others are freemen and a very few people belong to the ruling elite of born leaders such as Bob Mathews and George Lincoln Rockwell. The minds of slaves and even some of the freemen are little more than computers. As such they are subject to the powerful programming techniques of the Zionist Occupation Government, which Wotanism must try to counteract by reprogramming the members of its own race.

In Lane's opinion the only hope for world peace is if the various races, cultures and nations of the world are allowed the freedom to pursue their own separate destinies. Progress towards globalisation and one world culture is anathema to him. He warns that if the Third World follows the Western path of mass industrialisation the fossil fuel reserves of the earth will be rapidly consumed and the resulting environmental pollution totally unmanageable.

In his *White Genocide Manifesto* he calls for the setting up of white homelands in Europe and North America where separatist communities can promote their own way of life free from outside interference. In order to initiate such a process he suggests that like-minded people should move in groups – as large as a few dozen families at a time if possible – to a sparsely populated county. They could then gradually take over the local political system, control local tax issues and employ a sympathetic sheriff, who could tap into the national crime computer system; this would greatly help the separatists gain access to the information they need to further their goals.

The American Ragnarok and Kinsland Defenders

His vision of how such communities could operate – even when 'at war' with the rest of America – is outlined in Lane's recent short novel, *KD Rebel*.[8] The story is set early in the twenty-first century in what was formerly the United States of America. Interracial marriage, mass immigration and propaganda directed against white males have led to the further decline of the white race. The Harmony Laws provide large cash incentives to interracial marriage and are the last straw for many disenfranchised white men. Thousands of them, mainly young, leave the cities behind and set up home in the Rocky Mountains. Their numbers allow them to gain a certain amount of autonomy from the System over a large area stretching across parts of the former states of Utah, Idaho, Colorado, Wyoming and Montana.

This territory is Kinsland and KD in the book title refers to the Kinsland Defenders, the separatist militia or guerrilla army which maintains its independence from the hated System. Most of the warriors are Wotanists (Odinists). The recruiting of females into the new community has been less than successful due to the power of propaganda and the lack of creature comforts in the scattered dwellings of Kinsland. The Kinsland Defenders are compared to the Vikings whose restlessness was supposedly partly driven by their desire to be free of the shackles of Rome and Judaea. KD raids into enemy territory in search of plunder and women are also modelled on the ways of their Viking ancestors.

The story begins in a sleazy nightclub owned by a Jewish pornographer and cocaine trafficker named Sid Cohen. On stage are two beautiful white girls performing mock-lesbian acts for the crowd. Among the onlookers are two Kinslanders who have taken the risk of entering System territory for a reason. The older of the two men, the community leader, is Trebor (Robert spelt backwards, as Lane himself says in the book, the name given to his character in honour of Bob Mathews) while the younger is called Eric. Like Bob Mathews, Trebor gives the bulk of his plunder to his own people and is portrayed as a kind of Robin Hood figure.

The two Kinslanders wait till the club closes and then follow Cohen, his bodyguard and the two girls back to the drug trafficker's luxury house. Trebor and Eric then dispose of the henchman and burst in on Cohen having kinky sex with the two girls, who are high on cocaine. They then beat Cohen until he gives them the location of his safe. Having got the information they slit his throat and leave with the girls in tow. Having fulfilled their mission to rob Cohen of his ill-gotten gains and to kidnap the two girls, who have been selected by Trebor to be his wives (leaders of the Kinsland community practise polygamy) they return home. Back in Kinsland in a small settlement called Mathewsville (another reference to the leader of the Order) the two girls are initially obsessed with getting hold of some cocaine and escaping from the primitive backwoods cabin which has been selected as their new home. The fact that Trebor does not force himself on them sexually comes as a surprise and they both begin to find him attractive.

The girls then find themselves in trouble when they steal some drugs from the community's nurse, who needs them to treat a wounded Kinslander who has just returned from operations in System territory. They are found out and a Thing (the traditional Germanic assembly where legal matters were dealt with) is called. The nurse asks that the punishment be severe and the assembled men, after consulting with their women, accede to her demands and order the two to be stripped naked and flogged. This punishment is meted out by the women of the community away from the eyes of the men. After their initial bitterness at the harshness of the world that they have been forced to join, the girls begin to settle in, overcome their cocaine habits and are deprogrammed. They are given books to study which prove to them that the propaganda they have been fed in the System schools and media is a pack of lies. As they get to know the taciturn Trebor better he teaches them about Wotanism, and the friendliness of the other women, many of whom were also 'liberated' from the System, helps them to accept, even enjoy, their new lives.

Events take an abrupt turn when System radio reports reveal that there has been a coup in Russia and that white nationalists have seized power. This signals that Ragnarok has begun and Russia, the Baltic states and the Ukraine have overthrown their Jewish overlords. This new Aryan power bloc delivers an ultimatum to the eastern European states to expel NATO and American forces from their soil or take the consequences. Coordinated revolutions by Islamic fundamentalists across the Middle East tip the balance of power further against Zionist–American interests by stopping oil supplies reaching the West. Trebor calls a Thing to announce to the Kinslanders the significance of these events to their own Aryan enclave. He tells them that most of America will be dead within weeks.

'Since nuclear-powered electrical generating plants were banned, and since KD shut down all western coal supplies from reaching the System, nearly ninety percent of all electrical power in North America comes from oil-fired plants. Most of the remainder comes from hydroelectric generation in the Northwest. Without oil the entire grid will shut down.

That means that gasoline and diesel fuel for trucks and cars won't be refined, and it won't be pumped in gas stations. Communications, computers, heating, traffic control, elevators and a thousand other wants and needs dependent on electricity will be shut down. That includes the food distribution system.

The cities will be starving in two weeks. All that pales into insignificance compared to the stoppage of water, especially drinking water. Not only will the water treatment plants cease to operate, but so will the pumps that transport water into the cities.'[9]

Kinsland on the other hand is well prepared for the catastrophe not only having a local supply of natural fresh water but also having hoarded food and fuel. Desperate outsiders will not be able to invade Kinsland because of lack of fuel to get there and because they have few weapons since the System crackdown on gun ownership. Only a few refugees will be accepted into KD society. They must be young and healthy and, needless to say, of good Aryan stock. Trebor estimates that of the 350 million people in America only five to ten million will survive. The novel ends with Trebor drifting contentedly off to sleep thinking that he must contact the Russians by radio to arrange the mass immigration of European Aryans to repopulate America.

The temple of Wotan: behind bars and beyond

Despite his continuing incarceration David Lane remarried in October 1994 and the following year with his new wife Katja he founded a small publishing company, 14 Word Press. Named after his well-known slogan, it soon started to publish books, pamphlets and a regular newsletter, *Focus Fourteen*. They were joined in this new enterprise by their friend Ron McVan. Born in Philadelphia in 1950, McVan moved to Washington State in his teens and became an artist, travelling widely across the continent with his paintings for a number of years. He was never interested in Christianity but explored Eastern religions before finding Odinism. In 1992 McVan and a friend, a lawyer named Michael (Reinhold) Clinton, founded an Odinist group named Wotan's Kindred. They ran courses together on traditional crafts, herbalism and healing, runes and archery, and performed blots (pagan ceremonies), but their relationship was not to last long due to both personal and ideological differences.

Clinton was to come to the attention of the media shortly after the discovery of a 9,200-year-old skeleton near Kennewick, Washington in 1996. The remains of Kennewick Man, as he became known, were thought to indicate that he was Caucasian rather than Native

American. In consequence some Odinists claimed him as their ancestor and a legal battle began between the scientists who wanted the bones for analysis, the local Native Americans who believed it was their ancestor and the Odinists. Clinton was the attorney for the Odinist faction in this high-profile case.

Clinton was later vilified by the Southern Poverty Law Center, a prominent anti-racist organisation in the States. In 1999 they published a report which described him as an anti-Semite. The grounds for this were that he had organised two lectures by David Irving, a British historian who has attained notoriety as a Holocaust denier, and had associated with the American Front, a group of racist skinheads. Clinton denies that he is a fascist, arguing that Irving was simply one of many guests of Wotan's Kindred, a number of whom were not white. His association with the American Front was short-lived and, according to researcher Mattias Gardell, unproductive – the skinheads denying Clinton was 'on their side'. Clinton also points out in his defence that he expelled McVan from Wotan's Kindred specifically because of the latter's racist views. However, McVan's racial ideology was no problem when he joined Lane's brand of Wotanism.

From its mountainside headquarters outside the small town of St Maries, Idaho the Wotansvolk machine soon became one of the most dynamic forces on the Aryan supremacist scene. It was managed by Katja Lane and McVan until September 2001 when the running of the organisation was handed over to others. In addition to being an outlet for Lane's writings, 14 Word Press also published other works, most notably those of McVan. Whilst most of Lane's work concentrates on the political and ideological side of their particular brand of Wotanism McVan's is more directed towards the religious aspects. His works *Creed of Iron* and *Temple of Wotan* contain detailed accounts of the seasonal festivals and other ceremonies of Wotansvolk along with studies of the runes and other symbols. The whole text of Jung's 1936 essay 'Wotan' is reproduced in *Temple of Wotan* and the book also contains a foreword by the ubiquitous Miguel Serrano, the man to whom Jung wrote his prophetic letter in 1960. Katja Lane has embarked on the translation of a trilogy of Serrano's works into English, a project which demonstrates the strong links between Wotansvolk and the Chilean.

In addition to his writings McVan has also used his artistic talents to produce wood carvings and many other objects inspired by the traditional crafts and images of the Norse and Anglo-Saxon worlds. He even built an intricately carved wooden temple (*Hof*) at the Wotansvolk headquarters and dedicated it to Guido von List. Contact with the Norse gods is achieved through rituals, this much is agreed by all Odinists. Wotansvolk follows the basic pattern of seasonal rites and blot ceremonies typical of Odinism but differs from most other groups in its constant emphasis on racial empowerment. Magical ceremonies and invocations are performed for a number of ends including attacking one's enemies. Curses have had a place in magic throughout the ages and across the world and Wotansvolk has its own – designed to weaken its foes through this traditionally inspired form of psychological warfare.

McVan has drawn heavily on Jung's ideas, especially his views on Odin as an archetype. He has developed a particular racial inter-pretation of Jung which argues that the archetypes can be revived by Aryan worshippers who perform the old pagan ceremonies. These archetypal forces are literally embodied in pure Aryan people, in their blood to be precise, and the pagan revival is essential to ensure the future of the white race. In his letter of 1960 to Serrano, Jung expressed his profound concern that a similar situation that had led to the Nazi era might recur. However, as Matthias Gardell puts it, 'What to Jung was a "risk" is to the Wotansvolk project a comforting forecast of the near future.'[10] McVan agrees with Jung that Odin's influence was pervasive in the Third Reich but, unlike Jung, believes the first Odinic experiment to have been a good thing, the most positive event in Aryan history since the pagan era of the Vikings. In developing his philosophy, McVan cites many of the figures associated with the occult side of Nazism, among them Guido von List, Karl Maria Wiligut and Heinrich Himmler.

In 2000 Wotansvolk realised one of its main aims when it achieved legal recognition as a church in the name of the Temple of Wotan. Due to the efforts of its small but dedicated core Wotansvolk has grown rapidly in influence. Through its publications and the internet it has managed to coordinate interested parties into active kindreds in both America and beyond. In 1996 a group was established in London and by the beginning of 2000 there were fourteen kindreds in Germany, eight in England, seven in Canada, six in Australia, five in Sweden and a number of other associated groups across the globe from Japan and the Philippines to South America. A total of forty-one countries have individuals or kindreds aligned to the Wotansvolk movement. Translations of Wotansvolk writings have also proliferated with works now available in numerous languages including Polish, Afrikaans and Finnish.

Both racist and non-racist Odinist groups have worked for official recognition of their religious status in order to be allowed to minister to the needs of prisoners by supplying them with literature, guidance on the conducting of ceremonies and general support. The development of prison outreach programmes has always been high on the Wotansvolk agenda and the organisation has been more successful in this endeavour than many other groups. One of the main reasons behind this success is the high profile of David Lane and the Order among 'Aryan' prisoners. Lane's continuing presence behind bars seems to make many prisoners empathise with his organisation.

At the beginning of 2001 it was estimated that more than 5,000 prisoners in US jails were in contact with Wotansvolk. The solidarity and strength that these prison kindreds developed in a number of different states led in some instances to the moving of prisoners to other penitentiaries in order to break them up. The effect of this however seems to have been the opposite of what was intended. Far from curbing the kindreds it has actually allowed their influence to spread. Many prisoners have probably joined up for their own protection as membership of one of the kindreds affords a certain safety in numbers.

Lane's Odinism is, as we have seen, more political and ideological than ceremonial and religious. This seems to be mainly down to temperament but also to lack of opportunity. Because interested inmates were largely cut off from the outside world, for a long time knowledge of pagan ceremonies was not available at the Florence Penitentiary where Lane is held. Then, in 1998 an Odinist *godhi* (priest) named Danny Johnson was transferred to Florence from another prison and he introduced the pagan prisoners to the ceremonial side of their religion. Despite, or perhaps in part because of Lane's incarceration, Wotansvolk has become the most prominent and successful separatist group advocating a pagan Aryan vision. Where once Aryan America was inextricably linked to Christian beliefs and unswerving patriotism now a significant part of it has rejected both Christianity and the federal government in favour of the objective of a separate and pagan Aryan nation.

Chapter 19

Journey to the South Pole

Jung had tried to find for modern man a myth . . . transcendent and vital . . . and in the end, after years of work, he revealed it in a statement which summarizes all his labours, namely, that man is needed to *illuminate the obscurity of the Creator*. His desire was to project the light of consciousness into the bottomless sea of the Unconsciousness, which is to say, into God himself. This is the living myth which Jung has passed down to modern man, although it is not, of course, for all men.

Miguel Serrano, *C.G. Jung and Herman Hesse*[1]

A Nazi yoga commune in northern California

In the ideological landscape of Aryan America not all those seeking pagan roots have looked solely to northern Europe for their inspiration. As had happened in Europe a few generations earlier, the Aryan civilisation was contrasted with the Judaeo-Christian world and was seen as extending from Iceland in the west to India in the east. The interest in Indian philosophy and yoga shown by more mystically inclined members of the racist right may seem bizarre and even contradictory to those unfamiliar with these byways of thought but the stereotypical view of what a white American racist professes is too simple. Whilst many of them just believe in white superiority and hate blacks, Jews and other non-Aryans, others ally themselves ideologically or even socially with other groups such as Arabs or Indians which it might be thought they would despise with equal fervour. That the Arabs and other Muslims are often at loggerheads with the Jews means that to some white supremacists they are potential allies, while the Indians like the Iranians belong to the Indo-European family and as such are seen by some right-wing mystics as acceptable Aryans.

The Viking-inspired ethos of Wotansvolk is only one aspect of pagan Aryan America; the National Socialist Kindred, founded by Jost Turner (1947–96), whilst claiming an Odinist heritage drew on the yoga traditions of India. Turner returned from active service in Vietnam traumatised and feeling out of place in the heady West Coast of the late 1960s and found a haven in an ashram in northern California where he stayed for two years studying yoga. During the 1970s he became interested in paganism and Nazism and made contact with two Odinist organisations, the Odinist Fellowship, founded by Else Christensen, and the Asatrú Free Assembly of Stephen McNallen. Turner subsequently married the sister of McNallen's first wife. McNallen had purged his organisation of its racist members whilst Turner set up his own group called the National Socialist Kindred and pursued his mystical aims at its Volksberg commune. This Nazi-inspired community lived on an eighty-eight-acre plot (88 = HH = *Heil Hitler*) in a mountainous and isolated part of northern California.

Turner hoped that the Volksberg commune would be a blueprint for a wider National Socialist society and he strove for self-sufficiency through farming and the craft production of clothes and other basic needs. A Wotanist primary school was set up so that the children of commune members could learn the ways of the Kindred rather than be indoctrinated into the ideology of wider American society.

Turner's aim was nothing less than the creation of the Overman – the more evolved form of humanity envisioned by the philosopher Nietzsche. This highly developed being was symbolised by Odin, and Turner's vision was fuelled by the ideas of Jung and Miguel Serrano.

Like many followers of both Nazism and New Age thinking Turner believed that city life was counterproductive for those seeking spiritual development. As centres of multiracial decadence the cities were to be left behind in favour of developing Aryan communes. Many of Turner's recommendations concerning lifestyle were stock yoga teachings – vegetarianism, macrobiotics, organic produce and daily meditation – whilst others, such as his advocacy of violent revolutionary actions as and when required, were not. The quest for mystical enlightenment in yoga involves the arousing of the inner energy source (*kundalini*) which, through meditation and other techniques, can be made to rise up from the base of the spine to the head via the spiritual centres (*chakras*) of the body. For Turner such practices would lead to the development of the Overman and the final goal of becoming Odin. By following this path he believed that the resulting enlightenment of the individual had the added effect of aiding the positive transformation of the racial organism – the Aryan collective soul – and even the universe itself. Turner himself died at the age of fifty from a heart attack which struck him down during meditation. His unusual synthesis of yoga and Nazi ideology has, however, outlived him and is practised by a few followers scattered across North America and Europe.

The mysterious doctrines of the German F.K.

The Jung letter quoted in Chapter 1 of this book was sent to Miguel Serrano in 1960, who reproduced it in his *C.G. Jung and Herman Hesse: A Record of Two Friendships*. The original Spanish title of Serrano's book, *El Círculo Hermético*, is revealing as it shows that he considered himself and his two illustrious friends to be part of a hermetic circle, an elite who shared a deep understanding of spiritual matters. Whether Hesse, the Nobel prize-winning author of *The Glass Bead Game, Siddhartha, Steppenwolf* and numerous other novels, or Jung would have seen their mutual relationship in these terms is a matter for speculation. What is clear is that neither of them were aware of Serrano's real orientations and political beliefs. To trace these we have to explore his formative years in Chile.[2]

Serrano was born into a prominent family in Santiago in 1917. His forebears included a number of notable poets, diplomats and political thinkers. Miguel was to combine these three fields in his own life and imbue them with his mystical obsessions. The school he attended had a marked German flavour and Serrano was later to acknowledge that this had a profound effect on him. He believed that his blue eyes and blond hair were the result of an Aryan bloodline which he could trace back to its origins in northern Spain. In the 1930s his budding literary interests were brutally interrupted by the realities of political strife when a friend who had supported the socialist cause was killed in a violent conflict with members of the Chilean Nazi party. Serrano reacted by becoming a Marxist but this was not to last. He soon came to believe that the Chilean communists were being manipulated by outside forces including Soviet Russia and the CIA. He turned to the other side and became a staunch supporter of the Chilean Nazis at the end of the 1930s, writing and publishing journals for the cause.

Soon after the outbreak of the Second World War Serrano made contact with the German embassy in Santiago. According to Serrano it was through the embassy that he subsequently met an SS officer who had previously worked in Berlin. This man told him that during the invasion of France, the prominent Nazi Alfred Rosenberg had discovered documents in Masonic lodges in Paris proving the extensive power of secret societies. Serrano's interest in conspiracy was sparked by these apparent revelations and in 1941 he came across the *Protocols of the Elders of Zion*. From then on he was a staunch believer in the world Jewish conspiracy, which, as we shall see, he took to truly cosmic proportions. The year after he first read the

Protocols he was initiated into a Chilean occult order. This order had been founded and was led by its German founder known only by the initials F.K. who claimed that his lodge had contact with secret Hindu masters based in the Himalayas. The practices of the order included ritual magic and tantric yoga.

His German master taught Serrano that such practices were the Eastern counterpart to the Nietzschean will to power and the goals of Nazism. Within the order Hitler was revered as a saviour of the Aryan race, and Serrano's guru even described the Führer as a *bodhisattva*, an enlightened being who had chosen to be reincarnated for the sake of others. These bizarre quasi-religious ideas were to remain with Serrano throughout his life. After the war F.K. also claimed to have telepathically contacted Hitler who was supposedly hidden deep inside the earth. Thus, he was certain that Hitler had not died in his Berlin bunker but lived on. This was the Hitler survival myth with an occult twist. Speculation that Hitler may have survived was rampant in Latin American newspapers in 1945. Serrano entertained the possibility that Hitler had sought refuge either in some warm region of Antarctica or deep under the polar ice cap.

This was an interesting inversion of the Thule mythology (see Chapter 12) of the northern hemisphere, which held that the original Aryan homeland was a long-lost land in the far north which, in some variations of the myth, could be a way into the subterranean world, or hollow earth. Now, in the southern hemisphere, Serrano was proposing that a new Aryan homeland had been founded in Antarctica and that it too had its subterranean realms.

In 1947, Serrano joined a joint Chilean army–navy expedition to Antarctica as a journalist, setting out from Chile on a voyage that would take him past Tierra del Fuego and across the Beagle Strait and Drake's Sea. On the journey he began to read a book that he had brought with him. He was later to write his recollections of this unusual physical and psychological journey:

It was finally there, amongst gigantic icebergs reverberating with thunder as huge slabs of ice cracked off and fell into the sea, in an atmosphere of total whiteness burning with cold, that I turned my attention to Jung's book [*The Ego and the Unconscious*]. There, in almost total isolation from the rest of the world, I began to look for something which would close that other gap which separates the Ego from the Sub-conscious in modern man.[3]

Serrano's pilgrimages to Europe and Asia

Serrano first visited Europe in 1951, making a pilgrimage to the ruins of the Berlin bunker, the remains of Hitler's Bavarian retreat and to Spandau prison where Hess and other leading Nazis were incarcerated. It was during this period that he struck up the friendships with Herman Hesse and Jung which became the subject of his book. Unlike most other occultists, whose interests in yoga and Indian mysticism were second hand (and largely derived from Theosophy and other European sources), Serrano was determined to personally experience the Indian tradition. In 1953 he began his diplomatic career with a posting to India, where he became his country's ambassador. He stayed there nearly ten years, pursuing his interests in yoga and searching for the Himalayan base of the secret Brahmanical order that F.K. had first told him about many years earlier in Chile.

In 1962 Serrano moved back to Europe, spending two years as ambassador to Yugoslavia and a further six as his country's representative in Austria. During these years he also worked for the International Atomic Energy Commission. In 1970 his diplomatic career came to an abrupt end when a Marxist government came to power in Chile. He decided to base himself in Switzerland and continued to write mystical allegories which contained no trace of his ever-growing obsession with Hitler and Nazism. As one commentator on Serrano's ideas puts it, 'While his poetry sang of unity and spiritual integration, Serrano became a hostage to the idea of opposing archetypes of light and darkness.'⁴ Serrano then began to write what was to become a trilogy of books on his personal mythology, which he described as Esoteric Hitlerism.

One of the few neo-Nazis to share both Serrano's interest in India and his belief that Hitler was an incarnate god was the racial mystic Maximiani Portas (1905–82), alias Savitri Devi. She, like Serrano, believed that Hitler was an avatar of the Indian gods Vishnu and Shiva and also of Odin. Serrano eulogised her as a herald of Esoteric Hitlerism and 'the priestess of Odin'.⁵ For both Serrano and Devi, Hitler and Odin were inseparable. Drawing on Jung's idea, Serrano saw Hitler as an embodiment of the racial unconscious of the Aryans. Serrano believed this to be a good thing whilst Jung saw Hitler's unconscious possession by the archetype as a serious danger to the stability of the world and warned against its possible recurrence in a second Odinic experiment. Jung believed that the archetype should not be suppressed – indeed it could not be suppressed – and that its power should be made conscious as Hitler's unconscious possession by it had led to disaster.

Unlike many occultists, whose social position is often obscure and marginal, Serrano has for many decades moved freely through circles of power and influence, particularly after the Second World War. In addition to his personal associations with Jung and Herman Hesse he sought out the American poet Ezra Pound, well known for his fascist views. Many contacts were also made through his diplomatic career, including with Nehru, Indira Gandhi and the Dalai Lama. Serrano believed occult connections existed between Esoteric Hitlerism and the tantric Buddhist tradition. The Austrian mountaineer Heinrich Harrer, whose book *Seven Years in Tibet* was made into a Hollywood film starring Brad Pitt, was, as the book describes, the friend and teacher of all things Western to the Dalai Lama. It has recently emerged that Harrer was also a member of the SS.

Not surprisingly Serrano was also in touch with surviving figures from the Third Reich, neo-Nazis and others on the far right active after the war. Italy's leading right-wing esotericist Julius Evola (1898–1974), SS veteran Wilhelm Landig (1909–97), who wrote a number of fantasy novels imbued with neo-Nazi mysticism, and Hermann Wirth of the Ahnenerbe were three of the most prominent of these contacts. Also among them was Otto 'Scarface' Skorzeny (1908–75), an SS colonel who played a key role in restoring authority following the failed assassination attempt on Hitler on 20 July 1940.[6]

Serrano has also kept in close contact with a number of prominent neo-Nazis and right-wing occultists in North America. Matt Koehl of the New Order is a long-term contact while Katja Lane's translation of Serrano's works will undoubtedly increase his readership considerably. He was also a particularly important influence on Jost Turner as Serrano was one of the few neo-Nazi mystics to share Turner's intense interest in yoga. Serrano has become one of the leading figures of neo-Nazi occultism; the fact that he has been able to inspire American groups as diverse as Wotansvolk and the National Socialist Kindred of Jost Turner attests to his wide influence across the ideological landscape of modern Aryan mysticism.

Jung predicted that the second Odinic experiment would be global. We have already seen that the narrower nationalist concerns of Nazi Germany have given way to a neo-Nazi network of groups spread far beyond the confines of Europe to, for example, the white separatist movement in North America and the South American Aryan mythology of Miguel Serrano. Serrano's neo-Nazi mythology is actually cosmic in scale, dealing as it does with themes of interstellar communication, vast aeons of time and the vilification of the Jews as the embodiment of the cosmic principle of evil. This has led Joscelyn Godwin to compare it for imaginative scope with *The Secret Doctrine* of Blavatsky and Tolkien's English mythology, particularly as described in *The Silmarillion*.[7] But, as Godwin goes on to say, it is not possible to read Serrano's work in a detached way. It is no simple work of fiction but an attempt to rewrite both history and myth according to his extreme political views.

By merging traditional mythological imagery with elements of science fiction Serrano seeks to transform the brutal reality of the Third Reich – which he never experienced – into a cosmic fantasy in which the Nazis are recast as heroes fighting the great Jewish demon supposedly responsible for all the economic, social and ecological ills of the contemporary world. In doing so Serrano makes use of a cluster of modern myths which only became current after the demise of the Nazi regime – Hitler survival, UFOs, Holocaust denial and the deification of Hitler. As Nicholas Goodrick-Clarke points out, it is this that makes his mythology so dangerous to young minds eager for alternative explanations of the world around them.[8]

Ironically Serrano's interpretation of Jung's theory of the Odinic archetype and its influence over the present era has become part of what Jung feared for the world. As has been mentioned, Jung believed that Hitler was unconsciously possessed by Odin and that this represented a great danger to mankind. But for Serrano Hitler's possession was a good thing; Hitler was an avatar and should thus be the focus of worship. Serrano and his neo-Nazi mythology represent, in the light of Jung's theory of the Odinic archetype and its role in the modern world, the shadow of Jung and his quest for the pagan renewal of Western man.

Chapter 20

Lord of the Spear

The general perception is that the Thule of myth and magic
has been defeated once this century, that the defeat of the
thousand-year Third Reich was the defeat of Thule as well.
But this was simply a manifestation of an unbalanced aspect
of Thulian doctrine, and the Nazi Thule was the reverse of a
coin which has still to reveal its obverse for our inspection.

Bernard King, *Ultima Thule*[1]

The mythology of Thule returns

The mythological legacy of Thule was to reach South America with
Nazis fleeing in the aftermath of the Second World War. The Gestapo
captain Klaus Barbie, known as the Butcher of Lyon, managed to
escape to South America in 1951 despite being sentenced by the
French in his absence to death for war crimes. The Americans seem
to have turned a blind eye as Barbie slipped away through the
Vatican ratline to Bolivia as he had already been used by the CIA as
an anti-communist spy. In the early 1950s he actively espoused
Nazism among the military establishment in Bolivia within a
clandestine neo-Nazi lodge named Thule.[2] The Chilean Miguel
Serrano's neo-Nazi fantasies also make use of Thulean mythology,

another route by which these ideas reached South America after the war.[3]

Thulean mythology has also made its way into North American neo-Nazi circles. The White Order of Thule was founded in 1994 as the American branch of the New Zealand-based Black Order.[4] According to Joseph Kerrick, one of the founders of the American group, Thule was an extraterrestrial civilisation of god-men from which the present-day Aryan race is descended. Other members advocated terrorism as a catalyst to hasten Ragnarok and stressed the importance of Loki as Odin's shadow-self. The founder of the Order (Silent Brotherhood) has been honoured by Nathan Zorn Pett of the White Order of Thule, who has conducted blots and swastika-burning ceremonies at the site of Robert J. Mathews' death in 1984 after his refusal to surrender to federal agents. Like its parent group in New Zealand the White Order of Thule dissolved after a few years.[5]

Back in Europe, the most prominent current organisation to identify itself with this tradition is the Thule Seminar, one of Germany's leading right-wing think tanks. Founded in 1980, the Thule Seminar has about fifty members described as 'élite, intellectual, and influential'.[6] Among its members is Sigrid Hunke, a student of the German philosopher Martin Heidegger, who has received the prestigious Schiller prize for 'German cultural works in the European spirit' and was also honoured by Egyptian President Mubarak for her work on Arabic thought and its relations with European culture. There is also a growing popular literature based on its own fictional and often highly imaginative accounts of the original Thule Society. The society has featured prominently, and somewhat creatively, in two classics of popular occultism, *The Morning of the Magicians* and *The Spear of Destiny*, as well as in the best-selling James Herbert novel *The Spear*.

Modern fantasies of Thule

In 1960 Louis Pauwels and Jacques Bergier published a book in French

J.R.R. Tolkien.

Poster of Gandalf on New Zealand Post Office building.

Gandalf's Garden shop in World's End, Kings Road, Chelsea, London, late 1960s.

Miguel Serrano.

Carl Gustav Jung.

Logo of the Odinic Rite.

Modern pagan ritual equipment.

Wooden carving of Odin with pagan holy book the Edda.

Odin on his horse Sleipnir in front of a panoramic view of the famous Royal burial mounds at Gamla Uppsala, Sweden.

Stav Altar.

Modern pagan rites at Thingvellir, Iceland.

Ivar Hafskjold,
leader of Stav organisation
with his Eagle Owl.

Brian Bates.

Modern Pagan
in Wolf Clothing.

Deer eating from
Yggdrasill, the World
Tree, carving on the
side of Stave Church
at Urnes, Norway.

later translated under the title *The Morning of the Magicians* (also *The Dawn of Magic*). This is a chaotic mosaic of all things weird and wonderful – fringe science, alchemy, occult conspiracies and bizarre coincidences and events. It became a best-seller and the ideas within it – a seamless mixture of fact, conjecture and outright fantasy – were widely disseminated. The supposed link between the Nazis and the occult is one of the recurrent themes of the book. The historical Thule Society that we have documented is embellished and transformed by these authors. Its membership was said to include not only Alfred Rosenberg and the early Nazi Dietrich Eckart (both of whom were associates but not actual members of the society) but also the geopolitician Karl Haushofer, who was said to have convinced his fellow initiates that the key to power lay in control over central Asia, the hub of supernatural forces.

The Thule Society was said to hold strange beliefs about two mystical centres in Asia, Agarthi and Shambhala – the first good and the other evil. Those who followed the 'right-hand way' had their centre in the subterranean Agarthi, 'a hidden city of goodness' deep under the Himalayas. Those following the 'left-hand way' dwelt in the city of Shambhala – a centre of 'violence and power'.[7] The success of *The Morning of the Magicians* resulted in a cluster of books on similar themes. Herbie Brennan in his *Occult Reich* (1974) described Pauwels and Bergier as 'those two superb historians of esoteric Nazism'.[8] He may have been wrong in his assessment of their historical merits but he was right when he went on to say that the real importance of Thule is not as a geographical location but as a myth. Brennan adds his own concoctions to the modern mythology of Nazism, linking Thule with black magic, hypnotism, witchcraft and Nostradamus.

Another sensational rewriting of the history of the Thule Society is to be found in Trevor Ravenscroft's *The Spear of Destiny* (1973). The book allegedly grew out of Ravenscroft's meetings with Walter Johannes Stein, an Austrian Jew and Holy Grail scholar who had fled Germany in 1933 to settle in Britain. Ravenscroft says that during the course of a series of long meetings at Stein's home in Kensington, London – some so long that Ravenscroft spent weeks at a time there – the secret occult obsessions of Hitler and others were revealed to him. Stein was said to have picked up a second-hand copy of the grail legend *Parzival* full of manic scribblings which he then found out to be those of none other than Adolf Hitler. Ravenscroft's book goes on to 'reveal' how through drug-induced visions, blood rituals and black magic ceremonies Hitler rose to power obsessed with the occult power of the spear of Longinus, the Roman centurion who had pierced Christ's side at the Crucifixion. The Thule Society is at the very heart of this occult fantasy. As Ravenscroft puts it, 'The inner core within the Thule Group were all Satanists who practised Black Magic. That is to say, they were solely concerned with raising their consciousness by means of rituals to an awareness of evil and non-human Intelligences in the Universe and with achieving a means of communication with these Intelligences.'[9]

Ravenscroft adds his own twist to the connection between Thule and Asia. Building on the fantasies of Pauwels and Bergier, he tells us of two very ancient sections of the Aryan peoples who turned to the path of evil. They set up their own communities in the mountain ranges of a land now submerged, as a result of the great flood, under the Atlantic somewhere near Iceland. Before the deluge engulfed them they travelled across Europe and Asia until they reached Tibet. The two groups then set up the 'twin resonators of evil', Agarthi and Shambhala, they prospered until the modern era when they were totally destroyed by the forces of materialism in the form of Maoism. We are told that all the surviving adepts were wiped out in the Chinese communist invasion of Tibet in 1959.

Elements of Ravenscroft's dramatic and fanciful account of black magic under the Third Reich reached an even wider audience when one of Britain's most popular horror writers, James Herbert, used similar themes in his fantasy novel *The Spear*, published in 1978 five years after *The Spear of Destiny* first appeared in print.[10] Harry

Steadman, the hero of Herbert's book, finds himself drawn back into the shadowy world of espionage he thought he had left behind when he is visited by two members of Mossad, the Israeli intelligence agency. He is soon on the trail of a leading arms dealer, the disfigured Edward Gant, who he later discovers had received his horrific injuries when he stepped on a mine whilst assisting Himmler to escape the ruins of Nazi Germany – Himmler's apparent suicide in Allied custody by means of a cyanide pill being down to the willing self-sacrifice of one of his doubles.

Gant is the present leader of the original Thule Society, which survived Hitler's ban on occult groups and secret lodges by being covertly integrated into the SS by Himmler. Gant and his powerful cabal of industrialists, politicians and other notables are on the verge of unleashing their plot to destabilise the world when Steadman foils their plans. But Gant is only the outer leader of the Thule; its true leader is the animated corpse of Himmler, who draws the life energy from Gant's minions and is sustained by the magic of the supernatural Spear itself. As Himmler had been able to keep the Thule Society thriving without Hitler's knowledge so he had also been able to switch the real Spear, leaving the Führer with a faithful copy. The book ends with Steadman plunging the spear into the hideous decaying cadaver of Himmler and casting the weapon of evil into the flames engulfing Gant's burning headquarters, thereby extinguishing its power.

Modern Thulean mythology, even in its most fantastical forms, seems to be directly concerned with Nazi and neo-Nazi political aspirations. From the Thule Society of fact to the Thule Society of fiction and fantasy the quest is for earthly power. Thule thus stands in opposition to Hyperborea, the archetypal sysmbol of spiritual attainment. Hyperborea is an illuminated sanctuary, the inhabitants of which, after the great winter that heralds the Ragnarok, will come forth again into the new world born out of the aftermath of this cataclysm.

As Jung predicted, the effects of the second Odinic experiment are worldwide.

At the heart of the issue is the ethnic consciousness of Europeans and their descendants in North America, Australasia and elsewhere in the world. Liberalism has tended to downplay the importance of ethnic identity for the white community whilst concentrating on social agendas designed to redress the economic and other inequalities experienced by non-whites. White ethnic identity has become a political hot potato and its discussion is almost taboo. Ignoring the issue however has not resulted in it going away; refusal to address this question has left the political far right as almost the only spokesman for the northern European heritage. This in turn has resulted in the further alienation of the mainstream, who understandably do not want to be associated with the violent racist agenda of fascist groups. This is a dangerous state of affairs. The pagan roots of ethnic identity, if not openly acknowledged, sink down to the unconscious level. There, out of the light of day, they fester and become poisonous.

A dangerous social abyss is opening up in both Europe and North America, and we are forced to wonder what role there is for the European heritage in the push for globalisation. A war is being fought deep in the European mind and the outcome remains unclear. What is clear is that the second Odinic experiment, as predicted by Jung, is already under way. Yet there is much cause for optimism. The modern growth of paganism, shows that the second experiment is entering a new and more positive phase. Certain practices and ideas which draw on ancient pagan sources have value and relevance to contemporary life, as will be seen in subsequent chapters. This is a phase in which the northern tradition has overcome the taints of Nazism and racism and created its own identity beyond the narrow confines of the amalgam of paganism, nationalism, social Darwinism, Christianity and anti-Semitism that was Nazism. There are still racist elements within the tradition but there are also anarchist and liberal groups. In its diversity paganism reflects Christianity, which also has groups, factions and cults across the whole spectrum of political allegiances.

I have already dealt in detail with the modern historical events and ideas which surrounded the first Odinic experiment and part of the second Odinic experiment. It will become clearer in the third part of this book that many cultural ideas often thought to be related to the rise of paganism such as anti-Semitism and extreme nationalism have no intrinsic relationship with it. It now remains to look at how the second experiment and the revival of paganism may come of age. But before turning to these matters it is only proper to ask what purpose a pagan resurrection can serve in the modern world.

A paganism which is merely a form of escapism into an illusory golden age – whether set in the Viking era or at some time earlier in history – can serve no meaningful purpose. Dressing up in Viking and Saxon clothing – physically and metaphorically – is important for historical reenactment groups but has little to do with spiritual authenticity. The traditional pagans of the northern world respected the past and the accumulated knowledge it represented but they did not wish to live in it. Neither should we.

Part Three

VISIONS OF
THE WEB

Chapter 21

Tribes of Odin

National socialism and Asatrú are diametrically opposed . . .
national socialism is against freedom, Asatrú is freedom, national socialism has a lot of dogma, Asatrú has none.
National socialism is centralization and Asatrú is radically
decentralized. You couldn't have any more individualistic
people than in Asatrú. And if the Nazis ever got into power,
the first thing they're going to do is to throw all the Asatrúers
in jail. The German Nazis appropriated the Asatrú ancient
symbols, like the swastika, so we can't use that now, and as
far as Wotansvolk and other fringe groups go, I wish they'd
just go away.

> Michael (Reinhold) Clinton, from an interview with
> Mattias Gardell[1]

One could be tempted to see some kind of synchronicity at work in
the dramatic resurgence of paganism in the early 1970s. The
Asatrúarmenn was founded in May 1973 in Iceland, the Odinic Rite
was formally set up in April 1973 in Britain and the Viking
Brotherhood in America was founded in 1972. Shortly after Stephen
McNallen founded the Viking Brotherhood it developed into a much
larger group, the Asatrú Free Assembly (AFA). The name Asatrú is

derived from the practice of worshipping the Aesir, the family of Norse gods which includes Odin. Stephen Flowers, speaking both as an academic and a pagan, remarks how fundamental the influence of Jung has been:

> The concepts of the *archetypes* and the *collective unconscious* have exerted a tremendous influence on the formation of the ideology of the neo-Germanic religion . . . divinities in Asatrú/Odinism are not seen as independent, transcendental beings, but rather as exemplary models of consciousness, or archetypes, which serve as patterns for human development. These entities are viewed as psychic realities present within both the individual and within society. They are not made the objects of worship in the Judaeo-Christian sense, but rather humanity and divinity are conceived of in a mutually dependent relationship, and as part of the same ultimate reality.[2]

The Asatrú Free Assembly was dissolved in 1987 and reformed in the mid-1990s as the Asatrú Folk Assembly is neither a monolithic entity nor a rigid hierarchical organisation; it is a loose network of affiliated communities with different views and no central body to which they are subordinated. As the leading Asatrú spokesman in North America, Stephen McNallen has made repeated efforts to distance the movement from right-wing extremists, who have on occasion sought to infiltrate the organisation.[3] It is possible to distinguish between adherents of northern paganism on the basis of their attitudes towards race. At one extreme are the racist pagans who see their religion as exclusively Aryan and typically believe in the superiority of their own racial origins over those of other peoples. At the other are those for whom race is not an issue and who believe that the way of northern paganism is open to all those who wish to explore it. Sitting often uncomfortably in the middle are those who may be described as ethnic pagans, who claim that their adherence to the faith of their pagan forefathers is a natural spiritual position and does not mean they are racist. It is this position which Stephen McNallen and the Asatrú Folk Assembly espouse:

> All indigenous or 'pagan' religions spring from the soul of a particular people. The religion of the Sioux comes from the depths of the collective Sioux experience – not just as it is today, but as it has been from the beginning. The Sioux religion is not separable from the people, and has no meaning apart from them. The same may be said of indigenous African religions, the tribal religions of Asia – and the native religions of Europe as well.[4]

Today in both American and British pagan circles practitioners generally divide themselves into three basic groups: Wiccans; Druids and those who follow some kind of Celtic religion; and Heathens, those who follow Germanic and Norse traditions. Heathens call themselves by this name for two main reasons. Firstly, they prefer the word (derived from 'heath', a wild part of the landscape, so similar to pagan, meaning 'from the remote countryside') as it is an indigenous term used by the northern peoples themselves as opposed to pagan, which is derived from the Latin. Secondly, it distinguishes them from other pagans whose ideas, beliefs and practices may be very different.[5]

The Odinic Rite: faith, folk, family

During the 1950s and 1960s there were a number of small and not very well organised groups of Odinists in England. The founders of two of these groups – Asbjeorn of the Frey Hof and Heimgest of the Heimdal League – subsequently became members of the Odinic Rite (OR). The OR itself was co-founded by John Gibbs-Bailey (alias Hoskuld) – who had been an Odinist since the thirties – and John

Yeowell (1918–), alias Stubba, who was for many years its Director.[6]

Yeowell traces his earliest encounter with the pagan gods to when he was five. One day a supply teacher came in to the Church of England school he attended in the 1920s. During the course of the lesson, the teacher told the children briefly about Odin and Thor. For many years he did not pursue this interest but gradually he began to study after being given a subscription to *The Odinist*, a periodical published in the United States by Else Christensen, which he found 'mildly interesting'. During the early 1970s he corresponded with Christensen and he, along with Gibbs-Bailey then founded the Odinic Rite on 24 April 1973. Yeowell felt that he was playing a part in restoring the indigenous religion that, in his opinion, had never been fully supplanted by the Christian faith. He said:

> 'Odinism has always existed. First of all, it's within us. It can't possibly be expunged. It can't be obliterated: everybody is born a heathen. So that every little English baby is born an Odinist and remains so . . . this is why what we have to do is to reawaken the living heathenism which is within every one of us. And when I say every one of us – I mean I see heathenism as an international religion. It's the only true international religion. It differs according to each racial group, according to that group's culture and history. So, we have more in common with Japanese Shinto than with the Methodists or the Anglicans.'[7]

The watch-words of the Odinic Rite are 'Faith, Folk and Family' and appear on the central symbol of the group which is a triskelion within a circle. The OR has a moral code that is embodied in the Noble Virtues, of which there are nine, in accordance with the sacred number most identified with Odin. They are courage, truth, honour, fidelity, discipline, hospitality, self-reliance, industriousness and perseverance. Also central to the OR code are the nine Noble Charges, eight of which were formulated by an earlier Odinist group to which Gibbs-Bailey had belonged. These Nine Charges are as follows:

1. To maintain candour and fidelity in love and devotion to the tried friend: though he strike me I will do him no scathe.
2. Never to make wrongsome oath: for great and grim is the reward for the breaking of plighted troth.
3. To deal not hardly with the humble and the lowly.
4. To remember the respect that is due to great age.
5. To suffer no evil to go unremedied and to fight against the enemies of Faith, Folk and Family: my foes I will fight in the field, nor will I stay to be burnt in my house.
6. To succour the friendless but to put no faith in the pledged word of a stranger people.
7. If I hear the fool's word of a drunken man I will strive not: for many a grief and the very death growth from out such things.
8. To give kind heed to dead men: straw dead, sea dead or sword dead.
9. To abide by the enactments of lawful authority and to bear with courage the decrees of the Norns.

The religious path of the OR is described as one that leads to the illumination of the Odin Consciousness. Runes are used in the OR and play a central role in their rituals and ceremonies. Like other religions and organisations like the Freemasons, the OR uses a different calendar to the conventional one, adding 250 years onto the normal Western calendar date (so that, for example, 2005 becomes 2255). The organisation expanded in the 1990s with branches in Germany, France and North America, the latter is known as OR Vinland, Vinland being the name the Vikings gave to the New World when they first sailed there one thousand years ago.

There are three grades or levels within the OR. The first is Apprentice Membership (Apprentice of the Odinic Rite or AOR) which is open to all who are interested in Odinism and involves no obligation to take the next step and become a Professed Member (who displays the letters OR in internal communications and in publications). To do so usually requires that the candidate has been an apprentice for at least a year and must be at least twelve years old. Those who do make the commitment by undertaking the ceremony of profession thereby become full members of the Odinic Rite, 'Odin's Holy Nation'. This is not to be taken lightly, it is a life-long commitment and it is not possible to resign as if it were simply a club. The organisation is governed by those belonging to the third grade – the Court of Gothar (CG) which is responsible for the spiritual guidance of the OR.

Various pagan festivals are observed by the OR and regular rites are performed in the Hearths (small groups roughly equivalent to the lodges of Freemasonry or the covens of the Wicca tradition). Yeowell explains the purpose and symbolism of the Hearth in the Odinic Rite: 'Hearth is the term that we apply to a group of friends meeting and worshipping the gods of our ancient faith in the domestic privacy of the home. It is the basic organisational unit of the OR. The hearth was at one time traditionally the central and most important part of the house. In saga poetry it is called "the fire table". It is emblematic of the captive sun presiding over the miniature world of the home, symbolising security, warmth and friendship.'[8]

In the Odinic Rite great emphasis is placed on the Folk (echoing the German concept of the Volk) and their continuity through time. The ancestors are revered and the living Folk are equally concerned to hand down their traditions to their as yet unborn descendants. In an article entitled *The Odinic Rite: a Radical Movement!* written by Heimgest (the present Director of the Court of Gothar) religious and social radicalism is defined as being in 'opposition to the establishment and prevailing codes of present Western society.'[9] The author describes the Judeo-Christian ethos as spiritually polluting in the way that a chemical works poisons the Earth. The idea of 'equality' that is promoted by Western governments is attacked as a subterfuge by which the separate identities of the various ethnic groups can be destroyed. The OR opposes these ideas on religious grounds believing that by the creating of a uniform mass of humanity politicians and financiers achieve their goals more easily as:

'A folk with no heritage, no proud past, is lost in the present and does not consider a future. In such a society, the population is far easier to control give them booze, porn and other material trappings and they will never seek to rise beyond that'[10]

Heimgest goes on to criticise many ecologically aware pagans for their lack of self-understanding. He notes that they will fight to defend a species of any other creature and protect its natural breeding grounds but that they do not extend this philosophy to the human species, caring little for the preservation of their own ethnic identity and traditions. As a folk religion Odinism is 'as concerned to preserve the diversity of race groups as we are to preserve the diversity of bird life.'[11] The importance of family life is also stressed in their motto, the watch-words 'Faith, Folk and Family'. Heimgest rues the increasing breakdown of the family in modern western society – leaving children more at the mercy of television consumerism and the state propaganda of the school-system. The wonderment of fairy stories (for those children still fortunate enough to have parents who have enough time to read to them) and other vestiges of the pagan tradition can give an early grounding in ideas that are not propagated by the State.[12] The Odinist religion concerns itself with all aspects of culture and relationships both within the community of believers and beyond to the rest of humanity. Each ethnic group is seen to have its own cultural traditions, that of the Northern Europeans being Odinism. It

is the Odinist belief that, until Northern Europeans regain their self-
respect, they are not truly able to respect others.

Allied to the OR is a group called the Circle of Ostara. It is named
after Ostara, the pagan Goddess of Spring (and the origin of the word
Easter). The Circle of Ostara describes itself as a magical order with
three main goals:

1. The furtherance of Odinism/Asatru,the organic spiritual
   expression of Northern Europe, as a living faith, relevant
   to the problems of existence which face us now, at this
   time of great change.
2. The development of the 'divine powers' which lie in each
   one of us, and which are the gifts of the Gods – not only
   physical and intellectual powers, but those psychic
   abilities that have for the last two millennia been distorted, damped down, and denied, by an alien ideology.
3. The total rejection of the pseudo-religion of Judeo-
   Christianity and all the belief systems which have grown
   out of it. The Circle struggles against it, seeing it as a force
   of chaos and evil, inimical to all the forms of life which live
   upon the Earth, and works towards its replacement by a
   religion which has grown from the Folk-Soul of our
   Northern Peoples, an organic social system, and an Earth-
   attuned technology.'[13]

The Odinic Pantheon (1996), an article published, by the Circle of
Ostara deals with the credibility problems that accompany their faith.
Its author is highly critical of the simplistic way in which the gods and
goddesses of the Norse pantheon have been represented by many
neo-pagans. To think of Odin as a one-eyed old man in a blue cloak
or Thor as a red-bearded and bad tempered character has reduced the
deeper meaning of the mythology to the level of a comic book.
Instead, in order: 'to build Odinism into a valid and inspiring religious

expression we must overcome this tendency to trivialise divinity. The gods are not Vikings . . . they are spiritual beings, potent forces of numinous power.'[14]

Chapter 22

A New Pagan Psychology

The fact that an archaic God formulates and expresses the dominant of our behaviour means that we ought to find a new religious attitude, a new realization of our dependence upon superior dominants. I don't know how this could be possible without a renewed self-understanding of man, which unavoidably has to begin with the individual. We have the means . . . to give him a new definition. We can see him in a new setting which throws an objective light upon his existence, namely as a being operated and manoeuvred by archetypal forces instead of his 'free will', that is, his arbitrary egoism and limited consciousness . . .

. . . In each aeon there are at least a few individuals who understand what Man's real task consists of, and keep its tradition for future generations and a time when insight has reached a deeper and more general level. First the way of a few will be changed and in a few generations there will be more . . . whoever is capable of such insight, no matter how isolated he is, should be aware of the law of synchronicity . . . if the archetype . . . is properly dealt with in one place only it is influenced as a whole, i.e. simultaneously and everywhere.

Carl Gustav Jung in Miguel Serrano *C.G. Jung and Herman Hesse*[1]

These powerful paragraphs are from the letter quoted in Chapter 1. This extract provides suggestions on how to avert the horrors manifested by the unconscious manifestation of the Odinic archetype. As Jung makes clear in the letter, interaction between an individual and the Odinic archetype reveals itself in our modern age not only through the unconscious motivations and influences in the psyche but also has external effects through the mechanism of synchronicity. Like the concepts of the archetype and the collective unconscious, the principle of synchronicity, as we will see, has also been integrated into the pagan world view and philosophy.

Today, alongside these Jungian ideas, there are other elements of genuine spirituality drawing on an authentic pagan heritage. Artefacts and other archaeological evidence, early mythological texts, shamanic practices and historical descriptions of trance states are among the sources of inspiration for modern pagans. They provide philosophies and practices which aid the process of spiritual and psychological self-transformation.

The Odinic inspiration of Dr Ralph Metzner

Jung has not been the only psychologist to have had a marked influence on the pagan revival. Dr Ralph Metzner, a psychotherapist and professor of psychology at the California Institute of Integral Studies, is another scholar whose interest in northern mythology is more than purely academic. He writes in *The Well of Remembrance*:

> The Odin myth seemed to describe many aspects of my own life path: my continuing interest in exploring nonordinary realms of consciousness, triggered by my first psychedelic experience in 1961, as well as my continuing fascination with cross-cultural studies of religion, mythology, and shamanism. The old legends say that the followers of Odin were 'seized' by the god, and often I felt as though I was seized, or inspired. I would think of Odin and get insights or

answers to my questions, including questions about the
meaning of certain myths. Or I would suddenly find pertinent
myths that I had not known before. Strange as it may sound,
I would have to say that much of what I am relating in this
book has been directly given to me by Odin.[2]

He describes his book as an exercise in ancestral memory, which
he believes to be an antidote to the alienation felt by modern man,
both from his past and from nature. Through an understanding of the
continuing relevance of the old pagan mythology contemporary
people can reconnect with their ancestral past and with nature herself.
He believes such a task must be undertaken to remove the 'Nazi curse
on Germanic mythology'. Metzner does not accept Jung's belief that
Hitler was possessed by the Odinic archetype and sees little to link the
old pagan god and the modern dictator. He does, however, concur
with Jung that the Odinic archetype and northern myths have a vital
role in transforming modern consciousness. Metzner believes that
embracing northern mythology is a therapeutic and conscious
process for the Germanic psyche and that by undergoing this, the
curse can be lifted.

Metzner spent the first few years of his life in Nazi Germany and
later found it hard to approach the study of Germanic mythology
because of the 'massive taboo' which surrounded its appropriation by
the Nazis. Yet he found once he delved into the myths that they
actually bore no resemblance to the ethos of under the Third Reich.
He describes the huge gap many Germans born during and straight
after the war felt existed between themselves and the generation to
which their parents belonged. In the late 1940s and the '50s both
teachers and parents would try to avoid talking about 'the past'. For
Metzner this created a generation gap of extraordinary significance –
a collective silence which effectively cut him and others of his
generation off from their ancestral past which had been so
traumatically hijacked by Nazism.

The new way of Wyrd

Alongside the revival of northern paganism during the 1970s, America and Britain saw another change in the spiritual landscape which altered traditional patterns of occultism almost beyond recognition. This was the increasing interest in shamanism and the cultures which still practised such spiritual traditions. The occult tradition has always looked for sources of ancient wisdom earlier than the religious traditions of the Bible. In the late nineteenth century dramatic archaeological discoveries made Egypt a prime candidate for the location of such wisdom. Simultaneously, the mystical traditions of India popularised by Blavatsky and her Theosophical movement also had a dramatic effect on the Western search, as we have already seen.

After the Second World War the Far Eastern traditions of Zen, Taoism and the martial arts also became more widely known in the West and gained many adherents. When all the spiritual traditions of the world's major civilisations had been investigated the search was continued by those who started looking to the 'tribal' cultures of the world previously dismissed as primitive. With the growing interest in ecological matters such cultures took on a new significance and their seemingly close relationship with nature gave them credibility as sources of ancient wisdom concerning the Earth. These societies and the shamanism which embodied many of their spiritual beliefs and practices became the dominant model among a new generation of seekers. The hugely successful books of the anthropologist Carlos Castaneda in which the author describes the spiritual teachings imparted to him by Don Juan, a Native American sorcerer or shaman, epitomise the popularity of this new wave of occultism.

For many this interest in shamanism and indigenous cultures was little more than a love of the exotic, and Native American societies were heavily romanticised. But others who looked deeper found that it was not the desire to 'go native' which was important but what people of European origin could learn from these other cultures about their own pagan past. Interest in the shamanism of exotic cultures led many, by a circuitous path, back to their own European roots. In Britain and beyond, the academic and psychologist Brian Bates has played a major role in popularising pagan Anglo-Saxon spirituality mainly through his powerful historical and psychological novel *The Way of Wyrd: Tales of an Anglo-Saxon Sorcerer* (1983) set in southern England during pagan times. In some respects this echoes the works of Carlos Castaneda, but in Bates' work the sorcerer's apprentice is not an anthropologist but a young idealistic monk eager to learn the ways of the pagan in order to convert him to the Christian faith.

The northern sorcerer communicated with spirits which were, according to Brian Bates, 'manifestations of forces pertaining to *wyrd*'.[3] To the average person these spirits were invisible but the more subtle perception and consciousness developed during the training of sorcerers meant that they were able to see them. The spirits each have their own place in the overall system; they represent particular aspects of the Web. The sorcerer who becomes the monk's guide in the pagan world plays a role similar to that of Don Juan. Bates' book was a turning point in that the exoticism typified by Castaneda was replaced by a spiritual journey which did not seek its goal in the East or in Native America but within the native traditions of pagan Europe.[4]

In his introduction to the book the author describes how his own explorations of Taoism and Zen during the 1970s led him to search for an indigenous European tradition which might have played a parallel role in our own culture. This then led him to an Anglo-Saxon manuscript in which he saw traces of a pagan sorcery with a mixture of medicinal and psychological techniques similar to those of shamanism. He sees the insights of pagan Anglo-Saxon sorcery as undergoing 'A dramatic resurgence in the last third of this century [the twentieth], particularly in the areas of medicine and healing, meditation and mysticism, parapsychology and personal trans-formation, ecology, and most recently in theoretical developments in the physical and natural sciences.'[5]

Such a view resonates strongly with Jung's idea of the return, in our modern era, of Odin – the archetypal Anglo-Saxon sorcerer. According to Bates the real purpose of his book is to bring back to life in an accessible way an indigenous path to 'psychological and spiritual liberation'. The way of Wyrd espoused by the sorcerer fundamentally challenges our views and even the 'very notions of body, mind and spirit'.[6]

It is no meaningless coincidence that the metaphor of the Web has assumed such cultural significance in recent years. The World Wide Web of interconnected computers has revolutionised communications on a global scale. Yet despite the apparent technological modernity of this concept the notion of a Web connecting all things is fundamental to the pagan cosmology of northern Europe. The pagan gods were not all-powerful but, like humans and other races of beings, were subject to the all-powerful Wyrd. As has already been suggested, the concept of Wyrd, personified as a woman, was a deeper and probably older aspect of pagan belief than even the gods themselves. Whilst most Odinist groups and related pagan organisations seek to venerate the old gods the concept of Wyrd must have an even more fundamental place in pagan philosophy. In order to do justice to this notion I have drawn on a number of strands of pagan speculation each of which sheds light on the mysterious and elusive Wyrd.

Brian Bates has done much to bring the notion of Wyrd back into modern consciousness and he recasts it in a way explicable to the modern mind, showing how it goes beyond the simplistic idea of cause and effect. It is also:

A way of being that transcends our conventional notions of free will and determinism. All aspects of the world were seen as being in constant flux and motion between the psychological and mystical polarities of Fire and Frost: a creative, organic vision paralleling the classical Eastern

concepts of Yin and Yang, and echoed by recent developments in theoretical physics in which the world is conceived
of as relationships and patterns. Following from the concept
of *wyrd* was a vision of the universe, from the gods to the
underworld, as being connected by an enormous all-reaching
system of fibres rather like a three-dimensional spider's web.
Everything was connected by strands of fibre to the all-
encompassing web. Any event, anywhere, resulted in
reverberations and repercussions throughout the web. This
image far surpasses in ambition our present views of ecology,
in which we have extended our notions of cause and effect to
include longer and more lateral chains of influence in the
natural world. The web of fibres of the Anglo-Saxon sorcerer
offers an ecological model which encompasses individual life
events as well as general physical and biological phenomena,
non-material as well as material events, and challenges the
very cause and effect chains upon which our ecological
theories depend.[7]

The concept of the Web of Wyrd has much in common with the
law of synchronicity mentioned by Jung in his letter to Miguel Serrano
at the beginning of this chapter. In his foreword to Richard Wilhelm's
translation of the I Ching Jung describes this famous Chinese oracle
as working according to the principle of the system he calls
synchronicity. Not only is the law of synchronicity related to the
concept of the web of Wyrd it also helps the modern mind to
understand the purpose of the runes. As we have seen in Chapter 3,
the northern European runes are comparable to the Chinese *I-Ching*.
There is a relationship between the runes as a form of divination
designed to 'read' the Web of Wyrd in northern pagan philosophy,
and the *I-Ching* as a system of divination based on the Tao. The idea
of Wyrd is the northern European equivalent of the Tao. Thus the
system of divination which seeks to understand the workings of the

cosmic Web is not so much an attempt to see the future but more a method of understanding the nature of synchronicity: 'a sense of parallel accidents: chance operating one way in observed bird or beast . . . may indicate a parallel in the case of something happening or about to happen in another sphere: a matter of good or bad luck applying to a series of events, circumstances or times, rather than a firmly directed course of future history'.[8]

Along with the concept of the Web of Wyrd, contemporary neo-pagans have expanded on another concept found in Old Norse lore intrinsic to the notion of Wyrd – the Orlog. The word is made up of two components. Or means first or primal and log is from the Old Norwegian *lagu* meaning law, lore, knowledge, wisdom. Glenn Magee, who has published some remarkable insights into the philosophy of the ancient Germanic peoples, compares the Orlog both with the Logos of Greek philosophy, and relates it to the Tao Stephen Flowers, who has written and translated a number of texts on northern European paganism, expands on the philosophy of the Orlog.[9] He defines it as the Germanic concept of fate, and says it is based on the idea that the present – and hence any contingent future – is conditioned by actions laid down in the past. Literally, Orlog means primal layers. He goes on to define Wyrd (Urd) as 'the process by which past actions (i.e. the Orlog) work through time to affect present experience'.

In the ancient Germanic world contemplation of the past was not a morbid or stagnant refusal to acknowledge present and future possibilities. Intriguingly, according to Glenn Magee, in the pagan world the past was a dynamic concept. Paradoxically the past is both changing yet unchangeable; it is forever expanding and changing but what has passed over into the past is unchangeable. The past is neither static nor fully formed, as things pass out of the hands of Verdandi (the present) and into the well of Urd.[10]

This emphasis on the past can be illustrated by two very different uses of the word 'original' in English – one which stresses the past, the more traditional meaning, and the other which stresses the future, a more modern understanding of the word which developed with the shift from an emphasis on the past to stress on the future. In the more modern sense of the word to be original is to innovate and create something new. Nowhere is this made clearer than in the writing of fiction. The very word 'novel' means new and the task for the author is to write something which has not been written before. Yet the older meaning of 'original' requires the opposite, a return to the source, to an archetypal origin. This is the basis of traditional myth, that ancient form of 'fiction', which concerns itself with the origin of things – the creation of the world, the first people and so on. Myth seeks originality not through innovation – which is future-based – but in its return to an archetypal past.

Chapter 23

Navigating the Web of Wyrd

Every Rune can be taken from the Web of Reality, and therefore each one can be seen as being [a different aspect] of Reality. This is the main concept behind their more magical and divinatory uses: the fact they make up Reality means they can be used as signposts, or keys, to read what Reality actually is, or even to re-write it as something we want.

David Stone, *The Principles of Stav*[1]

The mystical notion of the Web of Wyrd, the codes embodied in the runes and the collective levels of the mind reveal a living philosophy which can be adapted to the needs of the individual in the modern world. The traditional practices of the pagan world, including meditation, magic, divination, trance and physical exercises, are shown to be the elements of a living philosophy, a system of mind, body and spirit training that, through an 'inner technology' taps into the energies that flow through both the cosmos and the individual.

Stav: a northern system of mind, body and spirit

Stav is an important organisation which came to Britain in the 1990s. 'Stav' literally means knowledge of the rune staves but also denotes a staff in the sense of a walking or fighting staff – which is used in both physical exercises and in martial arts training within the Stav system. Stav has no racial agenda whatsoever and its leader had family members who fought in the Norwegian resistance against the Nazi invaders. Ivar Hafskjold is a Norwegian who has lived in Yorkshire, England for many years. After studying languages and psychology at the Universities of Oslo and Leeds he lived in Africa for several years. On his return to Norway he joined the army and specialised in guerrilla warfare and intelligence.

When he was thirty-four he moved with his Japanese wife to Japan. He spent fourteen years there and made an intensive and prolonged study of the Japanese martial arts of Kenjutsu and Jojutsu. He returned to Europe in 1991 having attained the level of 4th dan in Jojutsu from the Shinto Muso Ryu. He used this knowledge to augment the teaching he had received from members of his own family, particularly his grandfather Karl and his great-uncle Svend. According to Hafskjold, his grandfather taught him mainly about mythological matters and his great-uncle gave him some informal training in breathing techniques, chanting and runic exercises.[2] Hafskjold describes Stav as: 'A spiritual training system for learning to see the reality about ourselves and the world about us. From this Stav can help us learn how to use that reality for living in harmony with ourselves, our community and the natural world.'

Unlike some pagan Germanic groups, Stav does not have an agenda of exclusion. Hafskjold, whilst recognising it is most likely to appeal to those who share his northern European roots, also makes clear 'anyone with a desire to study will be welcomed, one's race or religion is of no concern to Stav. It might be somewhat more difficult to grasp concepts if you have a non-European educational background, but otherwise there is no problem.'[3]

In the early 1990s Hafskjold wrote an article for the martial arts magazine *Fighting Arts International* which outlined some of the basics of his system and attracted his initial students. 'Quality control' is strictly maintained and Hafskjold has only four long-term associates to whom he has given the title of Stav master, which authorises them to teach largely independently of his direction. The spiritual centre of Stav is called Heimbu, the home of Ivar Hafskjold in Beverley, Yorkshire. Below this are the teaching centres of the four Stav masters, each of which is known as a hov, a Scandinavian word often translated as 'temple'. A number of Stav practitioners, members who have a good working knowledge of the Stav system but who are still themselves training under a master, also run their own centres. A group under the direct guidance of a practitioner is known as a ve (shrine). In addition to its various centres in Britain Stav also has a number of branches in California, Texas, Australia and more recently in Germany, Sweden and Japan.

Unlike some pagan groups which stress the occult nature of their teachings, Stav has a much more direct approach. There are no secrets – all the techniques used in the system are openly taught. To master them is, of course, another matter and mere knowledge of the practices is not the same thing as understanding their deeper meaning. Hard work and long practice are the only means of gaining this level of insight. The particular style of martial arts taught is a major part of the system. Through the martial arts the practitioner's understanding of the principles of Stav is tested. The basic training and the core of Stav as a practical system is the performing of a sequence of physical exercises known as the stances. These involve the practitioner assuming various postures based on the shape of the runes.

Other advanced Stav courses involve not only martial arts but also woodcraft and survival skills, which are taught as aspects of its living philosophy. Herbalism, archery and traditional crafts are also taught in order to give a wider understanding of how Stav principles permeate various aspects of traditional life. The Stav system makes use of some traditional practices which once went under the name of magic but redefines them in terms more suited to the modern mind and in doing so removes any superstitious elements. For example, *galdr,* an Old Norse word meaning a magic chant or more generally magic, is explained as a traditional way of expressing the power of the spoken, sung or written word.

Rune casting on the fabric of reality

In the Stav system the Web of Wyrd is represented by a symbol consisting of three intersecting groups of three lines (see Figure 9) which is also connected to the meaning of the runes. All of the runes of the futhark can be extracted from the nexus of nine interconnected lines in the symbol. This is a graphic representation of the vision of the runes that Odin experienced after his nine nights on the tree. The symbol is a way of explaining that it is from the Orlog and the Web that the runes come and that Odin's vision was of the primal reality that underlies even the runes.

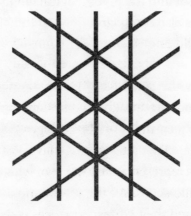

Figure 9: A graphic representation of the web of Wyrd

Like Bureus' Rune Cross, the symbol represents both the source of the runes and is a representation of the whole futhark in one image. According to Graham Butcher, one of the Stav masters, the runes are 'signposts to help us navigate within the web'. They are a means of communication between the conscious and unconscious parts of our mind, ways of bridging the gap which so often divides the intuitive and the rational. In the Stav system the Orlog is defined as the external law of the universe, a 'Primal Goddess' – an entity without beginning or end, older and superior to even the gods and giants. It was the pattern set by the Orlog that the Norns, the three Northern goddesses of fate, wove. Orlog is the ultimate purpose or grand plan of creation. Graham Butcher states that the purpose of Stav training is to discover how to live in accordance with the Web of the Orlog.

The Web of Wyrd by its nature is inscrutable, and since it cannot be grasped solely through reason other ways must be sought to divine its meaning. Mention has already been made of Jung's law of synchronicity in this regard. In the Stav system the purpose of giving rune readings is described not in terms of some magical means of revealing the future but as a type of counselling. This is at once both ancient and modern in its approach. To describe divination as a form of counselling brings it into the psychological language of the twenty-first century, but it is also firmly grounded in the old tradition for, as we have seen, the Old English word for counsellor is *rūnwita*, rune-reader.

We can see how the symbolic code of the runes is used in the modern world by looking at the Stav system of analogical classi-fication using the sixteen runes of the Younger Futhark traditionally used in Scandinavia. The attributes I have listed here are not exhaustive but give a representative sample of what kind of things are included in such runic codes. All the information included below in the list of the runes and their correspondences is drawn directly from the writings of Graham Butcher.

It can be seen from this index of correspondences that each of the three *aett*s, divisions of the futhark, is attributed to a particular god of the Norse pantheon. Each *aett* consists of five runes with Kreft, who is associated with the trickster god Loki, considered a kind of joker in the pack. The name of each rune is given along with some basic attributes traditionally assigned to it. This is followed by the god or goddess connected with it, its *fylgia* 'animal familiar' and some correspondences with the natural world. Finally each rune is accompanied by one of the short enigmatic texts known collectively as the Norwegian Rune Poem, which date from the twelfth century. Each of these short verses consists of two apparently disconnected lines. However, the relationship between them is deliberately obscure as they belong to a northern European tradition of poetic and artistic multiple meanings.[4]

Frey's *aett*

1. Fe

Money causes strife amongst kinsmen,
The wolf grows up in the woods.
Basic attributes: animals especially cattle, gold, riches, success
God or goddess: Frey
Fylgia: stag, boar, hog
Day: Friday
Tree: hazel
Herb, grain or berry: barley

2. Ur

Slag is from bad iron,
Oft runs the reindeer on the hard snow.
Basic attributes: slag from smelting ore, the primal forces of nature, the processes of purification and refinement necessary to strength and perfection
God or goddess: Vidar, the strong silent son of Odin
Fylgia: aurochs (wild ox)
Tree: pine/oak
Herb, grain or berry: plantain

3. Thurs

Thurs causes the monthly sickness of women,
Few are (sexually) aroused at this time.

Basic attributes: thunder, war, thorn, protection; symbol: Mjollnir (Thor's hammer), bolts of lightning
God or goddess: Thor son of Odin, protector of Asgard
Fylgia: goat (two goats are said to draw Thor's chariot)
Day: Thursday
Tree: rowan
Herb, grain or berry: burdock

4. As

The mouth is the way of most journeys,
But the sheath is that for swords.

Basic attributes: mouth, estuary, knowledge, wisdom, kingship
God or goddess: Odin, all-father of the Aesir
Fylgia: raven, wolf, horse, dragon
Day: Wednesday
Tree: ash
Herb, grain or berry: oats

5. Rei

Riding, it is said, is worst for horses,
Regin forged the best sword.

Basic attributes: wheel, road, ride, the wild hunt and process of death and transformation
God or goddess: Hel, queen of the underworld, daughter of Loki, half dead half alive
Fylgia: red rooster
Tree: elder/ash?
Herb, grain or berry: coltsfoot

6. Kreft

Canker is the curse of children,
Evil makes a man pale (as in death).

Basic attributes: canker, cancer, malignancy, fire, deviousness, evil

God or goddess: Loki, blood brother of Odin but rarely a true friend to Aesir

Fylgia: serpent, dragon

Tree: spruce/ash?

Herb, grain or berry: wormwood

Heimdall's *aett*

7. The Hagl

Hail is the coldest of grains,
Christ formed the world in ancient times.

Basic attributes: hailstones, the rainbow between heaven and earth, sudden and unexpected transformation

God or goddess: Heimdall, son of Odin, watchman of the Aesir

Fylgia: ram, otter

Tree: beech

Herb, grain or berry: bearberry

8. Nod

Need makes for a difficult situation,
The naked freeze in the frost.

Basic attributes: need, necessity, crisis, fate, compulsion, destiny

God or goddess: Norns, three wyrd sisters: Urd (past), Verdandi (present), Skuld (that which is to be)

Fylgia: owl (Urd), spider (Verdandi), carrion crow (Skuld)

Tree: alder (Urd), willow (Verdandi), elm (Skuld)

Herb, grain or berry: nettle (Urd), raspberry/strawberry (Verdandi), dandelion (Skuld)

9. The rune named Is

Ice we call the broad bridge,
The blind need to be led.

Basic attributes: ice, winter, the hunt, state of stasis

God or goddess: Skadi, daughter of Thiassi, sometime wife of Njord

Fylgia: polar bear, polar fox, ptarmigan

Tree: juniper

Herb, grain or berry: mugwort

10. Ar

A good harvest is the profit of men,
I say the Lord has been generous.

Basic attributes: good year, fertile land, harvest, plenty, the earth, bounty of nature

God or goddess: Jord, mother of Thor

Fylgia: honeybee

Tree: holly/apple

Herb, grain or berry: bilberry

11. Sol

The sun is the light of the lands,
I bow to the holiness.

Basic attributes: sun, the peaceful warrior who brings harmony and justice

God or goddess: Baldur, son of Odin and Frigg; Forsetti, son of Baldur and Nanna

Fylgia: warhorse

Tree: oak

Herb, grain or berry: camomile

Tyr's *aett*

12. Tyr

Tyr is the one-handed amongst the Aesir,
The smith has to blow often.

Basic attributes: war, justice, victory, self-sacrifice, honour

God or goddess: Tyr, son of Odin, who lost his right hand
to Fenrir the wolf. Tyr as the embodiment of the social order
tethers Fenrir to a rock to keep control over the wild
instincts and destructive tendencies symbolised by the wolf.

Fylgia: war dog

Tree: linden/oak

Herb, grain or berry: comfrey

13. Bjork

Birch twig is the limb greenest with leaves,
Loki brought the luck of deceit.

Basic attributes: female energies, magic, childbirth, family
life

God or goddess: Frigg, wife of Odin, mother of Baldur

Fylgia: cuckoo, hare

Tree: birch

Herb, grain or berry: flax

14. Mann

Mankind is the increase of dust;
Mighty is the talon span of the hawk.

Basic attributes: mankind, moon, sexuality, witchcraft,
humanity, death

God or goddess: Freyja, sister of Freyr, daughter of Njord

Fylgia: cat, sow, hawk, falcon

Tree: hawthorn/ash

Herb, grain or berry: lily of the valley

15. Laug

Water is that which falls from the mountain as a force,
But gold objects are costly things.

Basic attributes: water, bath, lagoon, washing, bathing, coastal areas, wealth, gold; the sauna and its benefits
God or goddess: Njord, father of Freyr and Freyja, briefly husband of Skadi
Fylgia: geese, sea mammals
Tree: apple
Herb, grain or berry: leek (garlic or onion)

16. Yr

Yew is the greenest of wood in the winter;
There is usually, when it burns, singeing.

Basic attributes: male energies, bow and arrow, shield, archery, single combat, protection
God or goddess: Ull, a patron of skiers and hunters
Fylgia: brown bear, brown fox
Tree: yew
Herb, grain or berry: yarrow

This table of analogical correspondences allows us to understand the multiple layers within which the specific powers and attributes of the runes manifest themselves. It is only by being able to see the runes working through these layers that the extent of the Web of Wyrd can be comprehended. The runes along with their correspondences symbolise the elements of the pagan mind of northern Europe.

Different cultural codes stress particular numbers as symbolically more important than others. The key numbers in the northern tradition are three, five and nine, and here in the use of the Younger Futhark sixteen (divided into three groups of five plus the rune Kreft).

Although Stav writings do not mention Jung there are a number of concepts compatible with his psychological observations. Jung's geology of the mind is echoed in the Stav system, which talks of the *hamingja*, a psychic force running through the family which is thus a form of collective psychological experience shared by family members. The runes, which as we have seen were used in Jungian analysis, are also described in Stav as symbols uniting the unconscious and conscious parts of the mind.

Chapter 24

Inner Technology

Careful reading of the texts suffices to show that the experiences in question are transphysiological, that all these 'centers' represent yogic states . . . the yogins performed their experiments on a 'subtle body' . . . they became masters of a zone infinitely greater than the 'normal' psychic zone, that they penetrated into the depths of the unconscious and were able to 'awaken' the archaic strata of primordial conscious-ness, which, in other human beings, are fossilized.

Mircea Eliade, *Yoga: Immortality and Freedom*[1]

The primal energy of the pagan cosmos
The Web of Wyrd was explained in the last chapter to be the theory or philosophy underlying a complex series of analogies which structure the collective pagan mind. In this chapter the Web is looked at from a different perspective – as an energy field tapped into by practical techniques used in the pagan system. The analogical system of thought outlined in the previous chapter represents the theory of paganism; the techniques covered in this chapter represent the practice.

As each culture or group of cultures has its symbolic codes based on the fundamental idea of analogical thought so each too has doctrines concerning a primal source of energy coursing through the universe. This energy not only flows through the macrocosm but also through the microcosm, the human organism itself. Each tradition has developed certain practices which amount to an 'inner technology' for working with this energy in its various manifestations. For example, in ancient Chinese thought the various acupuncture points on the body are a mirror of the energy points on the earth's surface. Therefore architects who wish to align their buildings with the positive energies of the earth consult a specialist in the art of *feng shui*, Chinese geomancy. Today *feng shui* is used in the construction of corporate buildings in Hong Kong.

This energy is known under many names. It is the *chi* of the Chinese, the *ki* of the Japanese and the *prana* of Indian tradition. In the northern European system it is known as *megin* or *ond*. There are also numerous modern names for it including the Odic force of Baron von Reichenbach and the Vril of Bulwer-Lytton. This underlying force is often symbolised by a serpent on account of its fluid and snake-like qualities. In the yoga systems of India this energy, when manifested within the human body in a particular way, is known as kundalini, which, as we have noted earlier, is symbolised as both a serpent and a goddess. The activation of this energy in order to enter altered states of consciousness has been achieved by a number of physically based techniques – yoga, t'ai chi and other martial arts, and shamanic dances among them.

Brian Bates states that for the Anglo-Saxon sorcerer this energy pervades the physical, psychological and spiritual dimensions of life, thus linking them all in a holistic system. Through working with the life force it is possible to reconnect with the rhythms of the Earth which most of us have lost contact with due to city life and the technological cocoon we typically live in.[2] In Stav the life energy is known as *megin* and is also described as the northern European counterpart to *chi* and *prana*. The Old Norse word *megin* is usually translated as might, power or ability. Other occurrences of the concept reveal further levels of meanings. *Ó-megin* means faintness and *jordmegin* means Earth energy. This chapter deals with a number of practices which make up the inner technology developed in pagan times to access this primal source of energy.

The cosmology and symbolism of the ancient north present us with a picture of a fluid and ever-changing world. The spirals, coils and endless winding patterns so characteristic of pagan and pre-historic European art reflect this vision. The fluid, cyclic, complex and cursive lines represent a very different view of the world to that of solid and stable universe.

In the pagan symbolism of the north there is an analogy between the central axis of the macrocosm – the World Tree – and the spine or central axis of the microcosm. Furthermore, as we have seen, Saxon tribes venerated a great wooden pole they called the Irminsul which was the axis of their cultural world. The world tree, the Irminsul and the human spine all represent the mystical centre of their own particular spheres.[3]

Brian Bates states that the life force used by the pagan sorcerers of the Anglo-Saxon world was concentrated in the spinal column and from there flowed through the whole body.[4] Drawing on Nordic traditions concerning bodily health, the Stav system recognises two aspects of the body. *Mott* refers to the strictly physical body – bone, muscle, blood and so on. The other aspect is the *megin* body – the body of energy, the force which distinguishes the living body from a corpse. Good health is based on the free flow of *megin* through the body and illness is often the result of blockages in this flow. Such blockages can be caused by bad posture and muscular tension hence physical exercise does much to improve its flow. Special exercises and martial arts based on the runic system are recommended as ways to release the *megin* energy.

The runic stances of Stav

The most complete system of runic exercises to have emerged in the modern era is that taught by Ivar Hafskjold as the basis of the practice of Stav. Each of the sixteen runes of the Younger Futhark has its corresponding posture or stance as it is called in the Stav tradition. Unlike the more static sequence of postures of Marby and Kummer the sixteen stances are dynamic, being performed one after the other, one flowing into the next. In this sense, these runic exercises have more in common with the Chinese tradition of *t'ai chi* than with yoga. The purpose of performing the Stav stances is to improve health, still the mind and align the body with the Web, the energy field of the cosmos. According to Graham Butcher the stances work on many different levels:

> For the physical body they stretch and tone joints and muscles and align the skeleton and posture. The stances also cultivate deep and natural breathing using the whole of the lungs. On a mental level they fix the runes in the mind and clear and focus thought processes. They also provide daily feedback on one's state of mind. If you perform the stances well then you are probably relaxed and focused; if not, then you need to unwind and let go of tension . . . the stances also cultivate the *megin*, the intrinsic energy called chi by the Chinese. This is your life force and the stances will strengthen it and encourage its flow through all parts of your body. The stances also provide the basis for all other activities. Martial arts, healing, even crafts depend upon the awareness that comes from regularly practising the stances.[5]

The practitioner is advised to perform the complete set of stances twice daily, ideally once in the morning and once at the end of the day. The first set begins by standing and facing to the north. After bowing once and taking nine slow, deep and even breaths and clapping twice, the practitioner forms the Fe rune stance followed by the other fifteen stances of the runes in the sequence. The breathing technique used is very simple – a breath in for each stance and out at the end of each. During the sequence there are a number of turns between the north and the east and at the end of the last (Yr) stance the practitioner should be facing east. The second daily set of stances is a mirror image of the first and so begins with the practitioner facing east and ends facing north.

This is a brief description of the simplest method of performing the stances. More advanced practitioners of Stav use a number of more difficult procedures some of which involve alternative sequences of runes, chanting in the pentatonic scale – the traditional scale of northern European music – and various breathing techniques.[6]

Runic exercises are the northern European equivalent of the postures of the East, but there are other elements to these mind-body-spirit systems. Yoga has its own spiritual counterpart to modern Western anatomy and physiology, and modern pagans have described their own systems of subtle anatomy and what we may call paraphysiology – the physical counterpart to parapsychology. Marby, the founder of rune gymnastics, and Kummer, the founder of rune yoga, both describe an inner technology. By inner technology I mean a system of operating with life energy according to a spiritualised subtle anatomy and its paraphysiological potential.

As we saw in Chapter 5, Johannes Bureus wrote about the hidden centres or nexuses of energy which can be found within the spiritualised body when he described the workings of the Rune Cross. He outlined a subtle anatomy based on seven centres in a vertical system from the feet to the head. On the basis of this he developed a system of magical techniques to use exploiting the paraphysiological potential of the human organism. In Bureus' time the highly developed techniques of the oriental traditions were unknown in the West but today we have the advantage of being able to investigate these in detail in order better to understand the meaning of the runic inner technology of the north and how it may develop in the future.

The Taoists of ancient China practised a number of practical techniques including special breathing methods, gymnastics and sunbathing. The aim of their controlled breathing was to reproduce the respiration of the foetus in the womb. They believed that this could be achieved by breathing in and out as quietly as possible. They also stressed the importance of holding the breath for as long as possible. From such techniques they developed the idea that a special kind of inner breath could be generated. This inner breath could be circulated within the practitioner and transformed by the controlled use of the imagination. Other Taoists, drawing on earlier shamanic techniques, sought to imitate the breathing of hibernating animals in order to preserve their life energy.[7]

Taoist beliefs concerning the physical and spiritual benefits of sunbathing corresponded with their cosmology. For men, exposing the body to the sun was beneficial and the naked Taoist would do so whilst holding a symbol of the sun enclosed in red ink on green paper; male, sun, red and green are all connected in this Chinese system with the Yang principle. Women, on the other hand, should stand naked before the moon holding a symbol of the moon enclosed in black on yellow paper; female, moon and black all correspond to the Yin principle.[8]

The human body (microcosm) was also seen to correspond to the macrocosm. The energy which flowed down the spinal cord from the head was likened by Taoists to the Yellow River. In their sexual techniques designed to invigorate each of the partners the male was advised not to ejaculate, which allowed the spiritual essence of his sperm to return to his brain. This technique was called 'making the Yellow River flow backwards'.

The seven *chakras* of Indian yoga have also inspired rune practitioners who have sought to align these psychic centres of the subtle anatomy of the Indian tradition with the specific gods, runes and worlds of the ancient Norse cosmology. In Indian tradition the *chakras* are centres within the body, but the body in question is not the physical one but a spirit body, a kind of double with its own subtle anatomy. The *chakras* are the spiritual organs of this mystical anatomy and the yogic practices which make use of these go far beyond the physical exercises of 'outer' yoga. The physiological powers displayed by some yogis are truly remarkable. It is well documented that highly advanced yogis have been able to suspend some of the functions of the autonomic nervous system, most remarkably breathing and heartbeat.

Yogis identify seven main *chakras*. Descriptions of these centres are often very detailed and each is part of an extensive system of correspondences comparable to the runic analogies of the northern pagan tradition described above. In the Hindu tradition the *chakras* are assigned particular gods and goddesses of the pantheon, colours, elements, Sanskrit letters, shapes, senses and so on. The centres are also described as lotus flowers, each of a different colour and with a different number of petals.[9]

Similar ideas and practices relating to inner centres and the workings of a higher body are also common in the writings of Islamic mystics, who have their own counterpart to the *chakras* of Indian tradition. For example, in the writings of the fourteenth-century Iranian Sufi Alāoddawleh Semnānī, a whole spiritual system is outlined.[10] Like other Sufis, he held that there were seven esoteric meanings of the Koran. He related these seven hidden levels of meaning to seven *latīfa*, organs or centres of the inner body of light. This was all linked to mystical notions of time. Outer, physical time, called horizontal time by Semnānī, was marked by the movement of the stars. It had its counterpart in the inner world of psychic time, a vertical ascent of the soul through the heavens within. The seven centres of the inner body each represent a higher state of consciousness and each is symbolised by a key figure in the Islamic tradition and a particular colour of the spiritual light.[11]

The Hindu yogi wakes the *kundalini* force within so that it will pass through the various centres of the inner body on its way to the top of the head in order to achieve highest enlightenment. The Iranian Sufi makes an inner spiritual journey, led by the guiding lights of the Islamic tradition to attain personal enlightenment. These spiritual paths differ in both techniques and beliefs; nevertheless, there are underlying similarities. Both involve the idea of an inner body and describe its anatomy and physiology. Both ascribe different functions to the centres as we ascribe functions to the various internal organs of the physical body, such as the liver, heart, kidneys and so on. Both yogis and Sufis also undertake an inner, vertical journey through the centres of the inner body or through the inner heavens to achieve enlightenment. This is the goal of these systems of inner technology.

This spiritual journey has taken us back to the ideas of the founder of the runic revival, the Swedish mystic Johannes Bureus. It was he who laid the foundations of the runic system of inner technology which he embodied in the form of the Rune Cross. At the heart of this system of transformation was a vertical journey through the human body, the mystical counterpart or microcosm of the outer world. If we see this inner pilgrimage as a psychological journey to a spiritual pole, we find ourselves back at the mystical notion of the lost continent of Hyperborea, the inner world of the pagan imagination in the north.

Conclusion

Ragnarok and After

Our journey through the ancient and modern psychological world of the northern pagan tradition of Odin is now complete. We have undertaken a detailed exploration of Jung's prophetic writings concerning the return of the Odinic archetype and have seen that it is having profound effects at the very forefront of consciousness. We have seen how Jung himself, far from being a dispassionate observer, had been an active participant in the pagan revival. He drew not only on reason in his work but also delved deep into the living world of mythology in his efforts to understand the spiritual predicaments of modern man. In many ways this book could be described as an ethnography of the imaginal, an exploration of the cultural history of the myths of the northern European mind. In the modern era, the once sacred imaginal faculty has been trivialised by secular rationalism.

To most people today myth is mere fantasy; typically the word is used to mean something not true. We refer to something false as 'just a myth'. But it was once seen as the sacred repository of cultural wisdom, was venerated and imbued with poetic and spiritual truth. Myth is looked down on in the contemporary world because the modern mind devalues the power of its own imagination, which is an inner cosmos as real as the mundane world. Mythology may be poorly recognised today but its power remains undiminished. It is an essential and unavoidable aspect of cultural life which cannot be eradicated and is ignored at our peril.

The realms of the imaginal are vast and diverse, home to the beautiful and breathtaking, the wise and the benevolent. But these realms are home to darker things as well, things which are dangerous to dismiss. Jung identified the Odinic archetype as the single most influential force at work in the collective unconscious of the northern European mind. We have seen various manifestations of the Odinic archetype as it has resurfaced in the minds of individuals, groups and nations. The modern wanderings of the archetype have been traced back to its roots, as it surged forth from its survival on the fringes of European culture, back into the mainstream in the German Romantic movement, in the speculations of Karl von Reichenbach and the philosophical ideas of Nietzsche. The Odinic inspiration which heralded the social experiments at Ascona and among the German youth was a positive manifestation of the archetype, though frenzied nonetheless.

This frenzy grew and was to propel the German nation into mental epidemy. Jung's first Odinic experiment resulted in Hitler and the German people being unconsciously gripped by the god of war and violence. The ensuing turmoil in the collective unconscious of the northern world was constellated around the axis of Nazism and caused suffering on an unprecedented scale in the twentieth century. This struggle within the soul of Europe resulted in mass psychosis and war, and brought the Ragnarok, the apocalypse of the northern gods, to the modern Western mind.

This crisis in the collective mind has erupted again, and we have seen foreshadowed a second, this time worldwide, Odinic experiment in the Anglo-American world. Like the first, the second experiment began with the inspired frenzy of the god in its most positive form: an exciting period of ideas and expression with the social experiments of the 1960s in America mirroring those of German youth fifty years earlier. As the decline of the German youth movement led to its transformation into the Hitler Youth, so the end of the hippy era was sealed with the violence of Altamont and the frenzy of the Tate-LaBianca murders instigated by Charles Manson. The most psychotic unconscious manifestation of the Odinic archetype has been in the random violence of American serial killers like Lucas and Toole, while in the racist terrorism of white separatists, neo-Nazis and 'Aryan warriors' Jung would surely have seen further proof of his prophecies.

The key to Jung's role as a neo-pagan thinker and practitioner is to be found in the prophetic traditions of the pre-Christian European mind. At the very core of this book is Jung's letter to Serrano – his warning of the dangers of ignoring Odin and the myths of the *Volk*, the warning that the Nazi era was just a foreshadowing of a potentially greater Odinic experiment to come. Throughout this book we have seen that even though rational societies may ignore and even undermine their mythical and pagan pasts, they are still potent forces in the world. Christians burned witches on Biblical pretexts just as the Nazis justified their Holocaust through the fictional modern mythology of the *Protocols*. Heinrich Himmler and the rituals and ideologies of the SS were influenced by modern myths born of forgeries and the minds of madmen. In the same way Miguel Serrano has built an entire system of esoteric Hitlerism, picking and choosing from a diverse range of ideas, systems and myths.

The one thing that all these myths have in common is that they are blueprints for action in the real world – they are akin to prophecy. It was a 'master race' with supposed ancient origins and a manifest destiny which fuelled the ideologies and motivations of the first Odinic experiment. It was a prophetic vision of an apocalypse which motivated Manson. It was the future fantasy of *The Turner Diaries* which inspired the Oklahoma bombing. Whether anyone believes in prophecy as a genuine glimpse of the future is, on one level, irrelevant; the fact is people act on such prophecies, using them to guide their actions in the real world.

Jung's notion of the two Odinic experiments echoes the ancient northern myth of Ragnarok and so we come full circle, for it is the Norse myths which provide us with the key to understanding the final outcome of the experiments and the fate of their ancient archetype.

In one such mythological text, *Voluspa: The Prophecy of the Seeress*, we are told that the Ragnarok was not the end. Odin himself does not survive; he is devoured by Fenrir, the mythological wolf and the embodiment of chaos, during the cataclysmic battle of the Ragnarok. It is his son Vidar who avenges him. Vidar pins the wolf down by stamping on its lower jaw with his foot and then kills it. According to the *Voluspa*, Vidar (Silent One) inhabited a place called Idavöll, the location of Asgard, before the latter was destroyed at the Ragnarok. Idavöll is the plain which makes up part of the home of the gods. The meaning of the name is obscure but may be translated as 'field of activity' or 'rejuvenating field'. We are also told that after the Ragnarok the surviving human beings come out of hiding from the trunk of the world tree Yggdrasill, a new land rises out of the sea, a green and fertile Hyperborea, and the world enters a new golden age.

Like all myths, this prophecy contains many levels of meaning. Directed at the phenomenal world, the myth may be applied to history. The culmination of the inspirations and expressions of the Odinic archetype produced the rise of the Nazis, mental epidemy, war and destruction – a mass psychosis which shook the world resulting in a Ragnarok for Europe. Jung predicts in his letter that if the influence of the Odinic archetype is not recognised and reconciled in the northern European collective awareness, a second, this time worldwide, Odinic experiment will result, a frightening prospect in the light of technological advances.

Yet the Ragnarok can also be viewed at the level of the individual, as symbolic of explorations on a personal level into the depths of the unconscious. For Jung personal development lay in uniting the unconscious and the conscious parts of the mind. The unconscious is represented by the vast store of images to be found in the deeper levels of the mind and their exploration is not without its dangers.

This process is a difficult one, and inevitably reaches a personal catharsis, a dark night of the soul or Ragnarok, when the old, unintegrated self dies off, to be replaced by the new, integrated individual. The dangers of this psychological undertaking are well illustrated by the fact that various forms of mental disturbance may be explained by the potential of the unconscious to override the conscious mind. In psychotic individuals the unconscious is said to dominate entirely. By implication, groups – families, nations, alliances of nations – can also be dominated by unconscious forces, which can lead to outbreaks of collective mental disturbance and war.

This enlightening, frightening and sometimes dangerous process can be understood in the light of Jung's and Hesse's explorations into the geology of the mind. In this model of the mind each ego rising like a mountain out of the ocean of the unconscious seems like a separate entity, but this is just an illusion. Beneath each summit are numerous layers in which, stage by stage, the individual gradually merges into increasingly collective minds. The various layers of the group mind exist both in time and space. In time we may perceive ourselves in a seemingly endless line which includes both our most distant ancestors and the generations of beings who will become our equally distant descendants; in space we are linked to a vast network of relationships, not just with those immediately around us but with other peoples and even other species.

According to Jung, the only way to avoid the second Odinic experiment turning into a psychotic episode in the history of the twenty-first century is to harmonise the conscious mind with the deeper levels of the psyche, which, for Europeans, are buried in the mythology of paganism. In this sense Jung is calling for a new paganism which is much more than a simple revival of dead forms of worship and cultural traits belonging to societies such as pagan Germany or the Viking world which have long since passed into history. Modern paganism is not about imitating the art and magic of ancient times by following the form but not the essence of the old ways. Even if it were possible to revive paganism fully intact in its old forms, that would be neither desirable nor authentic. Our modern world differs in fundamental ways from the world our ancestors knew and so the paganism of today must differ from that of the past, but this does not mean that it has no connection with the original pagan world.

Thus we may read the myth of the Ragnarok and the new world which comes after it in the light of what Jung said about the two Odinic experiments. Although Odin himself dies, Vidar his son survives the cataclysm. Perhaps Vidar can be understood as Nietzsche's new man perfected in the form of a new paganism born from the old pagan ways. Jung also called for a new man to befit a supposedly new age, but what are the qualities of this new kind of humanity? Jung spoke of the need for a transformation of consciousness which, inevitably, must begin within the individual. He spoke of a new religious attitude in which our view of what it is to be human must be changed. No longer can the arbitrary egoism of the individual be seen as a valid model; the notion of the Web of Wyrd teaches us that we as individuals are, whether we like it or not, part of a wider network of energies and relationships which extends far beyond our own species. Our own minds, which we like to believe are free and independent agents, are neither. Separatism, whether it manifests on the individual or on the collective level – as some racially orientated Odinist groups desire – can only cut us off from the wider web, which leads, via humanity as a whole, into a greater network which includes other species and the Earth itself. For it is through the web that we are all connected.

The return of the Odinic archetype in the modern era should not be seen as the whole story of the pagan revival. Odin, unlike the Christian God, never ruled alone; the ancient northern pagans were polytheists. For Odin to manifest alone necessarily leads to imbalance. We have seen how he is the god of frenzy, of various altered states such as battle rage, poetic inspiration and magical trance. Such states of mind are not part of the everyday workings of the mind. Frenzy is an extreme and overwhelmingly powerful state of mind and, at both the individual and collective level, cannot be sustained for long without leading to madness. To live in a perpetual state of Odinic inspiration would therefore be neither desirable nor even possible.

Odin is but one element in the pagan system; it is only if the power of this god is seen as part of the pantheon that the holistic nature of paganism can be truly understood. Each rune relates to a different pagan god or goddess. Each is connected with the others through the Web of correspondences, and each represents a particular aspect of our individual and collective minds. As a whole they give us a complete map of the mind and its capacities. These ancient blueprints are still active in our modern minds. The exploration of this wider picture is beyond the scope of the present book. We must rely on future investigations for the unfolding of this story.

Epilogue

As Jung predicted, the effects of the second Odinic experiment would be worldwide and we can see this in the wholesale destruction of traditional cultures across the globe. Many societies are on the verge of annihilation as global monoculture absorbs them, a process often described blandly as acculturation. Cultural diversity is as valuable to the world as the diversity of species of plants and animals. Ecologically speaking, the destruction of these cultures, their languages and knowledge is disastrous. Globalisation – the goal of a monolithic, secular and materialistic monoculture – is abhorrent. The very cultures which stand closest to the precipice of extinction – many small societies on the fringes of the modern world including the Amazonian Indians, the Pygmies of the African rainforests and many of the inhabitants of New Guinea and the South Seas – face this prospect together with those who live in so-called Fourth World conditions in the very heart of the modern world – Native Americans and the Aborigines of Australia.

Many such cultures have already disappeared or been changed beyond recognition. Countless languages have been lost; numerous epidemics have decimated the populations of native groups; traditional spirituality has been exterminated by missionary zeal; local wisdom, crafts and environmental knowledge have been dumped in favour of Western education, Western crops and Western goods. Even the most optimistic expect only a few to survive despite the fact that the twentieth century saw a marked change in the status of such indigenous peoples. At its beginning many were mere chattels of the great European empires and were scientifically classified on the lowest rung of the human ladder. By its end they had become, at least those who had made it through a long and arduous century, embodiments of ecological and tribal wisdom for many young Westerners.

What is the role of paganism in the modern world? The notion of the Web of Wyrd and the cosmology it implies is antagonistic to the ongoing project of globalisation, which has its roots in monotheism not paganism. In the pagan view all things are connected through the fabric of the Web so what affects one part of the globe affects what happens everywhere. In this respect this ancient doctrine is also very modern. Global awareness, fundamental to the ecological movement, is not the same thing as globalisation. Ecologists seek to maintain the diversity of ecosystems, plant and animal life, and, if extended into the human sphere, this should mean diversity of cultures. Among others, the anthropologist and ethnobotanist Wade Davis has spoken eloquently of the ethnocide occurring across the world. As native cultures disappear it is not simply they who lose. For example, their knowledge of the medicinal plants of their own environments is of value to us all; numerous cures have come from tropical species sourced through indigenous peoples.

Campaigns to save the Amazonian basin and other rainforests are an extension through global awareness of the ancient pagan veneration of the European forests epitomised by the sacred groves destroyed when Charlemagne cut down the sacred Irminsul pillar. So the pagan movement should strive to preserve cultural diversity, not just maintain its own. It is misguided to assume that because pagans wish to preserve and renew their own northern culture they therefore hate other cultures. Nazi doctrines of racial supremacy and ethnocide are antithetical to paganism. So too is globalisation, whilst global awareness is fundamental to it. A global monoculture is neither good nor inevitable. The death of languages and cultures is no more a natural process than is the destruction of animal and plant species; it is a political process.

Some pagans feel that their believes have much more in common with polytheistic traditions than with Christianity and the other monotheistic faiths. This has been most marked in relation to Hinduism due to the Indo-European connection. Some pagans who feel such a link explain that Hinduism is a living and unbroken tradition and believe that Westerners can learn a great deal from studying its spiritual ideas and practices, ideally in India itself. Other neo-pagans have sought to establish links with indigenous peoples and still others with polytheistic religions such as Shinto and Taoism in the Far East. One reason for this attraction is that Hinduism, Taoism, Shinto and various other indigenous spiritual traditions do not actively seek to convert others, as is the case with Christianity and Islam. In the Western World pagan traditions were replaced by Christianity so long ago that the intellectual flowering occurred within the uninterrupted pagan traditions of Taoism and Hinduism failed to take place in northern Europe. The revival of pagan thought in the modern era suggests that such a flowering may yet come to pass.

Notes

Preface

1. Henry Corbin, *Mundus Imaginalis: or the Imaginary and the Imaginal*, Golgonooza Press, Ipswich, 1972, 3–4

2. Ibid. *9*

INTRODUCTION – ANCIENT BLUEPRINTS IN THE MODERN MIND

Chapter 1 – Jung – The Pagan Prophet

1. Richard Noll, *The Aryan Christ: The Secret Life of Carl Gustav Jung*, Macmillan, London, 1997, xv

2. Ibid.

3. Ibid. xvi

4. Ibid. 18–21

5. Ibid. 21

6. Ibid. 146–7

7. Carl Gustav Jung, 'Wotan', 179–93 in *Civilization in Transition*, (second edition), translated by R. F. C. Hull, Routledge & Kegan Paul, London, 1970, 184

8. Ibid. 191

9. Ibid. 189

10. Ibid. 192

11. Ibid. 179

12. The text of this letter appears in Miguel Serrano, *C.G. Jung and Herman Hesse: A Record of Two Friendships*, translated by Frank MacShane, Routledge & Kegan Paul, London, 1966, 85–6.

13. The Icelander Snorri Sturluson (1179–1241) wrote down many of the myths which have been translated in Jean I. Young's *The Prose Edda of Snorri Sturluson: Tales from Norse Mythology*, University of California Press, Berkeley, 1992. See also Lee M. Hollander (translator), *The Poetic Edda* (second edition), University of Texas Press, Austin, 2000. There are a number of fine books on the myths in general including, H.R. Ellis Davidson, *Gods and Myths of Northern Europe*, Penguin, London, 1990, and Rudolf Simek, *Dictionary of Northern Mythology*, translated by Angela Hall, D.S. Brewer, Cambridge, 1993.

14. For a comprehensive list of the names of Odin see Neil S. Price, *The Viking Way: Religion and War in late Iron Age Scandinavia*, Aun 31, Uppsala, 2002, 100–107.

15. This was also the case among medieval knights, as expressed in the code of chivalry, and amongst the Japanese samurai and various other warrior traditions.

16. H.R. Ellis Davidson, *Gods and Myths of Northern Europe*, Penguin, London, 1990, 213–14

Chapter 2 – The Pagan Family Tree

1. H.R. Ellis Davidson, *Gods and Myths of Northern Europe*, Penguin, London, 1990, 9

2. A theme which is echoed in the mead of Celtic and Germanic myth, the Indian *soma* and the Iranian *haoma*.

3. C. Scott Littleton, *The New Comparative Mythology: An Anthropological Assessment of the Theories of Georges Dumézil* (third edition), University of California Press, Berkeley, 1982, 231

4. Hel is the subterranean realm of the dead – damp, cold and inhabited by a goddess also called Hel. She is said to be half white and half black, half dead and half alive. Her hall is called the damp place,

her bed is illness and her bed curtains are poetically described as 'bleak misfortune'. Etymological evidence points to the Norse realm of Hel being a mythological version of ancient family burial places in the form of the megalithic mounds dating back to the Bronze and even Stone Age. See Rudolf Simek, *Dictionary of Northern Mythology*, translated by Angela Hall, D.S. Brewer, Cambridge, 1993, the entry 'Hel'. It is not to be confused with the Christian hell.

5. Brian Branston, *The Lost Gods of England*, Thames & Hudson, London, 1957, 57–8

6. The Norns of Old Norse myths have their parallels elsewhere in the pagan traditions of Europe. The three Greek fates were also female. In Greek myth it is Clotho who spun the thread of life, Lachesis who measured it out and Atropos who cut the thread, so ending the individual's life. Comparisons can also be made with the Roman tradition of the Parcae – three mythical sisters named Nona, Decima and Morta.

The Norns also represent the three aspects of a single goddess, hag, mother and maiden respectively. The triple goddess of time may be connected to the lunar cycle, the new moon being the virgin or maiden, the waxing moon the nymph or sexually active woman and the waning moon the crone. It is the three Norns who weave the web of fate and rule over the destiny of mortal men. It is not clear whether or not the three Norns was a later myth which developed from an original concerning only Urd (Wyrd) as the sole personification of destiny or fate. It is however significant that of the three Norns only Urd plays more than a passing role in Norse mythology, perhaps suggesting that the past was of more significance in the pagan world view than either the present or the future. We see this reflected in the fact that not only is Wyrd a very powerful goddess but that she is also said to be older than the gods themselves.

Chapter 3 – Ancestral Visions

1. Rudolf Simek, *Dictionary of Northern Mythology*, translated by

Angela Hall, D.S. Brewer, Cambridge, 1996, 249

2. Joseph Needham, *Science and Civilisation in China, Volume 2: History of Scientific Thought*, Cambridge University Press, Cambridge, 1962, 280

3. The conjunction of the two genders male and female is a fundamental and recurrent theme in the most archaic layer of myths. Dating from prehistoric times, the symbolism of Indian religion has been underpinned by the lingam (phallus) and the yoni (vulva). In the rituals of the ancient Indians the altar was perceived as female and the sacred fire as male, their sexual union being seen as a creative act. Fire making, one of the earliest acts in the history of technology, was often achieved by the use of a fire drill and this too was permeated with sexual imagery. Both surviving tribal myths and terms reconstructed from prehistoric languages reveal this. Fire was generated as a result of the (sexual) heat caused by the rotating of a stick (phallus) into a notch on a piece of wood (vulva).

4. It should be noted here that while this comparison seems fairly straightforward, attempting to reconcile the symbolic correspondence tables of one culture's system with those of another can be problematic. And while there seem to be many continuities between such systems, the actual symbolic meaning of particular phenomena can vary. The example given here is somewhat simplistic, dividing phenomena into only two categories; these tables can consist of dozens of categories and the reader should not assume that creating these tables is easy; it is in fact a very complicated process.

5. Another symbolic classification system, tied to divination and numerology, can be found in Semitic traditions. The origins of the Jewish mystical doctrines known as the Kabbalah are unknown but can certainly be traced to the pre-Christian era. The earliest Kabbalistic text which outlines a numerological and alphabetical system of symbolic correspondences is the *Sefer Yezirah* (*Book of Formation*). Yet, despite its considerable antiquity, this system has even earlier roots. In the ancient Semitic world the number seven was

the most significant. In the astrological system of the ancient Near East there were seven planets (transmitted into later European cosmology as the Sun, Moon, Mercury, Venus, Mars, Jupiter and Saturn). Another example is the account of the seven days of creation in *Genesis*. Although we tend to take our seven-day week as almost a natural phenomenon it is actually an ancient cultural idea not directly connected with the solar, lunar or any other natural cycle. This symbolic cultural code was transferred to Europe with Christianity itself. Mystical groups and esoteric orders often structure themselves in correspondence with their cosmology. For example, the Golden Dawn had ten hierarchical grades each related to one of the ten *sefirot* or spheres of the Kabbalistic tree of life. As the initiate climbed the ladder of the grades so he or she was supposed to have an equivalently deeper knowledge of the cosmos.

6. Marie Soklund, 'The First Runes – The Literary Language of the Germani', in *The Spoils of Victory: The North in the Shadow of the Roman Empire*, edited by Lars Jørgensen et al., National Museum, Copenhagen, 2003, 172–9

7. Ralph W.V. Elliott, *Runes: An Introduction*, Manchester University Press, Manchester, 1963, 2, 63–5

8. *Egil's Saga*, translated by Hermann Pálsson and Paul Edwards, Penguin, Harmondsworth, 1976, Chapter 72, 191

9. Tacitus, *Agricola/Germania/Dialogues, Germania*, translated by M. Hutton, Harvard University Press, Cambridge, Mass., 2000, 145 and 147

10. Stephen Pollington, *Rudiments of Runelore*, Anglo-Saxon Books, ·Hockwold-cum-Wilton, Norfolk, 1995, 39

11. Elliott, op. cit. 67

12. Ibid. 13

13. Illustrated in Richard Rudgley, *Barbarians: Secrets of the Dark Ages*, Channel 4 Books, London, 2002

14. For a more in-depth account of the ship burial and its contents see Rudgley, op. cit. Chapter 21.

15. Christiane Eluère, *The Celts: First Masters of Europe*, Thames & Hudson, London, 1997, 116–17

16. The Buddhist tradition identifies only four chakras – located in the navel, heart, throat and head regions. For Buddhist adepts the secret force of the kundalini lies in the lowest of these four centres, in the navel area. Buddhist texts describe its fiery power and explain the kundalini as 'transmuted' sexual energy.

17. Marija Gimbutas, *The Language of the Goddess: Unearthing the Hidden Symbols of Western Civilization*, Thames & Hudson, London, 1989, 17, Figure 28.4

18. Gimbutas, op. cit. 126, Figure 201

19. Ibid. 121

20. Richard Rudgley, *Secrets of the Stone Age*, Random House, London, 2000, Chapter 2

21. For a thorough worldwide survey of the practice see Theodore Besterman, *Crystal-Gazing: A Study in the History, Distribution, Theory and Practice of Scrying*, University Books, New York, 1965.

22. Audrey L. Meaney, 'Women, Witchcraft and Magic in Anglo-Saxon England', in *Superstition and Popular Medicine in Anglo-Saxon England*, edited by D.G. Scragg, Centre for Anglo-Saxon Studies, Manchester, 1989, 9–40

23. Thomas Karlsson, *Uthark: Nightside of the Runes*, translated by Tommie Eriksson, Ouroboros, Sundyberg, Sweden, 2002, 31

24. The ancient Iranians believed that the sky was an empty shell, perfectly round and made of stone enclosing everything, passing beneath the earth as well as framing the space above it. The idea that the sky was made of stone appears to be part of a prehistoric level of Indo-European mythology. In both Iranian and Norse cases the stone was often identified as rock crystal (see also the Greek cosmological theory of crystal spheres). See Mary Boyce, *A History of Zoroastrianism, Volume One: The Early Period* (third impression with corrections), E.J. Brill, Leiden, 1996, 132.

25. See Michael Harner, *The Way of the Shaman*, Harper, San

Francisco, 1990, 108–12 for an interesting discussion on the role of quartz in shamanism.

26. Hilda Ellis Davidson, 'The Germanic World', in Michael Loewe and Carmen Blacker, *Oracles and Divination*, Shambhala, Boulder, Colorado, 1981, 133

27. Neil S. Price, *The Viking Way: Religion and War in Late Iron Age Scandinavia*, Aun 31, Uppsala, 2002, 217

28. See the detailed discussion of the sources in Price, op. cit. 216–23.

29. Ellis Davidson cited in Bill Griffiths, *Aspects of Anglo-Saxon Magic*, Anglo-Saxon Books, Hockwold-cum-Wilton, Norfolk, 1996, 40, Note 96

30 Griffiths, op. cit. 40–41

31. Richard Rudgley, *Barbarians: Secrets of the Dark Ages*, Channel 4 Books, London, 2002, 165

32. See Rudgley op. cit., especially Chapters 10, 15 and 20, also Erik Nylén, *Ships, Stones and Symbols: The Picture Stones of Gotland from the Viking Age and Before*, Gidlunds, Stockholm, 1988.

33. Flemming Kaul, *Ships on Bronzes: A Study in Bronze Age Religion and Iconography* (two volumes), National Museum, Copenhagen, 1998

34. Torsten Capelle, 'Bronze-Age Stone Ships', in *The Ship as Symbol in Prehistoric and Medieval Scandinavia*, edited by Ole Crumlin-Pedersen and Birgitte Munch Thye, National Museum, Copenhagen, 1995, 71–5

35. Thomas Karlsson, *Uthark: Nightside of the Runes*, translated by Tommie Eriksson, Ouroboros, Sundyberg, Sweden, 2002, 92–3

36. Many are large enough to accommodate groups of people and it is interesting to note that the Coast Salish people of British Columbia performed spirit journeys in which groups of shamans would form the crews of two imaginary canoes and undertake an imaginal voyage to the 'lowerworld' to retrieve the ailing spirit of one of their compatriots (Michael Harner, *The Way of the Shaman*, Harper, San Francisco, 1990, 70–71). Could similar practices have been part of the northern tradition?

37. Kirsten Hastrup, 'Iceland: Sorcerers and Paganism', in *Early Modern European Witchcraft: Centres and Peripheries*, edited by Bengt Ankarloo and Gustav Henningsen, Clarendon Press, Oxford, 1990, 391 and Footnote 29

Chapter 4 – Heathen Altars
1. Bill Griffiths, *Aspects of Anglo-Saxon Magic*, Anglo-Saxon Books, Hockwold-cum-Wilton, Norfolk, 1996, 97
2. Cited in Richard Noll, *The Aryan Christ: The Secret Life of Carl Gustav Jung*, Macmillan, London, 1997, 146–7
3. For a more detailed account of the flying ointments of the witches see Richard Rudgley, *The Alchemy of Culture: Intoxicants in Society*, British Museum Press, London, 1993, 90–95 and Richard Rudgley, *The Encyclopaedia of Psychoactive Substances*, Little Brown, London, 1998, entry 'Witches' Ointments' and references therein.
4. The persecution of the witches was largely directed against women and their traditional practices of healing and trance induction. This can be viewed perhaps as a continuation of the displacement and subordination of the female goddess we have already seen in prehistoric times with the arrival in Europe of the Indo-European peoples. The entire Judaeo-Christian ideology extended the patriarchal dominance in religion, and the role of the feminine in spiritual doctrine has been largely suppressed in favour of the male Trinity of Father, Son and the Holy Ghost, the latter being the original and logical position of the feminine principle in most spiritual triads.
5. These examples are taken from L.V. Grinsell, 'Witchcraft and Prehistoric Monuments', in *The Witch Figure*, edited by Venetia Newell, Routledge & Kegan Paul, London, 1973, 72–9. Grinsell also gives a number of other examples.
6. Kirsten Hastrup, 'Iceland: Sorcerers and Paganism', in *Early Modern European Witchcraft: Centres and Peripheries*, edited by Bengt Ankarloo and Gustav Henningsen, Clarendon Press, Oxford, 1990, 386

7. Ibid. 390

8. Stephen E. Flowers, *The Galdrabók: An Icelandic Grimoire*, Weiser, York Beach, Maine, 1989, 39

9. Ibid. 33

10. Pete Kautz, 'The Gripping History of Glima', *Journal of Western Martial Arts*, January 2000

11. Sven B.F. Jansson, *The Runes of Sweden*, Phoenix House, London, 1962, 165–6

12. Stephen E. Flowers, 'Revival of Germanic Religion in Contemporary Anglo-American Culture', in *The Mankind Quarterly*, vol. XXI, 3, Spring 1981, 282

Chapter 5 – Hyperborea: lost continent of the European imagination

1. Joscelyn Godwin, *Arktos, The Polar Myth in Science, Symbolism, and Nazi Survival*, Adventures Unlimited Press, 1996, 8

2. Henry Corbin, *The Man of Light in Iranian Sufism*, translated by Nancy Pearson, Shambhala, Boulder/London, 1978, 39

3. Ibid. 40

4. Ibid.

5. Godwin, op. cit. 33

6. Sven B.F. Jansson, *The Runes of Sweden*, Phoenix House, London, 1962, 165

7. Thomas Karlsson, 'The Rune Cross and the Seven Chakras', *Runa*, 14, Rune-Gild, n.d., 26–8

8. Ibid. 26

PART ONE – THE FIRST ODINIC EXPERIMENT: GERMANY

Chapter 6 – The Wanderer Returns

1. Karl von Reichenbach, *The Odic Force: Letters on Od and Magnetism*, translated by F.D. O'Byrne, University Books, 1968, 93

2. Richard Noll, *The Aryan Christ: The Secret Life of Carl Gustav Jung,*

Macmillan, London, 1997, 5–6

3. At the time of the *Thing* at Wartburg castle other groups had been founded such as the Gothic League, started in 1811 in Stockholm, and a Nordic secret society named the League of Manhem, founded in 1815 by the prominent author C.J.L. Amqvist (see Eldred Thorsson, *Northern Magic: Rune Mysteries and Shamanism*, Llewellyn, St Paul, Minnesota, 1998, 201–02.

4. Reichenbach goes on to say that if nature had endowed us with a clear perception of Od (which only sensitives – or mediums as we would call them today – have) we would be as angels and 'we should, as a further result, constitute a higher and noble order of beings'.

5. Jules Verne, *Journey to the Centre of the Earth*, translated by William Butcher, Oxford University Press, Oxford, 1998, 5

6. Ibid. 25

7. Joscelyn Godwin, *Arktos: The Polar Myth in Science, Symbolism, and Nazi Survival*, Adventure Unlimited Press, 1996, 108

8. Walter Kaufmann, *The Portable Nietzsche*, Penguin Books, Harmondsworth, 1982, 569

9. Ibid. 126

10. Carl Gustav Jung, 'Wotan' in *Civilization in Transition* (second edition), translated by R. F. C. Hull, Routledge & Kegan Paul, London, 1970, 182

Chapter 7 – Lost Subterranean Tribes

1. Lord Edward George Bulwer-Lytton, *The Coming Race*, George Routledge & Sons, London, 1871

2. See the detailed study of S.B. Liljegren, *Bulwer-Lytton's Novels and Isis Unveiled*, Uppsala, 1957.

3. Lytton, op. cit.

4. Ibid. 20

5. Ibid. 43–4

6. On Max Müller see Eric J. Sharpe, *Comparative Religion: A History* (second edition), Duckworth, London, 1986, especially Chapter 2.

7. Interestingly, in the 1930s the German rocket engineer and popular science writer Willy Ley reported that there was a group in Berlin who, whilst realising that *The Coming Race* was fiction, believed that it gave clues to the real power of Vril. The occult writers Louis Pauwels and Jacques Bergier subsequently claimed that this group was known by two names – the Vril Society or the Luminous Lodge, the latter perhaps an allusion to the artificially lit world of the Vril-ya. That such a group did exist has recently been demonstrated by German researchers (see Nicholas Goodrick-Clarke, *Black Sun: Aryan Cults, Esoteric Nazism and the Politics of Identity*, New York University Press, New York/London, 2002, 166–9).

8. Karl von Reichenbach, *The Odic Force: Letters on Od and Magnetism*, translated by F.D. O'Byrne, University Books, 1968, 93

9. Quoted in Joscelyn Godwin, *Arktos: The Polar Myth in Science, Symbolism, and Nazi Survival*, Adventure Unlimited Press, 1996, 95

10. Joscelyn Godwin has traced the source of the term Agarthi to Jacolliot, see Godwin op. cit. 81.

11. Ibid. 84–5

Chapter 8 – Hollow Earth, Inner Worlds

1. Cited in Richard Noll, *The Aryan Christ: The Secret Life of Carl Gustav Jung*, Macmillan, London, 1997, 264

2. Richard Noll, *The Jung Cult: The Origins of a Charismatic Movement*, Fontana, London, 1996, 144

3. Ibid. 21

4. In this regard it is interesting to note that Robert J. Wallis, an archaeologist and practising pagan, talks in his own work of 'autoarchaeology', a method by which, as a researcher, he gains a deeper understanding of the various cultural and other influences on his ideas and practices. See Robert J. Wallis, *Shamans/Neo-Shamans: Ecstasy, Alternative Archaeologies and Contemporary Pagans*, Routledge, London, 2003.

5. Quoted in Richard Noll, *The Jung Cult*, 234–5

6. It should be noted that Herman Hesse was vilified by the Nazis and that he repudiated their doctrines entirely. He therefore represents an untainted stream of modern Germanic mysticism.

7. Quoted in Heidi Paris and Peter Gente, *Monte Verita: A Mountain for Minorities*, translated by Hedwig Pachter, *Semiotext, the German Issue*, vol. IV, 2, 1982, 1.

8. James Webb, *The Occult Establishment: Volume II The Age of the Irrational*, Richard Drew, Glasgow, 1981, 397

9. Gordon Kennedy and Kody Ryan, *Hippie Roots and the Perennial Subculture*, hippy.com/php/article-243.html, 7–8

10. Richard Noll, *The Aryan Christ*, 117–18

11. Carl Gustav Jung, 'Wotan', in *Civilization in Transition* (second edition), translated by R. F. C. Hull, Routledge & Kegan Paul, London, 1970, 180

12. Quoted in John Yeowell, *Odinism and Christianity Under the Third Reich*, Odinic Rite, London, 1993, 10

13. Ibid.

Chapter 9 – The Chosen People and the Master Race

1. Hans Thomas Hakl, *Unknown Sources: National Socialism and the Occult*, translated by Nicholas Goodrick-Clarke, Holmes Publishing Group, Washington, 2000, 21–2

2. Oddly enough the first Western occultist to reify the swastika as a powerful magical symbol was not a German at all but a British astrologer, Richard James Morrison (1795–1874), who wrote under the pseudonym Zadkiel (the name of an angel). He stated in his almanac of 1870 that he was reviving the Ancient Order of the Suastica – also known as The Brotherhood of the Mystic Cross – in England and from there he hoped it would spread to Europe, India and America. The order had three degrees modified from the grades of Freemasonry – apprentice brother, doctor of reason and grand master. He also provided a mythological background to the order by claiming that it had been founded around 1027 BC by a master named

Foe somewhere in Tibet. See Joscelyn Godwin, *Arktos: The Polar Myth in Science, Symbolism, and Nazi Survival*, Adventure Unlimited Press, 1996, 147–8.

3. Thomas Wilson, 'The Swastika: The Earliest Known Symbol, and its Migrations; with Observations on the Migration of Certain Industries in Prehistoric Times', in *Annual Report of the Board of Regents of the Smithsonian Institute for the year ending June 30, 1894 (Report of the US National Museum)*, Government Printing Office, Washington, 1896, 757–1011. Despite its early date Wilson's study is still a mine of information on the history and prehistory of the swastika.

4. Norman Cohn, *Warrant for Genocide: The Myth of the Jewish World-Conspiracy and the Protocols of the Elders of Zion*, Eyre & Spottiswoode, London, 1967, 34

5. There have been numerous editions, for example *Protocols of the Learned Elders of Zion*, translated by Victor E. Marsden, Britons Publishing Society, London, 1921.

6. On the origins of the *Protocols* and their complex history among the White Russians see Norman Cohn op. cit. and also James Webb, *The Occult Establishment: Volume II The Age of the Irrational*, Richard Drew, Glasgow, 1981, Chapter Four, 'The Conspiracy against the World'.

7. Quoted in Martin A. Lee, *The Beast Reawakens: The Chilling Story of the Rise of the Neo-Nazi Movement*, Little Brown, London, 1997, 129

8. Cohn, op. cit. 57–9

9. Paul Watzlawick, *How Real is Real: Confusion-Disinformation-Communication*, Random House, New York, 1976, 81

10. Cohn, op. cit. 17

11. From an account of conversations with Hitler by Hermann Rauschning published in 1939 cited in Cohn, op. cit. 183.

12. Cohn, op. cit. 254

Chapter 10 – The Blind One

1. Guido von List, *The Secret of the Runes*, edited, introduced and

translated by Stephen E. Flowers, Destiny, Rochester, Vermont, 1988, 46.

2. Ibid. 2

3. Quoted in Nicholas Goodrick-Clarke, *The Occult Roots of Nazism: Secret Aryan Cults and Their Influence on Nazi Ideology*, I.B. Tauris, London, 1992, 35

4. Richard Noll, *The Jung Cult: The Origins of a Charismatic Movement*, Fontana, London, 1996, 63

5. See Helena Petrovna Blavatsky, *The Secret Doctrine*, two volumes, London, 1888

6. Belief in the racial purity of the Germans is by no means modern. In his *Germania* the Roman historian Tacitus (*c*.55-*c*.120 AD) tells us that this was a question debated even in his time. He remarked, 'Personally I associate myself with the opinions of those who hold that in the peoples of Germany there has been given to the world a race unmixed by intermarriage with other races, a peculiar people and pure, like no one but themselves, whence it comes that their physique, so far as can be said with their vast numbers, is identical: fierce blue eyes, red hair, tall frames' (*Germania* 4). Tacitus then goes on to mention that Germans are ill-disposed to regular hard work, inferring that they are unlike the Romans in this respect. This is a variation on the myth of the 'lazy native' which was to become a stock notion in later colonial writings such as those of the British Empire. The Nazis and their forerunners played scant attention to this slur on their ancestors and found in his remarks on racial purity an ancient confirmation of modern biological racism. Tacitus' comments were cited in support of a eugenic programme. It should be noted however that the question of racial purity that Tacitus mentions was one debated in Roman circles and there is no support for the conclusion that the Germanic tribes themselves placed any importance on this issue.

7. Many other occultists claim past lives. For example, Aleister Crowley counted the nineteenth-century French occultist Eliphas Lévi and the founder of the Egyptian Freemasonry Cagliostro among his

previous incarnations. Another British occultist, the artist Austin Osman Spare (1888–1956), believed himself to have been Apeleius the first-century writer of *The Golden Ass* and also William Blake.

8. Nicholas Goodrick-Clarke, op. cit. 63–4

9. Guido von List, op. cit. 58

10. Richard Noll, *The Jung Cult*, 179

Chapter 11 – Rune Yoga

1. Siegfried Adolf Kummer, *Rune Magic*, translated and edited by Edred Thorsson, Rune-Gild, 1993

2. Guido von List, *The Secret of the Runes*, edited, introduced and translated by Stephen E. Flowers, Destiny, Rochester, Vermont, 1988, 88

3. For an in-depth discussion of Marby and his runic gymnastics see Edred Thorsson, *Rune Might: Secret Practices of the German Rune Magicians*, Llewellyn, St Paul, Minnesota, 1994, from which much of the present account of Marby's ideas and practices is drawn.

4. With its dismissal as a forgery the book sank beneath the waves of criticism. It briefly resurfaced in two works by Robert J. Scrutton (*The Other Atlantis: Astounding Revelations of the Secrets of Atland, Long-lost Imperial Continent of the North*, Neville Spearman, Jersey, UK, 1977 and *Secrets of Lost Atland*, Neville Spearman, Jersey, UK, 1978) published during the flood of Atlantis mystery books which deluged the public in the 1970s. Today it is barely remembered although one occult group, the Ordo Anno Mundi, sees it as an ancient magical grimoire and uses it as a foundation text for its witchcraft practices.

5. Steve Anthonijsz, *Internalizing the Runes or Rune Yoga Theory*, irminenschaft.net/internalizing_the_runes.htm, 2004

6. Ibid. 5

7. Kummer, op. cit.

8. Quoted in Edred Thorsson, *Rune Might: Secret Practices of the German Rune Magicians*, Llewellyn, St Paul, Minnesota, 1994, 74

Chapter 12 – Thule: Island of Darkness

1. R.F. Burton, *Ultima Thule; or, A Summer in Iceland*, two volumes, William P. Nimmo, London, 1875, Volume One, 32

2. On the voyage of Pytheas and subsequent historical discussions of the location of Thule see Christina Horst Roseman's translation of the surviving fragments and ancient commentaries in *On the Ocean*, Ares Publishers, Chicago, 1994 and also Barry Cunliffe's excellent and highly readable *The Extraordinary Voyage of Pytheas the Greek*, Allen Lane, The Penguin Press, London, 2001.

3. For a very detailed account of the ancient and medieval sources mentioning Thule and the convoluted history of the meaning of this word see Burton op. cit.

4. Ithell Colquhoun, *The Sword of Wisdom*, Neville Spearman, London, 1975, 84–7

5. Nicholas Goodrick-Clarke, *The Occult Roots of Nazism: Secret Aryan Cults and Their Influence on Nazi Ideology*, I.B. Tauris, London, 1985, 145

6. Joscelyn Godwin, 'Out of Arctica? Hermann Wirth's Theory of Human Origins' in *Runa*, 5, Rune Gild, n.d., 2

Chapter 13 – The Dark Lord of the Rings

1. Stephen E. Flowers and Michael Moynihan, *The Secret King: Karl Maria Wiligut, Himmler's Lord of the Runes*, Dominion/Rûna-Raven, Waterbury Centre Vermont/Smithville Texas, 2001, 25–6

2. For a translation of this text see Flowers and Moynihan, op. cit. 83

3. The name is a compound of Baldr and Christ. Baldr is one of the sons of Odin, whose myth has many parallels with that of Christ. See for example the entry 'Baldr' in Rudolf Simek, *Dictionary of Northern Mythology*, translated by Angela Hall, D.S. Brewer, Cambridge, 1996.

4. Mund, cited in Flowers and Moynihan, op. cit. 34

5. See Flowers and Moynihan op. cit. Appendix E: An Interview with Frau Gabriele Winckler-Dechend conducted by Manfred Lanz, 139.

According to at least one of those who visited Wiligut at this time he was also an opium smoker.

6. Nicholas Goodrick-Clarke, op. cit. 183

7. For a translation see Flowers and Moynihan, op. cit. 98–102.

8. Hitler's leading architect Albert Speer, *Inside the Third Reich*, Macmillan, New York, 1970, 94–5 quoted in Bettina Arnold, 'The Past as Propaganda: Totalitarian Archaeology in Nazi Germany', 464–78 in *Antiquity* 64, 1990, 469

9. See Goodrick-Clarke, op. cit. 185

10. Ibid. 186

11. See Flowers and Moynihan, op. cit., Appendix E, 142

12. Ibid. 34

13. Ibid. Appendix E, 149

14. Ibid. 135

15. Günter Kirchhoff, who knew both men, said that Wiligut denounced Lauterer as an English spy on the grounds that he had relatives in England. This accusation resulted in Lauterer being sent to a concentration camp. That Lauterer claimed to be revealing the ancestral wisdom of the Wotanist tradition, which Wiligut believed to be an enemy of the Irminist tradition, may also have had much to do with this enmity. It was probably through the influence of Wiligut that Kummer and Marby, who as we have seen were prominent in 1930s German occult circles, came to be seen in a bad light by the Third Reich. This is according to the 1982 article 'The Wiligut Saga' by Adolf Schleipfer published as Appendix D in Flowers and Moynihan, op. cit. 129.

Schleipfer also suggests that Lauterer's English relatives may have been connected to the flight of Rudolf Hess to Britain. According to this account Hess planned to go to England in order to make contact with 'noble circles' sympathetic to peace between Germany and England. However, he was captured before he could make such contact. Schleipfer also notes that with the departure of Hess from Germany the esoteric circles and the natural health movement which he had protected were snuffed out and their influence replaced by that of the pharmaceutical industry.

Part Two – The second Odinic experiment: the Anglo-American world

Chapter 14 – An English Mythology

1. J.R.R. Tolkien, 'Beowulf: The Monsters and the Critics', *Proceedings of the British Academy*, Volume XXII, 1936, 15

2. Cited in David Day, *Tolkien: The Illustrated Encyclopedia*, Mitchell Beazley, London, 1992, 6–7

3. Gary Valentine Lachman, *Turn Off Your Mind: The Mystic Sixties and the Dark Side of the Age of Aquarius*, Sidgwick & Jackson, 2001, 78

4. See *The Letters of J.R.R. Tolkien*, selected and edited by Humphrey Carpenter with the assistance of Christopher Tolkien, Houghton Mifflin, Boston, 1981, 55–6

5. Roger Griffin, 'The Blend of Literary and Historical Fantasy in the Italian New Right', *Literature and History* 11/1, 1985, 101–24

6. Richard Noll, *The Jung Cult: The Origins of a Charismatic Movement*, Fontana, London, 1996, 6

7. Lachman, op. cit. 365

Chapter 15 – The Possessed

1. Denis Duclos, *The Werewolf Complex: America's Fascination with Violence*, translated by Amanda Pingree, Berg, Oxford/New York, 1998, 27

2. Gary Valentine Lachman, *Turn Off Your Mind: The Mystic Sixties and the Dark Side of the Age of Aquarius*, Sidgwick & Jackson, 2001, 3–4

3. Ibid. 273

4. Ibid. 123

5. On mass killings and 'random' massacres see Mattias Gardell, *Gods*

of the Blood: The Pagan Revival and White Separatism, Duke University Press, Durham/London, 2003, especially 90–91, 358 footnotes 26 and 27.

6. Cited in Duclos, op. cit. 25

7. Ibid. 106

8. Ibid. 147

9. Ibid. 207–08

10. Ibid. 208–09

Chapter 16 – American Armageddon

1. Andrew Macdonald (pen name of William Pierce), *The Turner Diaries* (second edition), National Vanguard Books, Hillsboro, West Virginia, 1980, 23–4

2. FBI, *Project Megiddo,* US Department of Justice, Washington DC, 1999

3. Rockwell, quoted in Nicholas Goodrick-Clarke, *Black Sun: Aryan Cults, Esoteric Nazism and the Politics of Identity,* New York University Press, New York/London, 2002, 10

4. Macdonald (Pierce), op. cit.

5. Nicholas Goodrick-Clarke, op. cit. 24

6. Mattias Gardell, *Gods of the Blood: The Pagan Revival and White Separatism,* Duke University Press, Durham/London, 2003, 359–60, note 31

Chapter 17 – Armed Insurrection in Aryan America

1. Nicholas Goodrick-Clarke, *Black Sun: Aryan Cults, Esoteric Nazism and the Politics of Identity,* New York University Press, New York/London, 2002, 246

2. Mattias Gardell, *Gods of the Blood: The Pagan Revival and White Separatism,* Duke University Press, Durham/London, 2003, 193

3. Ibid. 194

4. Quoted in the introduction to *Project Megiddo,* 1999

5. For a detailed account see Alan W. Bock, *Ambush at Ruby Ridge:*

How Government Agents Set Randy Weaver Up and Took His Family Down, Dickens Press, Irvine, California, 1995.

6. Quoted in Graeme McLagan and Nick Lowles, *Mr Evil*, John Blake, London, 2000, 45

7. For the full story of this atrocity see Lou Michel and Dan Herbeck, *American Terrorist: Timothy McVeigh and the Oklahoma City Bombing*, Regan (Harper Collins), New York, 2001.

8. Martin A. Lee, *The Beast Reawakens: The Chilling Story of the Rise of the Neo-Nazi Movement*, Little Brown, London, 1997

Chapter 18 – Wotansvolk

1. David Lane, *White Genocide Manifesto*, Article 14, 4, e-text: whiterevolution.com/text/tgm

2. Carl Gustav Jung, Foreword to *The I Ching or Book of Changes*, translated by Richard Wilhelm (third edition), Routledge & Kegan Paul, London, 1974, xxiv

3. Interview with David Lane, e-text: whiterevolution.com/interviews/davidlane, 2

4. The book in question was *The Secret Teachings of All Ages* by Manley P. Hall (1928). Plate 145 in this work, according to Lane, reveals the secret of these links.

5. David Lane, *Wotanism (Odinism)*, e-text: mourningtheancient.com/dl-2, 3

6. David Lane, *What to Think vs. How to Think*, e-text: white revolution.com/text/wttvshtt, 1

7. David Lane, *Focus (Excerpts)*, e-text: 14words.com/focus_excerpts_1, 1

8. David Lane, *KD Rebel*, e-text: whiterevolution.com/racfic/kdrebel

9. David Lane, *KD Rebel*, e-text: whiterevolution.com/racfic/kdrebel5, Chapter 5, 2

10. Mattias Gardell, *Gods of the Blood: The Pagan Revival and White Separatism*, Duke University Press, Durham/London, 2003, 212

Chapter 19 – Journey to the South Pole

1. Miguel Serrano, *C.G. Jung and Herman Hesse: A Record of Two Friendships*, translated by Frank MacShane, Routledge & Kegan Paul, London, 1966, 109

2. The following account is largely based on biographical information in Nicholas Goodrick-Clarke, *Black Sun: Aryan Cults, Esoteric Nazism and the Politics of Identity*, New York University Press, New York/London, 2002, Chapter 9.

3. Serrano, op. cit. 45

4. Goodrick-Clarke, op. cit. 178

5. Nicholas Goodrick-Clarke, *Hitler's Priestess: Savitri Devi, the Hindu-Aryan Myth, and Neo-Nazism*, New York University Press, New York, 1998, 220

6. The powerfully built six-foot-five Skorzeny had earned his nickname from a scar which ran from his forehead across his left cheek and down to his chin. He had gained this whilst fencing and had had the wound stitched without any anaesthetic, as was the tradition in Austrian and German fencing fraternities. His unswerving loyalty, daredevil exploits and Austrian roots made him one of Hitler's favourites. Skorzeny's most famous wartime deed was the successful rescue of Mussolini in 1943 from the remote ski resort where Il Duce was being held by Italian forces. By 1944 many in the Nazi elite were already making preparations to ensure that funding and escape routes were in place before the Third Reich collapsed, which they realised was imminent. In one venture Skorzeny reportedly buried twenty-three million marksworth of jewels and other valuables in the Austrian Alps, this being the haul from what was then the world's biggest unsolved bank robbery – an undercover SS raid on the Reichsbank in Berlin.

American informers inside Dachau, where Skorzeny was held after his capture in 1945, found out that he was the leader of a secret band of ex-SS officers with escape routes and false papers. It was discovered that this group was part of a larger one named ODESSA

(Organisation for Former SS Members). Both Frederick Forsyth's best-selling book *The Odessa File* (1972) and the subsequent movie of the same name created imaginative reworkings of this historical organisation. The hidden web of the real ODESSA, also known as *die Spinne* (the Spider), organised the escape of tens of thousands of Nazis to South America, the Middle East and other locations across the world. Skorzeny had many irons in the fire – he went to Egypt to talk to a Colonel Nasser, later to become President Nasser, about commando training. The most notable of those who were subsequently trained was a young Palestinian refugee named Yasser Arafat, who was to keep in contact with Scarface for many years after their first meeting.

7. Joscelyn Godwin, *Arktos: The Polar Myth in Science, Symbolism, and Nazi Survival*, Adventure Unlimited Press, 1996, p. 72

8. Nicholas Goodrick-Clarke, *Black Sun: Aryan Cults, Esoteric Nazism and the Politics of Identity*, New York University Press, New York/London, 2002, 191–2

Chapter 20 – Lord of the Spear

1. Bernard King, *Ultima Thule: The Vanished Northern Homeland*, Asatru Folk Runic Workshop and Rune Guild UK, 1992, 42

2. Martin A. Lee, *The Beast Reawakens: The Chilling Story of the Rise of the Neo-Nazi Movement*, Little Brown, London, 1997, 184

3. For a speculative study of the role of neo-Nazi occultism in Chile and beyond see Peter Levenda, *Unholy Alliance: A History of Nazi Involvement with the Occult* (second edition), Continuum, New York/London, 2002.

4. The Black Order was co-founded by an occultist named Kerry Bolton who with his associates developed a strange amalgam of pagan and satanic rites around the dark beings of the Norse pantheon. Loki, who leads the enemies of the gods at Ragnarok, was evoked along with the Midgard serpent, the Fenris wolf and the fire giant Surt. This cult, designed to undermine society and precipitate a modern

Ragnarok, is now defunct, see Mattias Gardell, *Gods of the Blood: The Pagan Revival and White Separatism*, Duke University Press, Durham/London, 2003, 294–5.

5. Ibid. 313–17

6. Karla Poewe, 'Scientific Thought and the Extreme Right Then and Today: From Luddendorff's *Gotterkenntnis* to Sigrid Hunke's *Europas Eigene Religion*', *Journal of Contemporary Religion*, Vol. 14/3, 1999, 399, note 16

7. Louis Pauwels and Jacques Bergier, *The Morning of the Magicians*, translated by Rollo Myers, Mayflower, St Albans, 1975, 198

8. J.H. Brennan, *Occult Reich*, Futura, London, 1974, 76

9. Trevor Ravenscroft, *The Spear of Destiny*, Weiser, York Beach, Maine, 1982, 161

10. James Herbert, *The Spear*, Pan Macmillan, London, 1999 (first published 1978)

PART THREE – VISIONS OF THE WEB

Chapter 21 – Tribes of Odin

1. Mattias Gardell, *Gods of the Blood: The Pagan Revival and White Separatism*, Duke University Press, Durham/London, 2003, 276

Although Odinism returned relatively late to the English-speaking world there were a few pioneers before its revival in the 1970s. In Britain there were Odinists who were subsequently to be instrumental in the Odinic Rite (see later in this present chapter).

In Australia there was Alexander Rud Mills (1885–1964) and his small group of followers. Mills (who published some of his earlier works under the pen name Tasman Forth) was an Australian lawyer who sought to fuse his fascist and anti-Semitic ideology with paganism. He saw Christianity as an extension of Judaism and so believed it was an imposition on the Anglo-Saxon people. He published these ideas in a number of pamphlets and books. In *The First Guide Book to the Anglecyn Church of Odin* (published by the author, Sydney, 1936) Mills outlined his new creed along with various ceremonies and prayers.

Four principal festivals were to be performed to celebrate Anglo-Saxon and Norse culture. These were: a festival in honour of the Old English poem Beowulf (1st March), the Sagaman of the Edda i.e. the compilers of the Norse myths (1st August), Hengist and Horsa – the legendary brothers who led the invasion of the Anglo-Saxons into Britain (1st October) and a general festival in honour of other early British heroes (1st December). Lesser memorial days were also to be observed to give homage to other important British luminaries including King Canute, Shakespeare, John Locke, Captain James Cook, Florence Nightingale, Admiral Lord Nelson and Sir Isaac Newton.

Alongside this veneration of the Anglo-Saxon tradition Mills wrote various diatribes against the Freemasons whom he believed to be controlled by Jewish forces and Bolshevism. Jesus, Spinoza and Marx were all implicated in a millennia-long Jewish plot to undermine Anglo-Saxon culture. The various officers within his Church were also outlined in this book: Skalds (poets), Sagamen, Thulers, Spellmen and Henchmen. Officers of the Church are to be carefully selected: 'the qualifications of all regular officers shall be a degree of approved racial purity predominantly if not wholly British and wholly Nordic' (op. cit. 88).

Despite his attempt to distance himself from the Christian tradition it is not just Mill's description of his cult as a Church that shows the influence of Christianity. A series of prayers are modelled on Christian services with sections such as 'Morning Service' and 'Evensong'. He even gives his own version of the Ten Commandments – some Biblical in origin, others of his own devising. Another book soon followed – *The Odinist Religion Overcoming Jewish Christianity* (published by the author, Melbourne, 1939). It contained the texts of three pamphlets on the Odinist movement along with material taken mainly from lectures given by Mills to the Odinist

Society in Melbourne and Perth. With the outbreak of war Mills' political ideas drew the attention of the authorities and he was briefly imprisoned and his organisation seems to have dissolved. After the war he continued to propagate his ideas in later works such as The Call of Our Ancient Nordic Religion (published by the author, Melbourne, 1957).

Mills is said to have set-up a number of Odinist communes in Australia, Britain, South Africa and North America as early as the 1920s. These small communities apparently practised the polygamy Mills envisaged as part of traditional Anglo-Saxon paganism. In the 1950s Mills revived his Anglecyn Church of Odin as the First Church of Odin which soon fell into the same obscurity of its earlier incarnation (Nicholas Goodrick-Clarke, Nicholas *Black Sun: Aryan Cults, Esoteric Nazism and the Politics of Identity*, New York University Press, New York/London, 2002, p. 259). Mills, like Karl von Wiligut before him, seemed unable to disentangle Christianity (and its anti-Semitic legacy) from paganism.

Mills and his Odinist Church would probably have been completely forgotten had it not been for a Danish Odinist named Else Christensen (1913–2005). Although she was interested in Mills as an early pioneer of modern Odinism she found aspects of his creed not to her taste (Mattias Gardell *Gods of the Blood The Pagan Revival and White Separatism*, Duke University Press, Durham/London, 2003, pp. 167–168). She moved to North America with her husband after the Second World War firstly to Canada then to the United States and eventually back to Canada. In the late 1960s Christensen set up her own organisation, the Odinist Fellowship. Later, as a result of her own pioneering influence she became known as the 'Folk Mother' in some Odinist circles.

2. Stephen E. Flowers, 'Revival of Germanic Religion in Contemporary Anglo-American Culture', *The Mankind Quarterly*, Volume XXI, 3, Spring 1981, 288–9

3. Ibid. 280 and footnote 10

4. *The Asatru Folk Assembly: Building Tribes and Walking the Spiritual Path of our Ancestors*, website: runestone.org/flash/home.html (n.d.), 1

5. In pre-war Britain major occultists seem to have shown no interest in the traditions of northern paganism. For example Aleister Crowley (1875–1947), despite his wide-ranging magical interests – he drew on almost all the available traditions and practices including alchemy, the tarot, yoga, Kabbalah, the I Ching and Egyptian magic – expressed little or no interest in the pagan traditions of the north. Other members of the Hermetic Order of the Golden Dawn, Britain's leading occult group, displayed a similar indifference. Odinism is also conspicuous by its absence. The magician and artist Austin Osman Spare (1888–1956) claimed to have been initiated into a witch cult and experimented with trance techniques but showed no interest in Norse paganism. Gerald Gardner (1884–1964), the founder of the Wicca movement in modern witchcraft, naturally had an interest in paganism in a wider sense but, like Crowley and Spare, barely mentions the northern tradition.

On Wicca and Gerald Gardner, see the excellent Ronald Hutton, *The Triumph of the Moon: A History of Modern Pagan Witchcraft*, Oxford University Press, Oxford, 1999; and for the Celtic pagan revival and its relations with heathenism see Robert J. Wallis, *Shamans/Neo-Shamans: Ecstasy, Alternative Archaeologies and Contemporary Pagans*, Routledge, London, 2003.

6. I am grateful to Asrad and other members of the Court of Gathar in the Odinic Rite for making me aware of various facts concerning the origins and subsequent history of the group and correcting a number of errors that I had made in this regard. The biographical details concerning Yeowell are largely based on a two-part interview with him published as 'The Director's Cut', Part One *Runa* 8, 24–8 and Part Two in *Runa* 10, 7–13.

7. 'The Director's Cut', Part One *Runa* 8, 27

8. *The Odinist Hearth*, Information Committee of the Odinic Rite,

London, 1992, Foreword by John Yeowell (Stubba), 2

9. Stephen E. Flowers, 'Revival of Germanic Religion in Contemporary Anglo-American Culture', *The Mankind Quarterly*, Volume XXI, 3, Spring 1981, 280 and footnote 10

10. John Yeowell, *Odinism and Christianity Under the Third Reich*, Odinic Rite, London, 1993

11. Article published on the website: odinic-rite.org/radical, 1

12. Ibid. 2

13. Ibid.

14. Heimgest, *Continuing Tradition*, odinic-rite.org/tradition, 1–2

15. See odinic-rite.org/CoO/circle

16. See odinic-rite.org/CoO/pantheon, 1

Chapter 22 – A New Pagan Psychology

1. The text of this letter appears in Miguel Serrano, *C.G. Jung and Herman Hesse: A Record of Two Friendships*, translated by Frank MacShane, Routledge & Kegan Paul, London, 1966, 85–6.

2. Ralph Metzner, *The Well of Remembrance: Rediscovering the Earth Wisdom Myths of Northern Europe*, Shambhala, Boston, 1994, 10

3. Brian Bates, *The Way of Wyrd: Tales of an Anglo-Saxon Sorcerer*, Harper & Row, San Francisco, 1983, 12

4. There are other scholars in Britain who have pursued similar spiritual paths, for example Jenny Blain and Robert J. Wallis, both of whom have written on the experience of being both professional academics and practitioners of northern paganism. See Jenny Blain, *Nine Worlds of Seidr-Magic: Ecstasy and neo-shamanism in North European paganism*, Routledge, London, 2002 and Robert J. Wallis, *Shamans/Neo-Shamans: Ecstasy, Alternative Archaeologies and Contemporary Pagans*, Routledge, London, 2003

5. Bates, op. cit. 11

6. Ibid. 9

7. Ibid. 11–12

8. Bill Griffiths, *Aspects of Anglo-Saxon Magic*, Anglo-Saxon Books,

Hockwold-cum-Wilton, Norfolk, 1996, 75

9. Glenn Magee, 'The Well of Urth and the Will of Man', *Runa*, 9 (n.d.), 2

10. Ibid. 3

Chapter 23 – Navigating the Web of Wyrd

1. David Stone, *The Principles of Stav*, Stav Marketing & Publishing, Kidlington, Oxfordshire, 1999, 3

2. For further details see *Stav's Recent History & Practices* on the main Stav website: stavinternational.org/stavhist.

3. See untitled interview with Hafskjold stavinternational.org/ivarint.

4. One aspect of this tradition is the kenning, a means of manipulating language common in Norse myths and sagas and in Old English poetry. It involves naming one thing after another. For example, fish's bath = sea; brine horse = ship; storm of swords = battle. Double or even multiple meanings were an essential component of the pagan verbal art of kenning. This is also seen in riddles, which were once more than merely amusements, playing a role comparable to that of the paradoxical sayings of the Zen tradition known as *koans*. John Porter, who has compiled a collection of these old riddles, explains their purpose: 'The riddles' major mode for destabilising habitual perception is the anthropomorphic, by which the inanimate is animated, given a human voice and often human features, to suggest a continual interplay between the natural and human worlds.' (*Anglo-Saxon Riddles*, Anglo-Saxon Books, Hockwold-cum-Wilton, Norfolk, 1995, 7)

Some of these riddles also make use of runic anagrams, demonstrating their use as another means of encoding secret meanings. We see something very similar at work in the visual art of the pagan Anglo-Saxons, the famous Sutton Hoo helmet from a royal burial in Suffolk being just one example. The decoration of this magnificent artefact includes eyebrows which terminate in gilt-bronze boars' heads, features that in conjunction with the bronze nose and moustache of the helmet make another image – a bird in flight. The bird's tail is the moustache, its body the nose and its wings the eyebrows (see Richard Rudgley, *Barbarians: Secrets of the Dark Ages*, Channel 4 Books, London, 2002, 176–7 and plate facing 91). Such objects have been called 'visual riddles' by one scholar who has made a special study of them. He notes that they often appear on expensive pieces of jewellery produced for the elite of society and are therefore unlikely to be merely for entertainment. He sees in this art an important: 'Insight into at least one level of early Anglo-Saxon thought; for this ambiguity would exactly mirror what we know of the poetic tradition which relies so heavily on literary devices conveying multiple meanings, such as metaphors, kennings and riddles. The identification of this trait in not just one, but two, of the major surviving art forms points to an underlying characteristic of early Anglo-Saxon thinking' (David Leigh, 'Ambiguity in Anglo-Saxon Style I Art', reprinted from *Antiquaries Journal*, Volume LXIV (Part I), 1984, 40).

That such multiple and often hidden meanings are found in both the visual and the verbal arts is no coincidence. Both types of art belong to a cosmology, a view of the world, based on notions of flux and change. Fluidity, plurality and transformation are seen as being in the nature of both human beings and the cosmic Web itself; Anglo-Saxon art and decoration is full of cursive patterns, swirling interlaced designs which seem to reflect these ideas. It comes as no surprise to find the same ideology at work in mythology and the magical arts – Odin and the other gods and goddesses repeatedly transform themselves into animals.

Chapter 24 – Inner Technology

1. Mircea Eliade, *Yoga: Immortality and Freedom*, translated by Willard R. Trask, Bollingen Series LVI, Princeton University Press, Princeton, 1970, 234–5

2. Brian Bates, *The Way of Wyrd: Tales of an Anglo-Saxon Sorcerer*, Harper & Row, San Francisco, 1983, 12

3. The same basic analogy occurs in Indian spiritual traditions, in which Mount Meru, the world mountain and axis of the cosmos (macrocosm), is compared to the spinal column in the human body (microcosm).

4. Ibid. 12

5. Graham Butcher, *This is Stav*, Stav Marketing & Publishing, Kidlington, Oxfordshire, 2000, 11

6. For a complete description of the basic exercises with photographs showing the individual stances and a description of some aspects of the more complicated versions see Graham Butcher, *The Sixteen Stances of Stav*, Stav Marketing & Publishing, Kidlington, Oxfordshire, 2001.

7. The gymnastic techniques and martial arts known as *kung fu* and *t'ai chi* probably developed out of the shamanic dances of ancient China. Shamans, like martial artists, base many of their postures and movements on the observation of animals. As the shaman seeks to tap into the energy of a particular animal by imitating its movements and other characteristics so too does the martial artist. In the late eighteenth century a Jesuit with a detailed knowledge of China wrote an article on 'Cong-Fou' which had a marked influence on one of its readers, P.H. Ling, the Swedish founder of medical gymnastics.

8. Similar beliefs about the health-giving properties of the sun can also be found in other cultures. For example, the following is reported concerning the Aleutian islanders (cousins to the Inuit), who live off the coast of Alaska and are well known for their longevity: 'For health and physical strength and longevity, everyone had to perform the following custom or rule: not to sleep through the dawn, but at the first light, to go naked outside and stand facing the east or where the dawn appears. Opening the mouth wide, one should swallow the light and the wind' (Ivan Veniaminov, *Notes on the Islands of the Unalashka District*, translated by Lydia T. Black and R.H. Geoghegan, edited with an introduction by Richard A. Pierce, Limestone Press, Kingston, Ontario, 1984, 211).

9. The first or lowest *chakra* is located at the base of the spine between the anal orifice and the genitals. Its correspondences include the number four, a yellow square – symbol of the element earth – within which is a triangle with its apex down, symbol of the female sexual organs or yoni. It is also associated with the sense of smell. The second centre, at the base of the genitals or sacral plexus, is related to the number six, a white half-moon shape, the element water and the sense of taste. The third centre is located in the navel region and is associated with the number ten, a red triangle, the fire element and the sense of sight.

The fourth *chakra*, in the heart region, relates to the number twelve, golden triangles, the element air and the sense of touch. The fifth centre, located in the throat, has correspondences which include the number sixteen, a white circle and the subtle ether of cosmic space. The sixth is located between the eyebrows and is related to the number two, a white triangle with its apex down (symbol of the yoni), the cognitive faculties and supra-sensory perception. The seventh, located at the crown of the head, is visualised as a thousand-petalled lotus and is said to be beyond the confines of the body. See Mircea Eliade, *Yoga: Immortality and Freedom*, translated by Willard R. Trask, Bollingen Series LVI, Princeton University Press, Princeton, 1970, for a more thorough examination.

10. On Alāoddawleh Semnānī and the Sufis see Henry Corbin, *The Man of Light in Iranian Sufism*, translated by Nancy Pearson, Shambhala, Boulder/London, 1978, Chapter VI.

11. The first centre was called the mould and symbolises the embryonic form of the spiritual body in its most basic form. It is called the Adam of your being and, being only one step beyond the ordinary physical body, is perceived as still in a state of darkness and so black in colour. The next centre is the lower part of the soul in which dangerous desires and evil passions reside. Symbolically this is related to the struggle of Noah with his people. When the Sufi has overcome these lower appetites this centre becomes known as the Noah of your

being. Its colour is blue. The third centre is the heart, the true self (spiritual ego) within the practitioner and is represented by Abraham and the colour red.

The fourth centre is known as the secret threshold of super-consciousness and is symbolised by Moses and the colour white. The fifth is the noble spirit, the divine ruler within, symbolised by King David and the colour yellow. The sixth centre is described as the Arcanum through which the Holy Ghost's inspiration is communicated. It is symbolised by the Prophet Jesus and the mystical notion of the black light or luminous night. The seventh and highest is the divine centre of your being, embodied by the Prophet Muhammad and brilliant green light. The unfolding of the Islamic religion in history (outer time) is mirrored in the Sufi's imaginal journey through the soul's inner time. Thus the inner prophets are encountered in the same sequence in which they appeared in the history of the outer world: Adam, Noah, Abraham, Moses, David, Jesus and finally Muhammad.

Picture Credits

book *Galdbrok* by Nathan Johnson and Robert J. Wallis

Odin on his horse Sleipnir © Torgärd Notelid, Gamla Uppsala Museum, National Heritage Board, Sweden

Stav Altar – Courtesy of Summer Rose de Graffham

Modern pagan rites at Thingvellir, Iceland © IP-agency/Sigurdur J. Jolafsson

Ivar Hafskjold – Photo by Graham Butcher

Brian Bates – Courtesy of Brian Bates